Unfamiliar Flowers for Your Garden

A. W. DARNELL
Unfamiliar Flowers for Your Garden

With a New Introduction by
DANIEL J. FOLEY

DOVER PUBLICATIONS, INC.
NEW YORK

SB
407
.D35
1975

Copyright © 1963 by A. W. Darnell.
Copyright © 1975 by Dover Publications, Inc.
All rights reserved under Pan American and International Copyright Conventions.

This Dover edition, first published in 1975, is an unabridged republication of the work originally published by W. H. & L. Collingridge, Limited, London, in 1963. It is republished by special arrangement with The Hamlyn Group, Astronaut House, Hounslow Road, Feltham, Middlesex, England. A new Introduction has been written especially for this edition by Daniel J. Foley.

International Standard Book Number: 0-486-23213-1
Library of Congress Catalog Card Number: 75-13001

Manufactured in the United States of America
Dover Publications, Inc.
180 Varick Street
New York, N.Y. 10014

Introduction
to the Dover Edition

Here is an intriguing book for the avid gardener written in a most engaging style. It is filled with descriptions and cultural information covering a choice array of unusual, rare and little-known trees, shrubs, bulbs, perennials and annuals. Although the great majority are of comparatively easy culture, they have, for the most part, escaped the attention of amateur gardeners. Two hundred forty excellent line drawings by the author, who is an accomplished botanical artist, add immeasurably to the value of the text. With this handy volume based on an alphabetical list of plants classified under their botanical names, there is no need for the curious gardener to thumb through a lengthy encyclopedia in pursuit of treasures to grow. Actually, this "mini-encyclopedia" is the result of careful selection and evaluation by a versatile amateur gardener with extensive botanical knowledge who spent sixty years growing and studying plants. With this truly exceptional combination of talents, A. W. Darnell has produced a unique garden book.

Like all dyed-in-the-wool tyros, the author is aware that long ago the lure of exotic plants captured the imagination of all who cultivate the soil, and he shares this age-old enthusiasm with gusto. The Egyptian Queen Hatshepsut, more than three thousand years ago, sent forth an expedition of five sailing vessels to the land of Punt (now believed to be the Somali Republic) to bring back myrrh trees to plant around a temple she was building in the western cliffs of Thebes. No effort was spared to insure that the precious trees would be transplanted successfully. The root ball of each tree was wrapped carefully in woven palm fiber in the manner in which burlap and plastic materials are used today. In the centuries that followed, plant hunters and adventurers, sea captains, missionaries and curious globetrotters searched remote parts of the world for new and strange flowering plants that eventually were to delight prince and peasant alike. Cargoes of seeds, bulbs, roots and cuttings were as much treasured and coveted as were gold and precious metals. The appeal of exotic flowers was without limit or reserve and the search for them continues to this day.

Many of these plant treasures such as the rose, the lily, the chrysanthemum and the peony, were introduced from China; the marigold, the zinnia, the petunia, the geranium and a host of others, from other lands, have become so widely known and cultivated that they are commonplace in America. Yet there are countless plants of equal beauty, ease of culture and strong eye appeal, introduced a century or more ago, which are comparatively unknown. It is these lesser-known plants that A. W. Darnell would urge gardeners to try. For more than half a century he observed their habits of growth, their flowering characteristics and their special needs in his own gardens. Living close to the Royal Botanic Gardens at Kew, not far from London, he had the additional advantage of studying others which his garden would not hold. From this rich and extensive background he selected more than 250 kinds of ornamental plants to inspire and to challenge amateur gardeners to grow for their own pleasure. His choices are related to the needs of the small- and medium-sized garden in town and suburb where space is limited. Furthermore, the plants described have been evaluated for their texture, their distinctive form, the beauty of their blooms and their performance throughout the growing year.

England has long been a prime testing ground for newly introduced plants, because of its comparatively mild climate and the love of flowers shared by the English in all walks of life. Consequently, they have produced an extensive collection of garden literature, written by amateurs and professionals, conspicuous for its sound appraisal of ornamental plants suited to home gardens. Naturally, with differences in climate, soil conditions, and other factors, not all of the garden books published in England are suited to American conditions. Occasionally, titles appear that spark the imagination of American gardeners and this book is one of them. Mr. Darnell writes out of wide experience with a conciseness and thoroughness that enables the reader to visualize each plant he describes. In addition he has extensive knowledge of American native plants which provides a common bond with his readers on this side of the Atlantic.

A significant feature of this book is the impressive list of American plants which the author considers of prime garden value. Those interested in native plants for use in wild gardens or for restoring areas of natural landscape, will find his list of more than fifty trees, shrubs, hardy perennials and bulbs of special significance. Mr. Darnell focuses attention on their merits with a fresh approach. Gardeners with a flare for ecology are bound to take a new look at them and be inspired to plant them in greater quantities. These plants are:

Amelanchier grandiflora *Arabis blepharophylla*
Anaphalis margaritacea *Asclepias tuberosa*

Callirhoe involucrata
Camassia leichtlinii
Celastrus scandens
Chionanthus virginicus
Clintonia andrewsiana
Cypripedium reginae
Delphinium cardinale
Delphinium nudicaule
Dodecatheon meadia
Erythronium grandiflorum
Eucharidium concinnum
Fendlera rupicola
Fothergilla monticola
Fremontia californica
Halesia carolina
Helonias bullata
Houstonia caerulea
Iris cristata
Itea virginica
Kalmia polifolia
Layia elegans
Lewisia heckneri
Liatris pycnostachya
Lilium superbum

Limnanthes douglasii
Lysichitum americanum
Mimulas cardinalis
Mimulas primuloides
Oenothera fruticosa
Oenothera missouriensis
Orontium aquaticum
Penstemon cordifolius
Phlox adsurgens
Physostegia virginiana
Pieris floribunda
Rhexia virginica
Rhus aromatica
Ribes aureum
Robinia kelseyi
Romneya coulteri
Sanguinaria canadensis
Sarracenia purpurea
Sedum pulchellum
Sisyrinchium douglasii
Sisyrinchium filifolium
Stylomecon heterophylla
Trillium grandiflorum
Zenobia pulverulenta

A careful perusal of several seed and nursery catalogs will turn up sources of supply for many of the plants described, most of which are seldom illustrated and generally only briefly described or merely listed in American catalogs. Others which may be considered somewhat rare and are not found commonly in garden centers and greenhouses may be purchased from specialists. Classified advertisements in garden magazines and garden pages of newspapers are often the clue to specialty plant sources. In some instances, botanical gardens and specialized plant societies publish lists of seeds, bulbs and roots which are available, often at modest cost. Tracking down sources can be almost as much fun as growing these little-known treasures. Sometimes sources of supply are to be found in the most unexpected places, since many small growers often develop a business from a pursuit that began as a hobby.

The English winter climate is considerably milder than that of the Northeastern United States. As a result, some of the plants described as hardy in England will prove to be hardy in the United States only south of Washington and along the West Coast. However, the entire collection described is so extensive that there is hardly a garden in America where some of these treasures cannot be made to thrive and flourish.

Salem, Massachusetts
April, 1975

DANIEL J. FOLEY

Foreword

This little book has been compiled to bring to the notice of amateur gardeners, especially those who reside in the suburbs of large towns and whose gardens are of limited area, a number of exceedingly beautiful plants with which they are perhaps quite unfamiliar. I have endeavoured to include in the space available descriptions and recommendations for the successful cultivation of the cream of the flowering plants that may be truly called unfamiliar flowers which present little or no difficulty with regard to their successful cultivation in the open air.

In dealing with the genera containing only a limited number of species, it has not been a difficult task to decide which species stands out pre-eminently above the others and is worthy of inclusion in these pages, but with regard to the larger genera of shrubs and trees, the size to which they normally grow when mature has been my guiding principle. All the plants included in the following pages are in cultivation and may be obtained from nurserymen who specialise in such subjects and who frequently advertise in the gardening press.

Over the past sixty years as an amateur gardener, I have grown with varying degrees of success a very considerable number of decorative plants, amongst which, with but very few exceptions, are the plants described in this little book. With regard to those that I have not grown, I am fortunate in residing within a short distance of Kew Gardens and have been able to observe the behaviour of these plants in that unique collection. Also since I possess an extensive library of the gardening press publications, extending over many years, I have had the opportunity of learning from the experience of others, in widely separated localities in this country, with regard to plants that are not among the easiest to grow and retain.

1963   A. W. DARNELL

The Plants

ABELIA FLORIBUNDA (*Caprifoliaceae*) [PLATE 1]
In choosing subjects to describe in this little book from among the very decorative plants one but rarely sees in amateurs' gardens, it has been my practice to include, with only a few exceptions, those that are perfectly hardy with regard to the number of degrees of frost they will survive throughout the British Isles. The comparatively small number of plants needing protection has been included on account of their superlative beauty and this Mexican evergreen shrub is one of the most desirable. Given the protection of a west wall, it has been grown with complete success in several localities in eastern Scotland. In the warmer counties of southern and western England it thrives without protection.

It is an ideal shrub for the amateur's garden, for it is of moderate dimensions, very floriferous and has larger and more brightly tinted blossoms than any other Abelia in cultivation. In an open position it forms a bush rarely more than 4 feet tall, with many slender, weeping branches, clothed with small, oval, deep green, entire or toothed leaves. The lovely blossoms have a funnel-shaped tube from $1\frac{1}{2}$ to 2 inches long, cleft upwards into 5, rounded lobes, forming a corolla $\frac{3}{4}$ inch wide, of a rosy crimson. The flowers are produced from June to August in the greatest profusion, all along the arching stems of the previous season's growths. It thrives in a compost of loam, peat and leaf-soil and is increased by layers and cuttings.

ABELIA SCHUMANNII
Where sufficient space is available to allow the inclusion of another Abelia in the garden, this species should be chosen for, with the exception of the preceding species, it is in my opinion the best of the abelias yet introduced into cultivation in this country. It is somewhat more robust in habit than *Abelia floribunda* and is definitely more hardy than that species, but needs some shelter from searing north and east winds, so damaging to plants that are otherwise hardy in this country. It is a native of temperate China, having been introduced into cultivation here in 1908.

It is a deciduous or semi-evergreen shrub, forming a very attractive and graceful bush, normally about 5 feet in height, with slender, arching, purplish-brown branches, clothed with rather small, ovate leaves, which are sometimes obscurely toothed but more frequently entire. They are of a darkish green and are smooth above, paler and downy on the midribs beneath, and are usually more densely placed on the branches than those of the preceding species. The lovely blossoms are a little over an inch in length and have broadly funnel-shaped tubes, inflated towards the base which expand at the mouth into 5, rounded, more or less spreading lobes. In the best forms they vary in tint from rose-pink to a beautiful shade of mauve-lilac and are borne in clusters of about half a dozen at each node of the old wood from June to September. It thrives in good, friable loam and is increased by cuttings.

ABELIOPHYLLUM DISTICHUM (*Oleaceae*) [PLATE I]

At present there is but one known species of Abeliophyllum, namely the above mentioned deciduous shrub. It was introduced into this country nearly forty years ago and should appeal to amateur gardeners whose gardens are too limited in area to allow the cultivation of many of the more robust though desirable flowering shrubs. It does not occupy a great deal of space and is so sparse in habit that it is no menace to light-loving plants growing beneath its branches, like the witch hazels which it very much resembles in habit but not in flower.

It is of slow growth, but fortunately bears its elegant, fragrant blossoms when quite small. The square brown branches, which are rather twiggy, are clothed with opposite, medium-sized, entire, ovate to elliptic leaves, pointed at their tips and covered on both surfaces with minute, flattened hairs. The flowers, which are borne in short racemes on the previous season's growths, are pale pink in the bud, slightly tubular below, expanding at the mouth into 4, lance-shaped, pointed segments, forming a creamy white corolla about $\frac{1}{2}$ inch wide, with an orange centre. They are produced from January to March and are followed by flattened fruits with a distinct wing. It is quite hardy and is rarely more than 5 feet tall when it is mature. It flourishes in good, light loam and is increased by cuttings taken in late June.

ABUTILON MEGAPOTAMICUM (*Malvaceae*) [PLATE I]

Only two members of this interesting genus of evergreen shrubs have proved sufficiently hardy to have been grown successfully in the open air in this country. No protection, or only a little, is required in mild locations but in bleak districts it should be given the shelter of a wall, if possible facing west. The other species of Abutilon are apparently stove and greenhouse plants. The species under consideration inhabits the extreme south-eastern corner of Brazil and is also found in Uruguay, and has been in cultivation for nearly one hundred years. It is a remarkable fact that quite a number of Brazilian plants have proved hardy or almost so in the open air in this country with little or no protection.

Abutilon megapotamicum is a very elegant, slender-branched shrub of loose, almost weeping habit. The attractive heart-shaped, long-pointed, coarsely toothed, deep green leaves are comparatively small. The beautifully coloured blossoms are produced from the end of April onwards, all along the branchlets; each consisting of an inflated, blood-red, 5-lobed calyx about 1 inch long and a more or less balloon-shaped, bright yellow, 5-lobed corolla about 1 inch in diameter. The red and yellow stamens and the style form a club-shaped mass, which projects beyond the mouth of the corolla. This shrub needs a compost composed of fibrous loam and peat and is increased by seeds and cuttings.

ACANTHOLIMON VENUSTUM (*Plumbaginaceae*) [PLATE 1]
Some botanists consider that the botanical characters on which the genus Acantholimon is based are not sufficiently distinct from those of the genus Statice for its retention as a separate genus. According to this ruling the lovely little plant described below should be known as *Statice dianthifolia*. I have retained the name under which this plant is listed in catalogues for the sake of convenience. All the 'prickly thrifts' as these plants are called are worth growing for they are quite hardy and given the correct cultural conditions are not difficult to grow. These desirable little plants are natives of the mountainous districts of Asia Minor, from Turkey to Armenia, where they grow on rocks and in clefts up to 8,000 feet above sea-level.

Acantholimon venustum has a tough, deep-delving rootstock which produces dense, spreading, evergreen tufts of rather short, linear, spine-tipped, rich dark green leaves. The rather slender flower-stem reaches a height of 6 to 8 inches and is naked, except for a few small bracts with very long points. Similar bracts are found at the base of each flower. The flowers are borne in a loose, one-sided spike from 3 to 5 inches long, composed of 10 to 12 very lovely rose pink blossoms, each measuring about ¾ inch across its 5, ovate, spreading segments. They are at their best in June and July in most seasons. In cultivation it needs a thoroughly well-drained gritty soil in full sun and is increased by layers and seeds.

ACONITUM CARMICHAELII (*Ranunculaceae*) [PLATE 1]
The reason why the Monk's Hoods are not very frequently seen in small gardens may be due to the fact that their roots, foliage and seeds are

extremely poisonous. The two species described below are probably the best of all these plants for furnishing the herbaceous border. *Aconitum carmichaelii*, perhaps better known under its former name of *A. fischeri*, is a native of Kamschatka and like the following species is quite hardy. Its tuberous root-stock produces rather stout erect stems 2 to 4 feet high, clothed with medium-sized leaves, divided into many lobed and toothed segments. The handsome flowers are borne in loose, leafy, many-flowered, branched, terminal racemes. The blue and purple flowers are about $1\frac{1}{2}$ inch long and are produced in July.

Aconitum wilsonii is a native of eastern China and is in my opinion the best of the Monk's Hoods yet introduced. It is a robust perennial from 5 to 7 feet tall, with branched stems, furnished with rather large, much divided leaves of a rich green. The beautiful blue and violet flowers, each about 2 inches long, are borne in a many-flowered pyramidal inflorescence, frequently 18 inches long, in September and October. The Monk's Hoods require a rich, moist, rather heavy soil for their well-being and will thrive in shady places, but not under the drip of trees. They are increased by careful division in the spring and by seeds sown as soon as they are ripe.

ADONIS AMURENSIS (*Ranunculaceae*) [PLATE 1]

Adonis amurensis is chiefly desirable on account of its habit of producing its flowers in normal seasons from about the middle of December to the end of February; these are large but normally far from showy. When in a thriving condition this species produces several thick somewhat fleshy stems from the stout root-stock. These reach a height of 9 to 18 inches and like those of most of the perennial species, are bare of leaves below but are clothed with long, sheathing scales, which gradually evolve upwards into much divided leaves, composed of numerous lance-shaped, pointed, toothed leaflets, eventually forming an attractive clump of dull green, feathery foliage. Each leafy stem ends in a solitary flower about 2 inches in diameter, composed of a varying number of oval-oblong segments of a greenish-yellow colour. There is a double form in cultivation and the Japanese have produced specimens whose flowers range in colour from golden yellow to orange and bright red.

This species is a native of north-eastern Asia, including northern Japan and was introduced into this country in 1895. It is perfectly frost proof in this country and like the following species thrives in full sun or slight shade in any good, deep, sandy loam that is never allowed to become dry. Propagation is effected by careful division and by seeds, which usually take a long time to germinate unless they are sown as soon as they are ripe.

PLATE 1

1. *Abelia floribunda*   2. *Abeliophyllum distichum*
3. *Abutilon megapotamicum*
4. *Acantholimon venustum*   5. *Aconitum carmichaelii*   6. *Adonis amurensis*

PLATE 2

1. *Aethionema grandiflorum* 2. *Akebia quinata* 3. *Allium caeruleum*
4. *Allium narcissiflorum*
5. *Amaryllis belladonna* 6. *Alstroemeria Ligtu*

ADONIS VERNALIS
The Spring Adonis is one of the most attractive of our flowers which may be gathered in the late winter days, for in mild seasons its welcome flowers may be cut for table decoration in late February, although it is at its best in April and May. It has been in cultivation in this country for nearly 150 years but is still far from common in small gardens. It is a native of the limestone districts of central and southern Europe, the Caucasus and Siberia.

It is a hardy perennial which produces several, branching stems from the root-stock, reaching a height of from 9 to 18 inches. These are clothed with scales below, which are gradually replaced upwards by well-developed leaves, whose blades are cleft almost to the base into numerous, entire, pointed lobes of a bright green colour. The glistening, bright golden yellow, cup-shaped flowers measure about $2\frac{1}{2}$ inches in diameter and are composed of 10 to 12 lance-shaped or oblong segments. They are borne on the tips of the stems and their branches.

There is a charming white-flowered form and one termed *sibirica* with golden yellow flowers 3 inches across. Another desirable perennial species of the genus is *Adonis pyrenaica* which resembles the preceding species in habit, but its stems are leafy from top to bottom and its flowers are golden yellow. It is quite hardy and flowers in June and July. Both species thrive under the same conditions as *A. amurensis* and are increased in the same manner.

AETHIONEMA GRANDIFLORUM (*Cruciferae*) [PLATE 2]
Several species of this small genus of rock garden plants are most attractive little sub-shrubby perennials and it is somewhat difficult to choose one or two species which excel the others in beauty. *Aethionema grandiflorum* is without doubt amongst the most desirable members of the genus. It is found on the mountains of Lebanon, growing in exposed rocky places and ranges eastwards to Persia.

It is a rather loose-growing, sub-shrubby perennial with erect and spreading, unbranched stems from 1 to $1\frac{1}{2}$ foot tall, forming a rounded little bush when mature. The stems are clothed with rather small ovate-oblong, glaucous, more or less blunt leaves, which render the plant quite attractive when it is out of bloom. The lovely blossoms are of a rich rose colour, each measuring nearly $\frac{1}{2}$ inch in diameter. They are borne in crowded terminal racemes, which are very freely produced during the months of May and June.

Aethionema pulchellum is another beautiful perennial species, inhabiting the mountains of Asia Minor and Persia. The root-stock produces stems from 4 to 6 inches high, furnished with numerous short branchlets, clothed with small linear leaves. The rose or rosy lilac flowers are borne in long, densely-flowered spikes, during late May to the end of June. Both species need a light, well-drained soil in full sun and are increased by seeds and cuttings.

AKEBIA QUINATA (*Lardizabalaceae*) [PLATE 2]

There are two species of these elegant twining shrubs in cultivation, the above mentioned species and *A. lobata*. *Akebia quinata* is the more desirable of the two on account of its hardiness and the fragrance of its flowers. It has slender, branching stems up to 40 feet long, furnished with smooth, long-stalked, medium-sized, light green leaves, which are not deciduous in mild winters; they are composed of usually 5, rarely 3, oblong or egg-shaped leaflets, borne on stalks of varying length, springing from the apex of the leaf-stalk. The flowers are carried in long pendulous racemes, which are composed of male and female flowers, for the plant is monoecious. The flowers consist of 3, oval, concave, spreading sepals. The males are pale purple and number a dozen or more and are about $\frac{3}{8}$ inch across. The females are chocolate-purple in colour, over 1 inch in diameter and are usually 2 in number, placed at the base of the raceme; they are produced in March.

The remarkable fruit is cylindrical, frequently slightly curved, rounded at the end and is of a pale greyish-violet colour. This species has been in cultivation for well over a hundred years. It is a native of China, Korea and Japan and needs a good, light loam for its well-being and is increased by layers, cuttings and seeds.

ALLIUM CAERULEUM (*Amaryllidaceae*) [PLATE 2]

Apart from *Allium moly*, one rarely sees any of the several species of this genus that deserve to be more widely grown, on account of their graceful habits and the beauty of their blossoms. All unfortunately possess the characteristic odour of garlic in their bulbs, stems and leaves to a greater or lesser extent, and but for this fault they might perhaps be more popular. The genus Allium is a rather large one and a dozen or so species are sufficiently decorative to be given a position in our gardens. The four species described below are, in my opinion, the best for small gardens.

Allium caeruleum formerly known as *A. azureum*, is very beautiful when grown in a raised bed, where the sun can shine through its azure bells. The rather small, globose bulb produces 3 to 6 linear, 3-angled leaves, about half the length of the flower stem, which is erect and from 1 to 2 feet tall. The very beautiful deep sky-blue flowers are borne in a globose, many-flowered umbel and are at their best in June. The individual flower is over ½ inch long; it is bell-shaped, with ovate, lance-shaped segments. This species is a native of Siberia and Turkestan.

Allium farreri is a Chinese species, with richly tinted flowers. The cylindrical bulb produces from 4 to 6 long, narrowly linear leaves and an erect flower-stem, about 15 inches high, bearing an umbel of 10 to 30 reddish-purple blossoms, in June and July. Both species flourish in well-drained loam and are increased by offsets and seeds.

ALLIUM NARCISSIFLORUM [PLATE 2]

The graceful habit and brightly tinted flowers of this charming species render it one of the most desirable of the genus for garden decoration. It is a native of the mountain meadows of Europe and western Asia, ranging from the Alps to the Caucasus, and normally flowers in July.

It is one of the clump-forming species, with ovoid or more or less globose bulbs with dark brown or blackish tunics. The bulbs quickly form clusters which produce tufts of narrow, linear, flat leaves, about half the length of the flower stem. The more or less erect flower stem varies in height from 4 to 12 inches and bears an umbel of delightful, bright rose-coloured, nodding flowers, numbering three to eight to the umbel. If but two species are desired, I would suggest that this species and *A. caeruleum* should be chosen.

The fourth species, formerly known for many years as *Allium ostrowskianum* and now as *oreophilum*, is quite a desirable border species and has been in cultivation in this country for about eighty years. It is a native of Turkestan and has a rather large, sub-globose bulb, clothed with a pale tunic. The leaves, which normally number 2 to a bulb, are broadly linear, pointed, rather flaccid and of a greyish-green colour. They are usually longer than the flower-stem, which measures about 15 inches tall and bears a rounded umbel of as many as 50 magenta-pink blossoms on long, slender stalks in July. All the alliums thrive in a good light soil in full sun and most species produce seeds freely.

ALSTROEMERIA LIGTU (*Amaryllidaceae*) [PLATE 2]

The only fault the alstroemerias have is that they are invasive, some more so than others; otherwise they possess all the attributes of the best of the decorative garden plants. Their flowers are large, brightly tinted, very freely produced and are very valuable as cut flowers for house decoration. Fortunately, some of the most beautiful species are sufficiently hardy to thrive in a warm, well-drained border in this country. Even so, it is advisable to protect the roots of the majority of the species from severe frost.

Alstroemeria Ligtu is probably the most useful of these charming herbaceous perennials. It has a fleshy, creeping root-stock, which produces several, more or less erect leafy stems, from $1\frac{1}{2}$ to 2 feet tall, clothed with medium-sized, narrow, linear-lance-shaped leaves, rather thin in texture. The inflorescence is a terminal, branched umbel, composed of twenty to thirty flowers and frequently measures 6 to 8 inches in diameter. The individual flower is from $1\frac{1}{2}$ to 2 inches long and is composed of a narrowly funnel-shaped tube and 6, recurved lobes. The general colour of the flower varies from pale lilac to red. The narrower two upper segments are usually yellow in the upper part with purple stripes. This species is a native of the highlands of Chile and flowers in August. All the alstroemerias thrive in a compost composed of light loam, leaf-soil and peat and should be planted 6 inches below the surface of the soil. Increase is by seeds and careful division.

AMARYLLIS BELLADONNA *(Amaryllidaceae)* [PLATE 2]

I would like to suggest to those of my readers who have a herbaceous border along the south or west wall of their house, that they experiment with a few exceptionally beautiful bulbous plants which thrive in the open air in this country under suitable conditions, but whose bulbs are reduced to pulp if subjected to severe frost. In addition to the Belladonna Lily, as the above plant is termed, such bulbous subjects as *Nerine bowdenii*, *Hippeastrum pratense* and *Galtonia candicans* etc., can be grown successfully at the base of a warm wall, even in districts that are far too cold for them if planted in an open situation.

The Belladonna Lily is a native of South Africa and has a large, more or less globose bulb which produces several, long, strap-shaped leaves, normally in late winter or early spring. The very stout, solid flower-stem reaches a height of $1\frac{1}{2}$ to 2 feet and bears a terminal, spreading umbel of about half a dozen flowers with funnel-shaped tubes and spreading recurved, lance-shaped lobes. They usually start to open in August and continue to do so until October. In the type they are rosy red. There is also a very beautiful pure white form and one known as *rubra maxima* with very richly coloured flowers frequently over 6 inches across. The Belladonna Lily and its forms should be planted at the foot of a warm wall in the spring at a depth of at least 6 inches in deep, light loam and well supplied with water in summer. Increase is by offsets.

AMELANCHIER GRANDIFLORA (*Rosaceae*) [PLATE 3]

Systematic botanists have now come to the conclusion that the two amelanchiers long known as *A. canadensis* and *A. laevis* do not differ sufficiently to be regarded as separate species, so have united them under the name of *A. confusa*. However, a hybrid between the two plants is in cultivation, under the name of *Amelanchier grandiflora* and it is to this plant I would like to draw the attention of my readers. It has larger flowers than either of its parents and its young leaves have a purplish tint and are covered with fine, cottony hairs, which disappear as the leaves mature. In an open, sunny position this graceful deciduous tree will reach a height of 20 or more feet.

It has an erect, rather slender trunk, bearing a rounded head of twiggy branches, clothed with alternate ovate finely toothed, fairly large, bright green leaves which gradually turn to bright yellow before they fall in the autumn. The dainty, pure white blossoms are composed of 5, narrow, strap-shaped, spreading petals, forming a corolla about $1\frac{1}{4}$ inch across. They are borne in graceful, arching racemes from 2 to 4 inches long, on the ends of the branchlets in April in the greatest profusion. It is quite hardy and is not particular with regard to soil, but seems to flourish and flower more freely when planted in a good, light loam in a fully exposed position; it is increased by cuttings and also by layers.

AMMOBIUM ALATUM (*Compositae*) [PLATE 3]

This Australian half-hardy annual is one of several annuals in cultivation which possess attractive everlasting flowers. The best known of these is probably *Rhodanthe manglesii*, also known as *Helipterum manglesii*, which was popular as a pot plant at the end of the last century.

The plant under consideration forms a spreading rosette of lance-shaped, rather long leaves and several broadly winged, branching stems from $1\frac{1}{2}$ to 2 feet tall, sparsely clothed with leaves similar in shape to those of the rosette but smaller. The flower-heads are terminal on the tips of the branches and measure in the type about 1 inch in diameter. They are composed of numerous overlapping bracts and ray-florets of a silvery white. As usual the tubular florets are yellow. The numerous flower-heads form a loose corymbose panicle and are very useful for winter decorations when dry.

The variety *grandiflorum* is much more desirable than the type for its flower-heads are whiter and up to 2 inches in diameter and the plant is more robust in habit.

Although this useful plant is not particular as to soil, a light, rich loam in full sun gives the best results. Propagation is by seeds, either sown under glass in March or April or in the open where the plants are to bloom, in May. If the flower-heads are required for winter decoration they should be cut before they are fully open and hung up in bunches with their heads downwards to dry.

ANAGALLIS LINIFOLIA *(Primulaceae)* [PLATE 3]

Several of the pimpernels from south-western Europe and north Africa are brilliantly beautiful, dwarf, extremely floriferous gems for the rock garden or a raised bed of light soil. *Anagallis linifolia* and its varieties are usually accounted greenhouse perennials but will quite frequently survive an ordinary winter with some protection in the open air. It has the annoying habit when treated as a perennial of sometimes collapsing when in full flower for no apparent reason, except perhaps over-flowering. Fortunately it may be successfully treated as a half-hardy annual and if raised under glass in March or April and planted out in a hot, sunny position will be in full flower in August.

The type has fibrous roots and is rather woody at the base. The spreading, 4-angled branches reach a height of 9 to 18 inches and are clothed with opposite or whorled (3 leaves to a whorl) small, narrow, linear-lance-shaped leaves, entire on their margins and pointed at their tips. The lovely bright blue flowers have a rotate corolla about $\frac{1}{2}$ inch across, with 5 spreading, egg-shaped entire lobes which are reddish beneath. They are solitary on slender stalks springing from the leaf axils.

There are several varieties the best of which are *collina*, with very rich rose to scarlet flowers, *monelli*, with blue or scarlet flowers with a red eye, and *breweri* with red ones. The type and its varieties seem to flourish best in a compost composed of two parts sandy loam and one part peat, and are increased by seeds and cuttings.

ANAPHALIS MARGARITACEA *(Compositae)* [PLATE 3]

It cannot be claimed that this hardy perennial member of the groundsel family is of any great value for the decoration of the garden, even when smothered with its small, white flowers, but as these are everlasting they are useful to associate with those of the popular statice for winter decorations. They were formerly much used for this purpose under the French name of Immortelles and were dyed various brilliant colours and used for

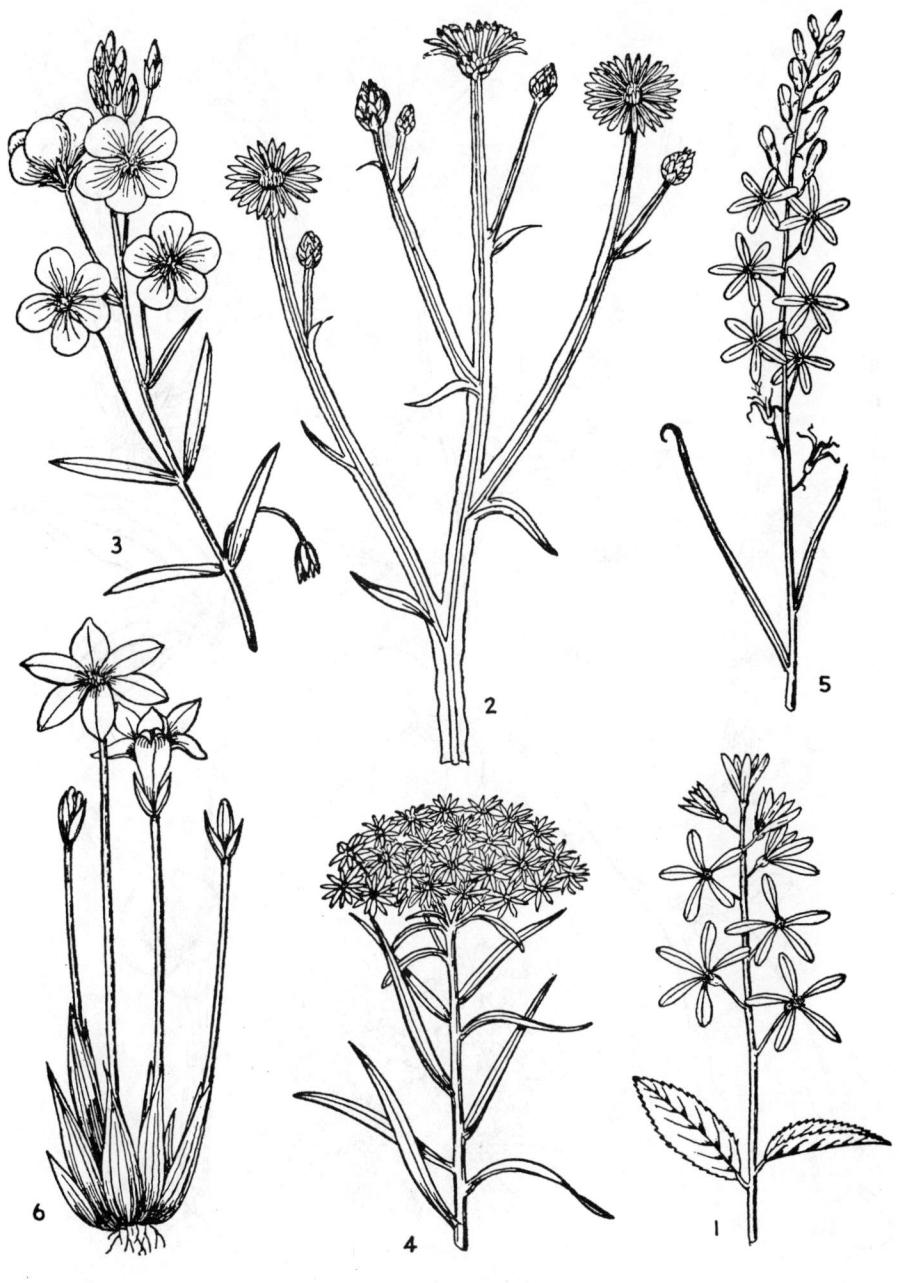

PLATE 3

1. *Amelanchier grandiflora* 2. *Ammobium alatum* 3. *Anagallis linifolia*
4. *Anaphalis margaritacea*
4. *Anthericum liliago* 6. *Aphyllanthes monspeliensis*

PLATE 4

1. *Arabis blepharophylla*   2. *Argemone platyceras*   3. *Arisaema candidissimum*
4. *Arisarum proboscideum*
5. *Aristolochia moupinensis*   6. *Armeria caespitosa*

making-up into wreaths. In these days of artificial flowers one does not see these useful subjects in cultivation as frequently as in former years although some everlastings are beautifully coloured naturally.

Anaphalis margaritacea is a native of North America and forms a dense, rounded, compact, bush 2 to 3 feet high. The branches and branchlets are clothed with numerous, fairly long, somewhat flaccid, linear-lance-shaped, pale green leaves, cottony on the under surface and sometimes on both. When in full flower in August the plant is a dome of pearly-white blossoms, each composed of very numerous, lance-shaped, very pointed segments, in several series, forming a very double flower, $\frac{1}{2}$ inch in diameter. This species thrives in any friable soil in full sun and is increased by division and cuttings.

ANTHERICUM LILIAGO *(Liliaceae)* [PLATE 3]

The reason why this handsome herbaceous perennial is not more frequently seen in amateur gardens may perhaps be because its flowers are less lasting than those of many other members of the lily family which are deservedly popular. It is known as the St Bernard's Lily and is a native of south-western Europe. The majority of the anthericums are greenhouse plants but this species is perfectly hardy.

It has thick, fleshy roots and a small root-stock which produces tufts of narrow, channelled, grass-like leaves which nearly equal the flower-stem in length. The rather stout flower-stem reaches a height of $1\frac{1}{2}$ to 2 feet and bears a long raceme of pure white flowers, each 1 to $1\frac{1}{2}$ inch across, with 6, recurving, pointed segments. Several flower-stems are produced from the same root-stock and the plant is daintily decorative when in full flower in June. The variety *major* is much superior to the type, being more robust, with longer racemes and larger flowers and if procurable should be grown in preference to the type. The once popular greenhouse plant with green and white striped, grass-like foliage, formerly called *Anthericum elatum variegatum* is now known as *Chlorophytum elatum variegatum* and is still used in conjunction with bedding plants in our London parks. The St Bernard's Lily needs a rich, well-drained loam in a sunny position and is increased by division immediately after the flowers have passed and also by seeds sown in a frame or greenhouse.

APHYLLANTHES MONSPELIENSIS *(Liliaceae)* [PLATE 3]

There must be some reason why this beautiful herbaceous plant is rare in small gardens but I have been unable to discover it, for it is quite hardy over the greater portion of the British Isles and is not fastidious with regard to soil. It is apparently the sole member of its genus and in a state of nature grows in peaty soils as well as one of a stiffer nature amongst dwarf shrubs and scrubby grass in the Mediterranean region of western Europe and north Africa, flowering from June to September. It is such a charming, compact little plant, occupying so little space that it is well worth any trouble taken to establish it and cultivate it successfully.

It has a short, branched rhizome with long white roots and short fibrous ones. The slender, stiffly erect flower-stems are grooved and of a deep green. They spring directly from the rhizome and in established plants may number a dozen or more to a rhizome and reach a height of 6 to 9 inches. Each stem is clothed at its base with a brownish sheath which is inflated below and tapers upwards to a narrow point. These sheaths are modified leaves. Each flower-stem bears from 1 to 3 pale or deep blue fragrant flowers subtended by chaffy bracts. The flowers measure about an inch across and have a short, wide tube and 6, spreading, oblong or ovate, pointed segments. A very sunny position is required with a plentiful supply of water when in growth and propagation is best carried out by seeds as it strongly resents disturbance.

ARABIS BLEPHAROPHYLLA (*Cruciferae*) [PLATE 4]
The chief attraction of this rock cress is the very unusual colour of its flowers. Most members of the genus Arabis have white blossoms or rarely purple ones. In the best form of this Californian species they are of an intense glowing carmine and are sufficiently large to render a well-grown specimen very decorative.

This species is a dwarf perennial with persistent foliage, forming rosettes of spoon-shaped leaves fringed with stiff hairs. The leaves are pale when juvenile but become greener and glossy as they age. The flower stem rises to a height of from 3 to 6 inches and is clothed with stalkless, oblong, blunt or pointed leaves. The flowers are borne in a similar manner to those of the popular *Arabis albida* and usually commence to appear in March in mild seasons and continue to do so until the end of May. The individual flower has 4, egg-shaped, spreading petals and measures over $\frac{1}{2}$ inch in diameter. The flowers of this species vary slightly in colour and in some specimens tend to become rosy purple, when they are not quite so attractive.

Unfortunately this beautiful rock cress is not found at a sufficiently high elevation above sea-level in California to enable it to survive a hard winter in the colder counties of this country without the protection of a handlight or cloche. It thrives in a well-drained friable soil and is increased by cuttings and seeds.

ARGEMONE PLATYCERAS (*Papaveraceae*) [PLATE 4]

I must confess that I have a weakness for these somewhat untidy Mexican plants on account of the exquisite texture of their flowers and their bold, handsome foliage, which is frequently veined and blotched with white. Of the several species of Argemone in cultivation, *A. platyceras* is perhaps the best, for it has flowers equalling in size those of *A. grandiflora* and is much more easily grown than that species. Most of the Devil's Poppies or Prickly Poppies, as these plants are called, are perennials in their native countries but give excellent results in cultivation when treated as annuals.

Argemone platyceras is a fairly robust herbaceous plant of loose habit and usually not more than 2 feet high. The stout, branching, spiny stems are clothed with large sinuately-pinnatifid, spiny, alternate, glaucous leaves, resembling those of some of our thistles. The beautiful, fragile-looking poppy-shaped blossoms frequently measure 5 inches in diameter and normally vary in colour from white to pale purple, but there is a beautiful form with pink or pinkish-white blossoms. To obtain the best results with regard to this species it should be treated as a half-hardy annual and raised in a greenhouse, if possible, in March or April and planted in their permanent quarters when they are large enough to handle. All it needs is a light soil and a sunny position.

ARISAEMA CANDIDISSIMUM (*Araceae*) [PLATE 4]

Only a few of the hardy members of the arum family possess flowers which are sufficiently brightly tinted to be of any value for garden decoration, but many species have very handsome foliage and are well worth growing in an odd, moist, shady spot where wood lilies thrive. The inflorescence of a member of the arum family consists of a large bract or spathe, which surrounds a poker-like structure termed a spadix; this bears below the middle both male and female flowers which consist of separate clusters of stamens and ovaries, usually with a few thread-like filaments above them. The whole structure is terminal on a stout stalk.

Arisaema candidissimum is a native of western China and is quite hardy. Its root-system consists of a flattened tuber furnished with a number of fleshy roots. A solitary, robust leaf is produced, with a stout stalk up to $2\frac{1}{2}$ feet long. Its blade is composed of 3, shortly stalked, broadly oval or almost sub-orbicular, rich green leaflets, 3 to 8 inches long. The quaint 'flower' which is produced in June has an inflated tube below, expanding at its mouth into an ovate-lance-shaped blade. The whole 'flower' is 2 inches wide and from 3 to 4 inches long, and is borne on a stoutish stalk of the same length. The spathe is pale yellowish-green, with a white mouth and blade, both of which are frequently tinged with pink. This species thrives in rich soil in a damp, shady position and is increased by seeds and offsets.

ARISARUM PROBOSCIDEUM (*Araceae*) [PLATE 4]

Possibly I owe my readers an apology for suggesting that they should introduce into their gardens a plant with so little claim to any decorative value as the little member of the arum family described below. But as it is so delightfully quaint both in the construction of its flowers and in its habits I have given way to temptation and have done so. However, it is not difficult to eradicate if it is eventually unwanted.

Arisarum proboscideum, also known as *Arisaema proboscideum*, is a very local plant on the wooded slopes of the Apennines. It has a shortly creeping root-stock, furnished with long whitish roots. The leaves and flowers spring directly from the nodes of the rhizomes. The former are arrow-shaped, comparatively large for the size of the plant, deeply veined and of a rich, shining green. They are borne on pale green succulent stalks, 6 to 9 inches long.

When the weird flowers first appear among the juvenile foliage all that can be seen is some thread-like chocolate brown filaments; these are the very long, slender, tapering, tail-like appendages of the hoods of the spathes, the other parts of which are typically arum-like. The spathe is inflated below and is white or pale green, thickly mottled upwards with chocolate-brown. This species flowers in early summer and is not particular as to soil, but must have moisture at the root and some shade. It thrives best beneath sparsely branched deciduous trees and is propagated by division and seeds.

ARISTOLOCHIA MOUPINENSIS (*Aristolochiaceae*) [PLATE 4]

There are many quite desirable hardy plants whose flowers though not sufficiently showy to render them of any use as decorative garden plants, are well worth cultivating on account of their handsome foliage or fragrance or quaintness of their flowers. The deciduous climbing shrub here described belongs to this category. It has slender, branching stems reaching a length of 15 to 20 feet, clothed with heart-shaped, pointed rather large leaves of a dark green above, paler and densely hairy below.

The quaint, curiously constructed flower measures about $1\frac{1}{2}$ inch long and consists of an inflated tube which is flattened upwards and bent back sufficiently to expose the tube's mouth, where it expands into 3, rounded, spreading lobes. The blossoms are yellowish-green, with a yellow mouth and some purple spots on the lobes. The flowers are either solitary or are produced in pairs, on slender, down-curved stalks, springing from the leaf-axils on the young branchlets, normally during June and July.

This species has been in cultivation in this country for slightly less than sixty years and is a native of western China. It is quite hardy and is not particular with regard to soil but seems to thrive best in a good, light loam, either in full sun or semi-shade. It is increased by imported seeds but where convenient layers are probably the best method of propagation for this plant.

ARMERIA CAESPITOSA (*Plumbaginaceae*) [PLATE 4]

Armeria caespitosa is a very charming and floriferous rock-plant and is a native of central Spain being found on the mountains at from 5,000 to 8,000 feet above sea-level and is perfectly hardy in this country. It is an evergreen perennial rarely more than 4 to 5 inches high when in flower. It forms dense flat-topped tufts of short, rather dark green, very narrow, linear, pointed leaves, which are 3-angled, rigid and recurved. The short-stemmed heads of comparatively large pale lilac blossoms are so freely produced that they almost hide the foliage. The individual flower measures about $\frac{1}{2}$ inch in width and is composed of 5, spreading, narrowly egg-shaped petals notched at the apex.

This delightful little plant flowers in June and is at its best when planted in a crevice between two rocks filled with gritty soil in a sunny spot. But it may also be successfully grown in a raised bed in soil of a similar nature. It is increased by seeds and by portions of the tufts carefully removed from the parent plant and rooted in pots of sandy soil in a frame. Several commercial horticulturists have produced a number of very desirable thrifts by selection and hybridism, noteworthy for their richly coloured flowers, close compact foliage and large heads of blossom on long flower-stems. Thrifts have long tap-roots and are not easily transplanted. Therefore seedlings should be planted in their permanent quarters as soon as they are large enough to handle.

ARNEBIA ECHIOIDES (*Boraginaceae*) [PLATE 5]

The Prophet's Flower is considered by many gardeners who specialise in herbaceous plants to be among the very best of our hardy border flowers, yet it is not commonly seen in small gardens. It has been given the name of Prophet's Flower on account of the legend that the five dark blotches at the base of the flower are the imprints of the fingers of the prophet Mahomet; these marks are at their darkest when the flower is quite expanded, after which they quickly fade and disappear.

This species is a perennial and forms a spreading bushy plant from 9 to 12 inches high. The rather long narrowly lance-shaped, roughly hairy leaves are stalkless and are fringed with spreading hairs. The bright primrose yellow flowers are shaped like those of a forget-me-not with spreading, rounded lobes and a short, broad tube. They measure about an inch in diameter and are borne in large terminal, secund spikes usually in the month of May.

It is a native of Armenia and seems to prefer a good friable loam when grown in the border but it must be well-drained and the position chosen for its cultivation should be a warm one in full sun. It is also a fine rock garden subject and thrives in a dry wall. Propagation is usually by root and stem cuttings. *Arnebia cornuta* is a handsome annual species which grows to a height of from $1\frac{1}{2}$ to 2 feet and bears erect, leafy racemes of deep yellow flowers, blotched with brown. It should be raised in heat and planted out in May.

ARTEMISIA LACTIFLORA *(Compositae)* [PLATE 5]

The genus Artemisia contains but few species of any horticultural value as decorative garden plants. The species under consideration is one of the exceptions to this rule, for it is a most valuable border perennial and when in full bloom always attracts attention. It has erect, stiff, deeply grooved, smooth stems from 4 to 5 feet tall, clothed with large, dark green pinnate leaves with ovate-lance-shaped, lobed and coarsely toothed leaflets. The leaves on the upper part of the stems are narrower and usually undivided. The inflorescence is composed of innumerable creamy or milk-white flowers about an $\frac{1}{8}$ of an inch in diameter, borne in crowded spikes springing from the leaf-axils. The whole inflorescence forms a panicle 1 to 2 feet in length.

The flowers are produced over a considerable period extending from July to November and the panicles of flowers last well when cut and placed in water, also they are sweetly scented. This artemisia is a native of western China and is also found in the Himalaya. It is quite hardy and thrives in a good, friable loam in the sun or in partial shade. Increase is by division in the spring and also by seeds. In *Artemisia sericea* we have one of the very best of the silvery-leaved plants in cultivation. It grows to a height of 6 inches and has greenish flowers. A very old fashioned species known as Southernwood, of shrubby habit with very finely divided fragrant foliage is not seen as frequently as it used to be.

ASCLEPIAS TUBEROSA (Asclepiadaceae) [PLATE 5]

One occasionally sees a specimen of this handsome herbaceous perennial in suburban gardens, but not nearly so frequently as its merits as a decorative plant deserve, considering that it has been in cultivation in this country since 1690. When planted close together and in full flower this Swallow-wort is a most arresting sight. It is a native of eastern north America and is considered by some horticulturists to be a difficult plant to establish, but be this as it may, when this is once accomplished it will thrive for years and grace the border with its heads of flaming blossoms.

As its specific name implies it has a tuberous root-stock and erect stems from $1\frac{1}{2}$ to 2 feet tall, clothed with rather long oblong-lance-shaped very shortly stalked, dark green, pointed leaves, frequently narrowed to a pointed base. The brilliant orange coloured flowers are borne in terminal umbels $1\frac{1}{2}$ to 2 inches in diameter on the apex of the branches and are produced from July to September. The blossoms have incurved lobes a little over $\frac{1}{2}$ inch long. This species should be given a sheltered sunny position in a dry well-drained spot and planted in a compost mainly composed of peat and sand. In cold localities it is advisable to protect the roots with a covering of ashes in the winter. The Swallow-worts are propagated by seeds sown under glass in the spring or when ripe, also by division in the spring.

AZARA MICROPHYLLA (Flacourtiaceae) [PLATE 5]

The azaras are evergreen trees and shrubs, natives of the temperate regions of South America. The majority are too tender for cultivation in cold exposed districts, even when given the shelter of a wall and are apt to be badly cut if not killed outright in severe winters. *Azara microphylla* is the only species that is definitely hardy in this country and will endure periods of severe frost quite unscathed if given a position where the early morning sun does not reach it in winter and spring. In its native habitat in Chile it is an elegant tree from 30 to 40 feet high, but here it is rarely more than a leafy shrub up to 15 feet tall and flowers freely when only 3 to 4 feet high.

It is rather stiff in habit, with erect and spreading branches, thick clothed with small, shining, dark green leaves, usually margined with small teeth. The leaves are densely arranged on the slender branches in two opposite rows, and thus resemble the fronds of a fern or palm. The inflorescence consists of a cluster of stamens with bright yellow anthers, subtended by green sepals, the petals being obsolete. The flowers are vanilla scented and are borne in clusters in the leaf-axils from February to April, and are usually followed by a crop of small bright red or orange berries. The azaras need a compost of good, light loam and leaf-soil and are increased by cuttings and seeds.

BERBERIDOPSIS CORALLINA (*Flacourtiaceae*) [PLATE 5]
The Coral Plant, as this lovely climbing shrub is called, is usually considered too tender for outdoor cultivation except in the maritime counties of south-western England and western Scotland. It has however been grown with complete success on west and even east and north walls, sheltered from hot sun and protected from searing winds in many parts of Great Britain even as far north as north-eastern Scotland. It is evergreen and twines around any support it may be given to a height of 10 to 20 feet.

The very slender, branching stems are clothed with alternate, leathery, ovate or heart-shaped, medium-sized leaves, armed with sharp spines on their margins and also on their tips; they are of a deep shining green above and greyish below. The brightly tinted blossoms are borne singly or in clusters in the leaf-axils on the ends of the shoots forming leafy racemes composed of 6 to 15 flowers. The flower varies from coral red to deep scarlet and resembles a miniature rose in shape and measures about $\frac{1}{2}$ inch wide. The flowers are borne on long, pendant red stalks and make their appearance in July, August and September. It is a native of southern Chile, inhabiting thin woodlands and thrives here in a lime-free compost of loam, peat and leaf-soil and is increased by layers, cuttings and seeds.

BERBERIS CALLIANTHA (*Berberidaceae*) [PLATE 5]
This very desirable barberry possesses larger flowers than those of any other species in cultivation, and owing to its dwarf habit is eminently suitable for the decoration of small gardens. It is a native of south-eastern Tibet, and is found in mountainous districts at 8,000 feet above sea-level. It has been in cultivation for about thirty-five years and is quite hardy. In a not too-rich soil and in an open situation it forms a more or less compact bush from 2 to 3 feet tall.

The rather slender brown branches are clothed with elliptic or oblong-oval, spiny margined, medium sized leaves of a dark shining green above and waxy white beneath. The flowers are about one inch in diameter and are composed of a number of egg-shaped or rounded, entire or cleft segments of a lemon-yellow colour and are similar in shape to those of our common barberry. They are borne in twos and threes on slender, curved stalks, springing from the leaf-axils on the branches and branchlets, in

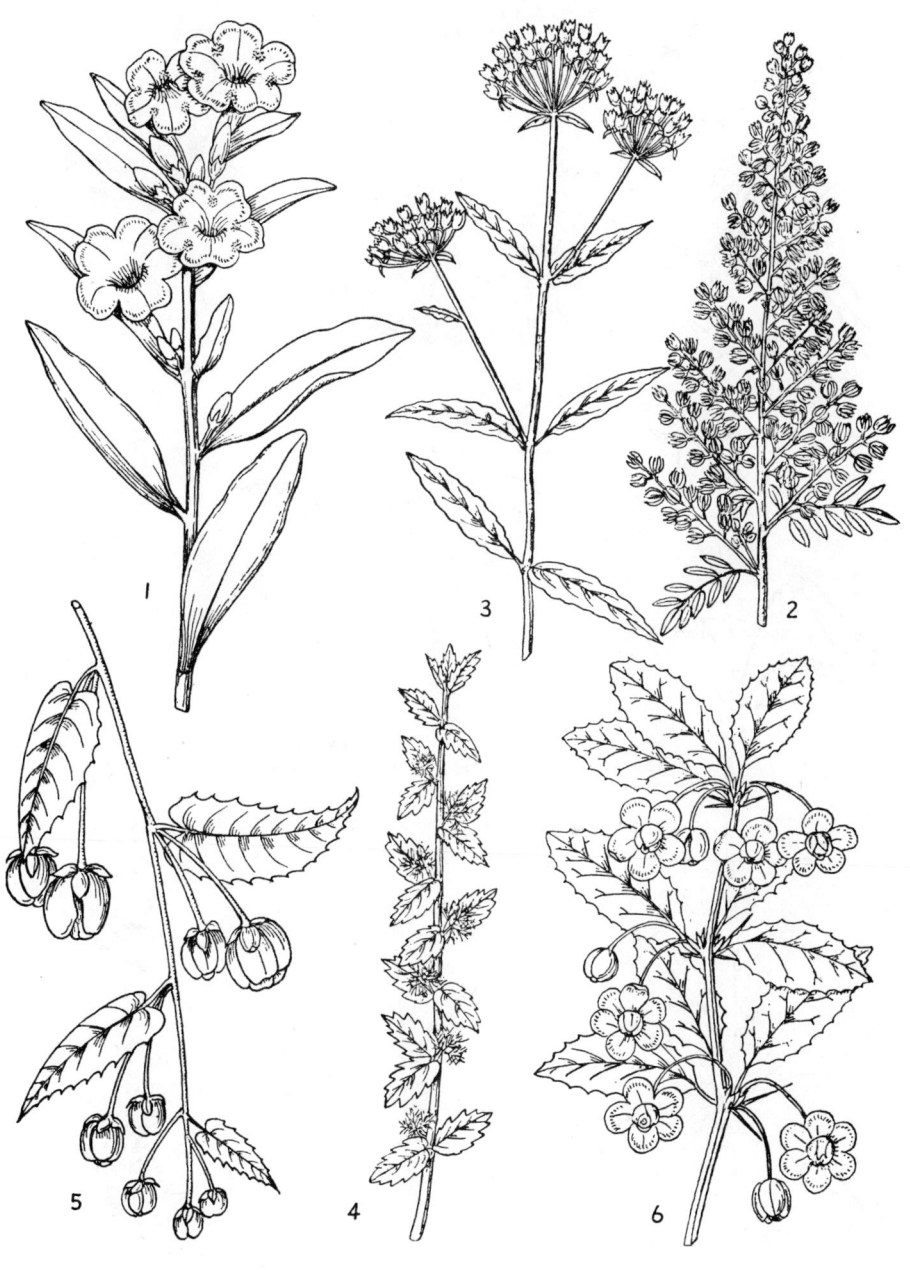

PLATE 5

1. *Arnebia echioides* 2. *Artemisia lactiflora* 3. *Asclepias tuberosa*
4. *Azara microphylla* 5. *Berberidopsis corallina* 6. *Berberis calliantha*

PLATE 6

1. *Berberis linearifolia*   2. *Bruckenthalia spiculifolia*   3. *Buddleia crispa*
4. *Calandrinia umbellata*   5. *Calceolaria polyrrhiza*   6. *Callirhoe involucrata*

May and June in normal years. The conspicuous ovoid fruits measure about ½ inch in length. They are black and are covered with an attractive greyish bloom and remain on the bushes for a long time after ripening. Like most barberries it thrives in light loam in an open position and is increased by seeds and by cuttings of firm young shoots taken in July.

BERBERIS LINEARIFOLIA [PLATE 6]

There is no doubt that this Chilean Barberry is the finest of all the evergreen species in cultivation with regard to its foliage and flowers but its habit perhaps leaves something to be desired. It is indeed a very beautiful sight in April and May when in full flower, with its wand-like branches wreathed in large, apricot-coloured blossoms. In addition to Chile it is also found in moist woodlands in Argentine.

Berberis linearifolia is hardy in most localities in this country and is a loose, more or less erect shrub from 4 to 8 feet tall of somewhat sparse habit. Its slender branches are clothed with medium-sized, broadly linear, usually entire, deep, rich green leaves, terminating in a sharp spine. The yellow flowers are produced in clusters, or corymbs, composed of 4 to 6 blossoms on rather long red stalks. They are nearly ¾ inch in diameter when fully open and are of a rich shade of orange in the centre. In most seasons these are followed by a goodly crop of black, ovoid fruits about ½ inch long, covered with a whitish bloom, and offer a ready means of increase although the flowers of seedlings frequently vary in colour. It thrives in well-drained loam and should have shelter from cutting winds. There is a natural hybrid between this species and *B. darwinii* in cultivation termed *B. lologensis*.

BERBERIS PRATTII

The majority of the vast number of barberries have black or blue-black fruits, usually with a white bloom on them. Of the several species with red or pink fruits *B. wilsoniae* is probably the one most frequently cultivated for although its berries are small they are very freely produced.

Berberis prattii has larger fruits than any of the other species in which they are pink or red, and is one of the most decorative barberries in cultivation. In a not too rich soil it reaches a maximum height of 7 to 8 feet. The spreading, grooved branches are clothed with medium-sized, egg-shaped or oblong leaves, beautifully reticulated and furnished on each side with from 3 to 8 spiny teeth. The leaves are yellowish-green on the upper surface and of an attractive glaucous green beneath and assume brilliant tints before they fall in the autumn. The yellow, more or less globular flowers measure about ⅜ inch wide and are borne in crowded panicles or corymbs 3 to 6 inches long, composed of 20 to 50 flowers which are produced in June. The ovoid, bright pink or coral red fruits measure up to ½ inch in length and are borne very freely and remain decorative for a long time.

This desirable species is a native of south-western China and has been in cultivation for about sixty years. Like most of the barberries it does not seem particular as to soil and is easily increased by seeds.

BRUCKENTHALIA SPICULIFOLIA *(Ericaceae)* [PLATE 6]

Personally I am not very enamoured of many of the heath-like dwarf shrubs except perhaps *Erica carnea* for the sake of its winter flowers and Maw's variety of *E. ciliaris*. There is a sameness about their habit of growth and the colour of their flowers, which if not white have a lot too much purple in them for my liking. However many of the garden forms have become very popular in gardens with a peaty, lime-free soil.

Bruckenthalia spiculifolia is the sole member of its genus and forms a spreading evergreen cushion of bright green verdure from which many slender flowering stems rise to a height of 4 to 6 inches. They are furnished with crowded, erect or spreading, very small linear, softly ciliate leaves dotted with small glands. Unlike those of most of the genus Erica the flowers are open bell-shaped, not urn-shaped. They have 4, rounded lobes and are about ⅛ inch long, varying in colour from bluish-pink to magenta-pink and the calyx is also pale pink. They are borne in crowded terminal racemes from May to July. The protruding pink stamens and style add to the attractiveness of the blossoms. It is quite hardy and is a native of south-eastern Europe and Armenia and thrives in a light soil or peat in situations where most other members of the heath family flourish. It is easily increased by the separation of a part of its growth in the spring.

BUDDLEIA CRISPA *(Loganiaceae)* [PLATE 6]

Of all the buddleias in cultivation in this country, the above species is in my opinion the most suitable for gardens of limited extent. A thriving specimen in full flower is a very charming sight, quite unfamiliar to many flower lovers. Moreover, it covers itself with great panicles of exquisite blossom when only 5 to 6 feet high. It ranges from Afghanistan through the Himalayas to China and is as hardy as the better known *B. globosa*.

It is a loose-growing, sparsely branched shrub, eventually reaching a maximum height of 12 feet. The square branches and branchlets are downy with rust coloured or pale hairs when young. They are clothed with rather long, lance-shaped or ovate-oblong leaves, heart-shaped at the base, pointed and strongly toothed. The dainty flowers are produced in terminal and lateral racemes from 4 to 7 inches long, the whole inflorescence forming a pyramidal panicle 1 to 2 feet long. The corolla is 4-lobed, $\frac{3}{8}$ to $\frac{1}{2}$ inch wide and of a beautiful shade of pale lilac, inclined to pink, with the mouth of its tube honey-yellow or white. In addition to their beauty the flowers are very fragrant.

This species sometimes commences to flower early in the year but is usually at its best in July and August. All the buddleias thrive in good, light loam and this species should, if possible, be planted in the shelter of a west wall. It is increased by layers, cuttings and seeds.

BUDDLEIA FALLOWIANA

As the flowers of this Buddleia are borne on the young growths, the previous season's branches can be cut down to the base in spring, thus enabling this elegant species to be grown in a comparatively restricted space, for if the previous season's branches are allowed to remain the bush may eventually reach a height of 12 feet.

Buddleia fallowiana is a native of China and was apparently introduced into cultivation in this country in 1906. It is of more or less erect habit, with slender branches arching over at their tips, clothed with long lance-shaped leaves drawn out into a long point and wedge-shaped at the base. Both surfaces are clothed with a silvery pubescence; that on the under surface being thick and felt-like and almost white. The elegant, very fragrant flowers are of a soft lavender tint with a yellow eye and are borne in a terminal panicle up to 15 inches in length, in dense, crowded clusters. The corolla measures about $\frac{3}{8}$ inch across and the tube is clothed with a white pubescence outside. When this shrub is cut down in early spring the flowers are produced on the new growths from August to October.

Another desirable species named *B. alternifolia* is seen now and again in suburban gardens. It is up to 20 feet high, with slender, arching branches, furnished with very small leaves with a dense cluster of very fragrant lilac-purple blossoms in their axils. All the above mentioned species are deciduous.

CALANDRINIA UMBELLATA (*Portulacaceae*) [PLATE 6]

I must confess to a predilection for plants whose flowers are intensely coloured and even admire those that are of a violent magenta, which usually clash with the flowers of every other plant in their vicinity, except of course those with white blossoms. These are a perfect background for their fiery flowers. *Calandrinia umbellata* is one of my favourites with brilliantly tinted flowers. Unfortunately it is only in hot, dry, sunny summers that it develops its full beauty, for the flowers remain closed in dull weather and are then of course very much less attractive. It is a true perennial in its native countries, but here is frequently of biennial or annual duration only.

The rather stout, fleshy root-stock produces several succulent trailing stems from 6 to 9 inches long, sparsely clothed with linear, fleshy, pointed, hairy leaves. The brilliant magenta-crimson blossoms measure about ¾ inch across when fully expanded and are borne in many-flowered corymbs, in summer or autumn, according to whether the seeds are sown under glass and the resulting seedlings are planted out when all danger of frost has passed, or whether they are sown in the open air in May where the plants are to bloom. The plant likes a hot, dry, sunny position and should be given a poor, gritty soil. In localities which normally have low sunshine records it is not a success. It is a native of Peru and Chile and is at its best when treated as a half-hardy annual.

CALCEOLARIA POLYRRHIZA (*Scrophulariaceae*)   [PLATE 6]
The genus Calceolaria is a quite extensive one and with the exception of a solitary species endemic to New Zealand, all are natives of the temperate regions of South America. Unfortunately a few only are sufficiently hardy to withstand the rigours of one of our severe winters, although several of the herbaceous perennial species will survive if they are given the protection of a hand-light. The genus comprises annuals, biennials, perennial herbs and shrubby species, many of which are very decorative.

The species under consideration is a perennial and is quite hardy. It is a native of southern Chile and Patagonia. In cultivation it forms low, close tufts or carpets of rich green foliage, springing from nodes on the widely creeping roots. The hairy, lance-shaped leaves are of medium size and taper to a stalk below. The flower-stem reaches a height of from 4 to 6 inches and bears from 1 to 5 quaint baggy blossoms of a canary yellow, frequently spotted with purple. They are freely produced from June to August. It is not particular as to soil, but does well in peat, leaf-soil and sand. It is imperative that the plant should be well supplied with water when it is in growth. Increase is by division and seeds. *Calceolaria tenella* is a very charming mat-forming species with small leaves and numerous small, golden yellow flowers spotted with red. It should be given the same cultural conditions as the preceding species.

CALLIRHOE INVOLUCRATA (*Malvaceae*)   [PLATE 6]
Although this brilliant-flowered member of the mallow family is fre-

quently considered to be unsuitable for cultivation in the colder parts of this country, which may be true after a sequence of wet, sunless summers, under normal conditions if it is provided with a well-drained position where it will be baked by all the sunshine available it will thrust up its long stems in the spring unfailingly for several years. It is not normally however a long-lived plant. It is a native of the central States of U.S.A. where it is known as the Buffalo Rose.

In cultivation it is a procumbent herbaceous perennial with slender stems, clothed with mallow-like leaves, divided almost to the base into from 3 to 5, narrowly lance-shaped lobes, each margined with from 3 to 5 teeth. The mallow-shaped, vivid magenta-crimson blossoms measure about 2 inches in diameter and are borne in loose panicles on the ends of the branches and branchlets in July and August. It is usually increased by seeds and must be grown in light stony soil in full sun to ensure its successful cultivation.

The annual species, *Callirhoe pedata*, is very decorative and grows to a height of 2 to 3 feet. It has numerous 3- to 7-lobed attractive leaves and panicles of cherry-red flowers, produced in August and September. The seeds should be sown under glass if possible in March or April to obtain as early a display of blossom as possible. It is a native of U.S.A. and is a useful plant for a hot, dry spot.

CAMASSIA LEICHTLINII (*Liliaceae*) [PLATE 7]

All the camassias are natives of western North America and have edible bulbs. That of *C. quamash*—formerly more familiar under the name of *C. esculenta*—was collected by the North American Indians and stored for winter use, under the Indian name of Quamash, forming a considerable part of their food. In their native habitat the camassias cover the moist meadows with their spikes of blue and white flowers in much the same manner as our native wild hyacinths do our woodlands. All are desirable plants for the herbaceous border and deserve to be much more widely cultivated than they are now.

Camassia leichtlinii is perhaps the best of the several species for garden decoration, but care should be taken to secure forms with the most richly coloured flowers as the plant is very variable in this respect. The large, more or less globose bulb produces long, broadly linear, pointed leaves, from the centre of which the stout flower stem rises to a height of 3 to 4 feet. It bears a long, loose spike of starry, 6-petaled flowers, each $1\frac{1}{2}$ inch across, varying from white and cream to azure blue and purple. The yellow or orange anthers add to the beauty of the flowers. This species flowers in

July and is perfectly hardy. The bulbs should be planted at least 3 inches deep and should be left undisturbed. An open situation and a moist, rather heavy loam gives the best results. Camassias are usually propagated by seeds as they rarely produce offsets.

CAMELLIA PITARDII (*Theaceae*) [PLATE 7]
There are three outstanding species of Camellia that should be afforded a position in every garden where conditions with regard to soil, etc., are suitable. In addition to the above mentioned species they are *C. reticulata* and *C. saluenensis*.

Camellia pitardii was discovered on chalky formations in south-western China and was introduced into this country in 1903. It is a sparsely branched evergreen shrub from 3 to 5 feet tall when growing naturally, but will grow much taller when trained on a wall. It has medium-sized, leathery, lance-shaped, pointed, finely serrate, dark green, leaves and very beautiful flowers borne on short stalks on the ends of the branches and in the leaf-axils in the spring. The flower measures from $3\frac{1}{2}$ to 4 inches in diameter and is of a lovely blush pink, with recurving petals, forming a trumpet-shaped corolla.

Camellia reticulata is the finest of all the camellias, but unfortunately is the most tender, although there are some fine specimens in the open air in the west country. It has the usual habit of growth of the camellias, but its glorious semi-double flowers are of a rich rose colour and sometimes measure as much as 6 inches wide.

The flowers of *Camellia saluenensis* much resemble those of the preceding species but are smaller and are of the same exquisite pink as those of the Dog Rose. It is quite hardy and like all the camellias needs partial shade, a peaty soil and plenty of water in dry weather. Increase is by seeds and cuttings.

CAMPANULA GARGANICA (*Campanulaceae*)
Campanula garganica is a most delightful little Italian species with all the attributes of the perfect rock garden plant and is even attractive in winter when its low mound of bright green foliage emerges from a mantle of melting snow, none the worse for its chilly experience. I have several plants of this campanula in my garden which have been in the same position for the past twelve years, never failing to flower profusely, and pictures of perfect health, each a foot or more across. They are growing in a raised bed in company with the somewhat invasive *Sedum spathulatum* with which they seem to agree very well. The secret of their longevity is the

poor fare that my hungry soil provides. Most authorities state that this charming little campanula should be propagated frequently in order to retain it in cultivation.

It is of tufted habit with small kidney-shaped basal leaves and trailing stems 2 to 3 inches long, clothed with smaller heart-shaped leaves. Both types of leaves are margined with rounded teeth. The dainty flowers are produced in clusters in the leaf-axils forming a cloud of pale blue, white-centred starry blossoms over $\frac{1}{2}$ inch across; they are produced in June and July but in some seasons continue to appear well into September. Propagation is by seeds and division in the spring. There is a hairy variety named *C. g. hirsuta* which is very beautiful, and also a pure white form.

CAMPANULA LACTIFLORA

In comparison with the desirable alpine and rock garden bellflowers, those of outstanding merit for cultivation in the herbaceous border are but few in number. Such species as *C. latifolia* and *C. persicifolia* are old favourites and are still popular in their many handsome garden forms. Although equally as decorative as the two above mentioned bellflowers, *Campanula lactiflora* is only rarely seen. It must be admitted that in rich soil and under conditions to its liking it has a strong tendency to encroach on other plants with which it is growing and is said by some to be more fitted for the wild garden than a select herbaceous border. Nevertheless, it is a grand bellflower and if it is dug up every two or three years and replanted in light, sandy soil its vigour will be kept in check without loss of floral beauty.

It is a perennial with a deeply buried root-system and erect, branching stems from 3 to 6 feet tall, clothed with fairly long ovate-lance-shaped, stalkless, sharply toothed leaves. The large flowers are borne in huge panicles with as many as a hundred blossoms open at one time. The corolla is open bell-shaped, deeply lobed and measures about $1\frac{1}{2}$ inch across its lobes, and is normally of a whitish-blue or mauvey-blue with a white base. There is a pink form and also a deep blue one. It is a native of the Caucasus and flowers from July to September and is useful as a cut flower.

CAMPANULA TOMMASINIANA [PLATE 7]

In habit this very graceful bellflower differs considerably from many of the dwarf species, being more compact and not invasive. It is not difficult to cultivate and should be more frequently seen in small gardens. Like several of our treasured rock-garden bellflowers it is a native of Italy and inhabits the mountains of Istaria; it is quite hardy.

It is a tufted perennial, without the creeping roots which many otherwise desirable alpine species possess. The rather small, linear-lance-shaped leaves taper to a slender point and are toothed on their margins. Several more or less leafy flower stems spring from amongst the tuft of leaves to a height of 6 to 12 inches. Each bears on its upper half a crowded cyme composed of very many pale blue blossoms. Each flower measures about ¾ inch long and has a slender tube which expands at the mouth into 5, small, ovate-triangular lobes. The flowers are produced in such profusion that their weight causes the flower-stem to curve over at the top. This species commences to open its flowers in July and continues to do so until September. It is not particular as to soil and will thrive in sun or semi-shade. Increase is usually by seeds.

Campanula pulla from the Styrian Alps is a most lovely dwarf species which produces a profusion of violet bells singly, on 3 to 6 inch stems, springing from a mat of shining foliage. It needs a limy soil and semi-shade for its well-being.

CAMPANULA ZOYSII [PLATE 7]

In the shape of its flowers this little gem is quite unique for no other bell-flower has a corolla in any way approaching them in form. It fulfills the specification for the perfect alpine plant, for its flowers are normally much larger than its leaves and it remains close and compact throughout its existence although its slender root-stock produces short underground stems bearing leaf-buds at their tips which slowly add to the diameter of the plant. It is a native of central Europe being found in rocky ground on the Alps of Carinthia and Styria up to 9,000 feet above sea-level.

In poor limy soil with plenty of grit it forms close, flat rosettes of oval or almost orbicular entire leaves of a rather deep green colour. A well developed rosette will produce as many as a dozen more or less erect, rather stiff stems from 2 to 4 inches high, each bearing from 2 to 4 very quaint yet beautiful pale blue-purple flowers. The corolla has an inflated tube, narrowed and constricted at the throat where it again expands into 5, pointed lobes, which are half closed over the hairy throat. They commence to open in early June and continue to do so throughout July into August. This species should be given a well-drained position in full sun and is increased by seeds, and also by detaching the rooted juvenile rosettes from the parent plant. Slugs are very fond of this species as they are of many choice campanulas.

CAMPSIS RADICANS (*Bignoniaceae*) [PLATE 7]

This magnificent climbing shrub is one of the most gorgeous sights

PLATE 7

1. *Camassia leichtlinii* 2. *Camellia pitardii* 3. *Campanula tommasiniana*
4. *Campanula zoysii* 5. *Campsis radicans*
6. *Caragana aurantiaca var. pygmaea*

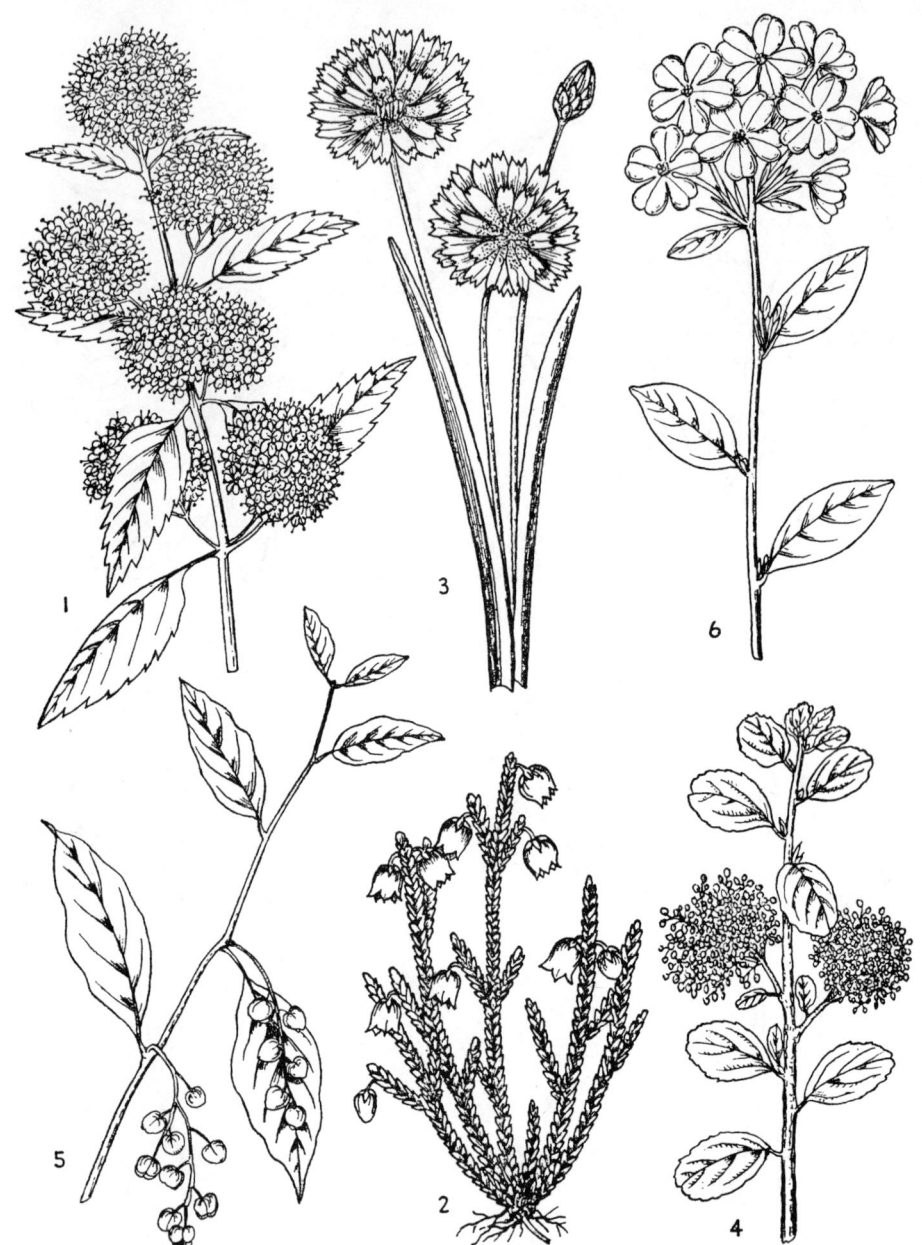

PLATE 8

1. *Caryopteris incana* 2. *Cassiope fastigiata* 3. *Catananche caerulea*
4. *Ceanothus × veitchianus* 5. *Celastrus scandens*
6. *Ceratostigma willmottianum*

imaginable when draping a wall with its handsome foliage and brilliant blossoms. It is a native of south-eastern U.S.A. and has been in cultivation in this country for well over three hundred years. Under good cultural conditions the branching stem will reach a height of 40 to 50 feet and cover a considerable space.

The dark green, rather large, pinnate leaves are composed of 7 to 11 lance-shaped, long-pointed, coarsely toothed leaflets. The flowers which are produced in clusters of from 6 to 10 at the tips of the current year's growths, during the months of August and September, have a trumpet-shaped tube about 3 inches long, expanding at the mouth into 5, rounded lobes, forming a corolla $1\frac{1}{2}$ inch in diameter. The flowers are of a beautiful orange-scarlet, gradually passing into clear orange at the base.

To flower this remarkably beautiful plant, which climbs by means of its aerial roots in the same manner as the ivy, it must be planted at the base of a south wall and allowed to climb unchecked. Its root-run should be somewhat restricted as this is conducive to the production of flowers. The branches should be pruned back to 2 to 3 buds in March or April in order to produce the long shoots which will bear the flowers later on. It needs a good light loam and a restricted root-run to give of its best. Increase is by layers and cuttings. This species is also sometimes known as *Bignonia radicans*.

CARAGANA AURANTIACA (*Leguminosae*) [PLATE 7]

Considering how suitable these very desirable deciduous shrubs are for small gardens it is puzzling to discover the reason why one never sees them, although such species as *C. arborescens* and *C. frutescens* have been in cultivation for over two centuries. All are perfectly hardy and range from central Asia through Tibet to China. The species and its variety described below are in my opinion the most decorative of the more dwarf species. An unshaded position in full sun and poor, stony soil suits them best.

Caragana aurantiaca is a native of central Asia and is a very delightful little shrub. It is from 4 to 5 feet tall, rather sparsely furnished with long, slender, arching branches, quite thickly clothed with small, attractive leaves, formed of two pairs of linear leaflets. The lovely orange-yellow pea-flower blossoms measure about an inch in length and are pendant on short stalks springing from the leaf-axils. They are produced in May and are sometimes followed by pods up to $1\frac{1}{2}$ inch long.

The variety *pygmaea* is from 1 to 4 feet high and has slender, pendulous branches, the lowermost becoming prostrate. The leaves are composed of two pairs of egg-shaped, pointed leaflets with spiny stipules. The beautiful bright yellow flowers, which measure 1 inch in length, are pendulous on short stalks all along the slender branches and are very freely produced. The caraganas are propagated by layers, cuttings and seeds which should be sown singly in small pots.

CARYOPTERIS INCANA (*Verbenaceae*) [PLATE 8]
This attractive member of the verbena family is one of a number of desirable shrubs, which although killed to the ground level in severe winters, will invariably push up new growths from below ground when warmer weather comes. That this should happen to shrubs which flower on their young wood is not altogether undesirable where space is limited, as it keeps the plants within bounds and at the same time does not deprive us of their flowers.

Normally *Caryopteris incana* is an evergreen bush of open, sparsely branched habit, up to 5 feet tall. The stems and under-surface of the leaves being clothed with grey, felted hairs gives the whole plant a silvery appearance. The medium-sized leaves which are opposite and not very numerous, are ovate, coarsely toothed and pointed. The bright violet-blue flowers are borne in rounded clusters in the leaf-axils on the upper parts of the terminal and lateral branches during September and October. The flower has a short tube, which is enlarged upwards and is divided at its mouth into 5 lobes; the upper are ovate and are smaller than the spoon-shaped lower one. *C. incana*, formerly known as *C. mastacanthus*, is a native of China and Japan and has been in cultivation in this country for well over one hundred years.

The hybrid *C.* × *clandonensis* has bright blue flowers and is very decorative. All these elegant autumn-flowering shrubs flourish in a hot, sunny position, in light, loamy soil and are increased by cuttings taken with a heel and inserted in a sand frame.

CASSIOPE FASTIGIATA (*Ericaceae*) [PLATE 8]
Considering that this little member of the heath family was introduced into this country over a hundred years ago, it is remarkable that one so rarely sees it in amateurs' alpine gardens, for it is not very exacting with regard to its requirements in cultivation, has an attractive and unusual habit of growth, and is also quite hardy. It is a native of the Himalaya, where it is found in damp moorlands, at 13,000 feet above sea-level and usually commences to flower in this country in May.

In an open position it forms an evergreen, much branched shrub, rarely more than 12 inches high, of spreading, erect habit. The branches and branchlets are completely hidden by very small, scale-like, deep green leaves, fringed with white hairs. The exquisite, pure white, bell-shaped flowers, wide-mouthed and shallowly cleft into 4 to 5 lobes at their tips, measure from ⅜ to ½ inch across and are borne in clusters, near the tips of the shoots, to the number of 3 to 6 on rather short, down-curved stalks.

Another beautiful species—*C. stelleriana*—forms dense mats of heath-like foliage, from amongst which numerous erect stems spring to a height of not more than 3 inches, each bearing a terminal pure white flower similar to that of the preceding cassiope. It is a native of British Columbia and Alaska. Both these plants should be grown in a cool, half-shady position in peat, leaf-soil and sand, with underground moisture if possible. Increase is by seeds.

CATANANCHE CAERULEA (*Compositae*) [PLATE 8]
It would be difficult to name a more floriferous plant and one whose flowers are more useful for cutting than those of this attractive hardy herbaceous perennial. Its flowers remain decorative for a long period and being semi-everlasting can be dried for winter decorations. It is a native of southern Europe and is common in Greece where it was used for making love potions by the women of ancient Greece; hence the Greek vernacular name for this plant of Cupidone. It is rather remarkable that such a useful plant is not more frequently seen in suburban gardens.

The many fibrous roots of this species produce a large, dense tuft or clump of long, narrowly lance-shaped, pointed, more or less erect, deep yellowish green, slightly hoary leaves and very numerous, erect, wiry, naked flower-stems from 2 to 3 feet long, according to the richness of the soil in which the plant is growing. Each flower-stem bears a solitary flower-head from 1½ to 2 inches in diameter, composed of between 20 to 30 ray-florets which are blunt and finely toothed at the apex. They are dark or lavender blue with a maroon-purple base. The flower-head is surrounded by a series of chaff-like coloured scales. It flowers throughout the summer months and has two varieties: *alba* and *bicolor*. It is not particular as to soil but needs full sun and is increased by division and seeds.

CEANOTHUS × VEITCHIANUS (*Rhamnaceae*) [PLATE 8]
All the species, hybrids and garden forms of Ceanothus are worth cultivating in gardens where space is not restricted but where there is room for only one of these beautiful shrubs my choice would be *Ceanothus × veit-*

chianus, for it has attractive foliage, beautifully coloured flowers and is one of the hardiest of these delightful Californian shrubs. It has a rather curious history. It was collected by W. Lobb in northern California when on a plant hunting expedition for Messrs J. Veitch & Son over one hundred years ago and has apparently never been seen in a wild state since it was first collected. It is believed to be a natural hybrid between *C. rigidus* and *C. thyrsiflorus*.

In an open situation it forms an evergreen, spreading bush from 8 to 10 feet high, furnished with numerous, rather small, egg-shaped or wedge-shaped leaves of a bright glossy green and greyish-green beneath. The beautiful, 5-petaled, rich, vivid blue flowers, each measuring about a $\frac{1}{4}$ inch across, are borne in crowded heads from $1\frac{1}{2}$ to 2 inches long in March and April, in great abundance when the shrub is well-established. It needs a sunny position in a well-drained soil and even flourishes in a poor stony one. In bleak localities it should have the protection of a wall and is propagated by cuttings.

CELASTRUS SCANDENS (*Celastraceae*) [PLATE 8]

It may not be possible to find room for this very handsome climber in gardens of very limited area, especially as normally the flowers are either male or female and are produced on separate plants; thus, in order to obtain a crop of fruits, which are the decorative part of the plant (the flowers are insignificant), it is necessary to grow a male plant near the female. However, a form has been recently offered in which both male and female flowers are found on the same plant. This may solve the space problem.

C. scandens and *C. orbiculatus* are two of the most decorative climbers we have when in full fruit in the autumn. They are closely allied to our native spindle tree and their fruits are similar in shape. An old decrepit tree draped with that grand vine, *Vitis coignetiae*, and a flourishing specimen of *C. scandens* should be a fine blending of autumn colouring.

C. scandens is a native of U.S.A. and Canada and was introduced into this country in 1736, but is rarely seen outside botanical gardens and the larger private gardens where such plants have room to develop. It is a vigorous climbing shrub, with slender stems and branches 20 to 30 feet long, clothed with medium-sized, ovate, sharply pointed, saw-toothed, rich green leaves. The orange coloured, 3- to 5-valved fruit, which is slightly smaller than that of the spindle tree, splits open when ripe and exposes the scarlet seeds. This climber is not particular as to soil and is increased by layers and seeds.

CERATOSTIGMA WILLMOTTIANUM
(*Plumbaginaceae*) [PLATE 8]
This very beautiful Chinese shrub is ideal for the decoration of the amateur's garden, for it is elegant in habit and foliage and lovely in flower. Moreover, it produces its charming blossoms over a long period and has the same desirable habit as our hardy fuchsias, for although like them it may be cut to the base in severe winters it will break from the ground in the spring and flower abundantly in the autumn of the same season, as the flowers are borne on the young wood.

When in a thriving condition it forms a leafy, rounded bush from 2 to 4 feet tall, with slender, rather zig-zag, dull crimson branches and branchlets. The medium sized leaves are of rather an unusual shape; they are lance-shaped, blunt at the apex, and are dilated above the middle into two broadly triangular lobes. They are of a rich green and are frequently suffused with crimson later in the season. At first sight the lovely flowers resemble those of a phlox. They measure from $\frac{1}{2}$ to $\frac{3}{4}$ inch across and are composed of 5 wedge-shaped, horizontal azure or ultramarine petals and are borne in compact, terminal clusters, opening in succession from early July to September and at times the greater part of October. This species is at its best in well-drained, light loam but will also thrive in one of a heavier nature provided it is not water-logged in the winter, and is usually propagated by cuttings, taken in late summer and struck in a sand-frame.

CERCIS SILIQUASTRUM (*Leguminosae*) [PLATE 9]
The common name of Judas Tree has been given to this remarkable and beautiful tree on account of the superstition that Judas Iscariot committed suicide by hanging himself on a branch of one of these trees. There are many trees native in Asia Minor which would have served his purpose equally well, although the branching habit of the Judas Tree is well adapted for that method of self-destruction.

In the tropics there are a considerable number of trees which normally produce their flowers on their trunks and larger branches such as the Cocoa Tree for instance, but the Judas Tree is one of the very few in the temperate regions that have this habit. It was introduced into this country nearly four hundred years ago, but is far from common. It is deciduous and has a comparatively short trunk and a head of widely spreading branches, clothed with handsome, medium-sized, deep yellowish-green, somewhat glaucous, rounded leaves, deeply heart-shaped at the base. The pea-shaped, clear purplish-pink flowers are produced before the leaves unfold; they measure from $\frac{1}{2}$ to $\frac{3}{4}$ of an inch long and are produced in clusters of up to half a dozen blossoms in May on the old and new branches as well as the trunk, in very great quantities. The fruit is a flat, rich brown pod 2 to 4 inches long, containing about a dozen seeds, which offer a ready means of increase. The Judas Tree is quite hardy and is a native of southern Europe and south-western Asia and thrives in a well-drained loam in a sheltered, sunny position.

CHIMONANTHUS PRAECOX *(Calycanthaceae)* [PLATE 9]
The Winter Sweet is one of the most difficult shrubs to propagate which may account for its scarcity in suburban gardens. Cuttings are quite hopeless, layers normally take a long time to root if they ever do (the method of layering with the help of hormone powder may be successful, but of this I have had no experience with this shrub), and seedlings take a long time to form flowering plants. Formerly better known as *Chimonanthus fragrans*, this very desirable deciduous shrub is a native of China, from whence it was probably introduced into Japan.

Normally it forms a bush of loose habit from 4 to 10 feet tall. The smooth, brown branchlets are rather sparsely clothed with longish lance-shaped, pointed leaves which commence to expand in April, and are of a deep, rich, lustrous green. The delightfully fragrant flowers are usually very freely borne on the short branchlets in pairs all over the bush, from November to March. As cut flowers they last for a considerable time if their stems are split before they are placed in water. The individual flower is from 1 to 1½ inch wide and is composed of a number of oval, pointed petals of a pale yellow colour, with the inner ones broadly edged with purple or dull red. There are several varieties such as *grandiflorus*, with larger flowers, *luteus* with deeper yellow flowers, minus the purple markings, and *luteus grandiflorus*, with flowers 2 inches across. The type and its varieties should be given the shelter of a west wall and planted in good, light loam, with plenty of moisture in dry weather.

CHIONANTHUS VIRGINICUS *(Oleaceae)* [PLATE 9]
Known as the Fringe Tree in its native country this very beautiful deciduous shrub or small tree does not seem to have become popular in this country, which it well deserves to be, although it has been in cultivation here for well over two hundred years. It is a native of U.S.A. and ranges from Texas, where it is known as the Snow Flower Tree, to Ontario, along the eastern side of North America. Over most of its range it is a small tree from 15 to 30 feet high. In cultivation in this country it is frequently a spreading bush with several stems 10 to 12 feet tall.

FOR YOUR GARDEN 39

The handsome, rich green, narrowly oblong or egg-shaped, large leaves, turn to a pleasing shade of yellow before they fall in the autumn. The elegant flowers are usually 4-petaled, but occasionally 5 or 6 are to be found; they are strap-shaped or linear, from 1 to $1\frac{1}{2}$ inch long, and are white, usually with a small purple spot at the base of each. The blossoms are pleasantly fragrant and are borne in loose, drooping panicles 4 to 8 inches long, springing from the leaf-axils on the preceding year's growths, in June. Like all the members of the olive family to which this plant belongs, its flowers have but 2 stamens. In favourable seasons the flowers are followed by decorative, egg-shaped, dark blue, berry-like fruits about $\frac{1}{4}$ inch long, each contains 2 or 3 seeds which provide the best means of propagation. The Fringe Tree is perfectly hardy and thrives best in a rich, well-drained, but rather heavy loam and is at its best when the preceding summer has been hot and dry.

CHOISYA TERNATA (*Rutaceae*) [PLATE 9]

One occasionally sees a specimen of this remarkably handsome evergreen shrub in suburban gardens, but not nearly so frequently as its sterling merits deserve. Although it is a native of Mexico it is hardy in this country, being found in elevated districts in its native habitat. Here, all it suffers in the London district is a slight browning of the tips of the leaves in hard winters in which drying winds prevail. Even if its flowers were less attractive than they are, there is no doubt that it would still be grown by those who are familiar with it for the sake of its very handsome foliage. It is known as the Mexican Orange-flower and is rather closely related to the orange.

In an open but snug position it forms a dense, rounded bush from 4 to 6 feet tall, occasionally reaching 10 feet. The stout branches and branchlets are clothed with opposite, rich, deep green shining leaves, usually composed of 3, egg-shaped, medium-sized, blunt leaflets, tapering to a stalkless base and are pitted with glands which emit an objectionable odour when the leaflet is bruised. The white, 5-petaled, hawthorn-scented flowers measure from 1 to $1\frac{1}{4}$ inch across and are borne in axillary corymbs during April and May. It thrives in good, light loam and is increased by cuttings.

CLEMATIS MACROPETALA (*Ranunculaceae*) [PLATE 9]

There are several very desirable species of Clematis that one rarely sees in gardens although they have been in cultivation for a considerable number of years. *Clematis macropetala* is one of them. It cannot be claimed that it is a showy plant but should appeal to those who appreciate flowers for their intrinsic beauty apart from their decorative value.

Clematis macropetala is a native of south-eastern Siberia and central China. It is deciduous and is not a rampant grower, being rarely more than 8 feet high. The numerous slender, brown branches are furnished with rich, glossy green leaves, usually composed of 9, stalked, lance-shaped, pointed, coarsely toothed leaflets, arranged in threes. The graceful, delicately tinted flowers measure about 3 inches in diameter and are of an exquisite lavender blue; they are composed of 3 to 4 lance-shaped, pointed sepals and a dozen or more petal-like segments, which give the flowers a double appearance. They are solitary on the tips of long stalks and are produced in May and June.

It should be grown in a sunny, sheltered position in a well-drained calcareous soil with protection to its roots during hard frosts. It is increased by seeds and internodal cuttings. The form *markamii* has lovely, clear pink flowers.

CLEMATIS TANGUTICA

This beautiful deciduous Clematis was formerly considered to be a variety of *C. orientalis*, which is a very much inferior plant, both in the size and colouring of its flowers and also in its foliage. *C. tangutica* is undoubtedly the best of the yellow-flowered species so far introduced into this country. It has been in cultivation for the past sixty years and should be more widely grown than it is. When several years old it may attain a height of 8 to 10 feet with adequate support and is admirable for clothing some decrepit fruit tree that is of but little value and is past bearing a useful crop of fruit. In such a situation it will almost hide its support in elegant glaucous foliage and large deep yellow flowers, in late summer and early autumn.

The leaves are pinnate, with large leaflets which are sometimes 3-lobed and are margined with regular teeth. The flowers, which frequently measure 4 inches in diameter, are nodding and solitary on long stalks which spring from the leaf-axils. They are composed of 4 narrowly ovate sepals from $1\frac{1}{2}$ to 2 inches long, ending in a slender point. The petals are rudimentary and the numerous stamens are yellow. The fruit is long and feathery. This species is a native of China and does not seem particular with regard to soil but like all the members of the genus should have its roots and the lower part of its stems shaded from hot sun. Propagation is by seeds and internodal cuttings.

PLATE 9

1. *Cercis siliquastrum* 2. *Chimonanthus praecox* 3. *Chionanthus virginicus*
4. *Choisya ternata* 5. *Clematis macropetala* 6. *Clerodendron trichotomum*

PLATE 10

1. *Clintonia andrewsiana* 2. *Colchicum speciosum* 3. *Colchicum variegatum*
4. *Commelina tuberosa* 5. *Convolvulus elegantissimus* 6. *Cornus kousa*

CLERODENDRON TRICHOTOMUM

(*Verbenaceae*) [PLATE 9]

Most of the clerodendrons are natives of the tropical regions and are among the most beautiful shrubs cultivated in hot-houses in former years. The contrast in colouring between the inflated calyces and the petals is usually very striking. Unfortunately only two or three are sufficiently hardy to withstand our winter climate if given protection from searing north and east winds. Of the two or three such species *C. trichotomum* is probably the most decorative. It is very essential that the position in which it is planted should be a sheltered one facing west if possible as a stiff frost in the autumn will frequently ruin the blossoms before they are fully open. The reason why a position facing west is preferable is because under such circumstances the sun does not reach the frosted blossoms until the afternoon by which time they should have thawed slowly and are usually quite undamaged.

It is an evergreen or semi-evergreen shrub from 6 to 9 feet tall with sparsely disposed, spreading, fairly stout branches, clothed with large, handsome, ovate, dark green leaves, pointed at the tip and tapering to a stalk below; when gently squeezed they emit a rather pleasant odour. The pure white flowers have maroon or reddish calyces and are borne in large, loose cymes in September and October. This species is a native of Japan and flourishes in a deep, well-drained loam and is increased by cuttings.

CLINTONIA ANDREWSIANA (*Liliaceae*) [PLATE 10]

Many beautiful hardy perennials flourish in damp, shady places and this handsome member of the lily family is one of the best of them. There seems to be about a dozen species of Clintonia, but apparently only two or three are stocked by nurserymen.

Clintonia andrewsiana has a short root-stock with several, thick, shortly creeping roots. The fairly stout, erect, cylindrical flower-stem reaches a height of about 2 feet and is clothed for the lower third of its length with large, handsome, rich green, broadly oblong or oblong-lance-shaped leaves, which become narrower and pointed at the apex. They are stalkless and sheath the stem below. The beautiful rose-pink, bell-shaped flowers measure $\frac{3}{4}$ to 1 inch wide and are produced in April. The perianth has a short, broad tube and recurving, very pointed, ovate-lance-shaped segments and resembles a miniature lily when fully expanded. The blossoms are borne in rounded, many-flowered umbels on the apex of the stem, with a few clusters of flowers, placed at regular intervals lower down. Like those of most of the lily family they last in good condition for some time.

In favourable seasons the flowers are followed by beautiful, oblong, blue berries. This herbaceous perennial is a native of North America and does best in a compost of peat and sand with continually moist conditions during the summer months. Propagation is by division and seeds.

COLCHICUM SPECIOSUM *(Liliaceae)* [PLATE 10]

The colchicums or Meadow Saffrons comprise a considerable number of species, ranging from Europe to the Himalaya and are frequently to be found in millions in the mountain meadows of their native countries like the true crocuses. *Colchicum speciosum var. album* is one of the most beautiful of all the bulbous plants in cultivation and should be given a place in every garden however small. The type and its form *bornmulleri* have beautifully tinted blossoms and differ mainly in the green-tinted tubes of the latter, which has much larger flowers than the type, also they are more richly coloured when mature.

Colchicum speciosum has a very large, long-necked, extremely poisonous bulb or corm, which produces 4 to 6 very large, broadly oblong, rich green leaves. These appear in spring and decay before the flowers are produced in September, from the apex of the corm, between spathe-like bracts. The flower has a slender cylindrical tube 3 to 4 times as long as the floral segments which measure nearly 3 inches in length. In the type they are of a beautiful rosy purple tint and pure white, stained with pale yellow at the base in the variety *album*. *C. speciosum* is a native of the Caucasus, Syria and Persia. *C. variegatum* is a handsome species with large lilac or purple, beautifully checkered blossoms, produced from September to November. The Meadow Saffrons thrive best in a rather heavy soil and are increased by offsets and seeds.

COMMELINA TUBEROSA *(Commelinaceae)* [PLATE 10]

The commelinas very much resemble the better known tradescantias both in habit and flower and are very closely related to them botanically, differing mainly in the fact that the tradescantias have 6 perfect stamens and the commelinas only 3. Some botanists consider that *C. tuberosa* is synonymous with *C. coelestis*; others make them separate species on account of slight differences which are of no horticultural value.

Commelina tuberosa was frequently cultivated in villa gardens in the latter part of the last century but seems to have now quite gone out of fashion. This is a pity as it is a really beautiful plant and although only half-hardy is quite easily accommodated. It is a herbaceous perennial and is a native of Mexico. The tuberous root-stock produces several, more or less erect stems, which reach a height of up to $1\frac{1}{2}$ foot. They are furnished with rather long, oblong-lance-shaped, pointed leaves, sheathing below and fringed on their margins with fine hairs. The beautiful sky-blue, 3-petaled flowers measure about 1 inch across and spring from ovate, pointed spathe-like bracts, borne on long stalks in the upper leaf-axils from June to October. The tubers should be lifted in the autumn and stored in pots of slightly damp sand and placed in a frost-proof building. Increase is by seeds sown under glass, the seedlings being planted out in May.

CONVOLVULUS ELEGANTISSIMUS
(*Convolvulaceae*) [PLATE 10]

The bindweeds formerly known as *Convolvulus althaeoides* and *C. tenuissimus* are now included under the above botanical name. *Convolvulus elegantissimus* well deserves its name for it has most attractive silvery foliage and very beautiful flowers. Unfortunately it has the same invasive habits as all the bindweeds for its widely creeping roots push up shoots where they are not wanted, in the same manner as our pestilent but beautiful *Convolvulus arvensis*. However, it is such an elegant plant that an attempt should be made to confine its roots to their allotted space by a stone border, sufficiently deep in the soil to mitigate if not prevent this undesirable habit.

Convolvulus elegantissimus is a twining herbaceous perennial, native in southern Europe. It is generally hardy but in severe winters in bleak localities it should be afforded some protection to its roots. The slender, much branched stems will reach a height of 6 feet and are well-clothed with comparatively small, much divided leaves, densely clothed in appressed white hairs, giving the whole plant a silvery appearance. The very lovely flowers are similar in shape to those of our common bindweed, but are smaller, usually measuring not more than $1\frac{1}{2}$ inch in diameter. They are a lovely shade of rich rosy pink, sometimes with a touch of orange in some seedlings. It flowers from July to September and needs a poor, stony soil, in full sun and is increased by seeds and division.

CORNUS KOUSA (*Cornaceae*) [PLATE 10]

Of the four species of cornel in cultivation with large decorative floral bracts, this is probably the best for small gardens. When in full flower and covered with a multitude of its snowy bracts it is indeed a very beautiful sight and again in the autumn when laden with its strawberry-like, brightly coloured fruits.

In this country it usually forms a loosely and sparsely branched, deciduous shrub but is occasionally of a more tree-like habit, reaching a height of 15 to 20 feet. Its spreading branches are clothed with medium-sized, opposite, shortly-stalked, ovate, acute, dark green leaves which are not very numerous. The very small, 4-petaled, green and red flowers are of no decorative value; they form closely-packed, semi-hemispheric clusters about ½ inch in diameter, subtended by 4, broadly lance-shaped, spreading, pure white bracts up to 1½ inch long and are borne on short spurs along the branches during May and June. The rich crimson globose fruits are about ½ inch in width and dangle on long, slender stalks from the branchlets. The variety *chinensis* is considered by some authorities to be superior to the type from a decorative point of view.

All the cornels thrive in good, light loam and are increased by seeds, layers and cuttings. The bracts of this species are sometimes browned by late, spring frosts. It should be given a position where the early morning sun does not reach it.

CORNUS MAS

The Cornelian Cherry, as this deciduous tree is called, is not in any way related to the cherries and its fruits are usually oblong, not globose. It is also known as Jew's Cherry and is a very old inhabitant of our gardens; it was formerly much more frequently seen than it is now. In the warmer parts of Europe it is much cultivated for the sake of its fruits, and many improved varieties are in cultivation there. A very potent liqueur brandy is made from their fruits and also a very palatable conserve, both of which are procurable in London.

Cornus mas is a small tree from 15 to 20 feet high, with a spreading, rounded head of twiggy branches. They are comparatively thinly clothed with handsome, rich yellowish-green, ovate, opposite, sharply pointed leaves of medium size. The flowers are produced in loose, many-flowered clusters from January to March. The 4-petaled corolla is not quite a ¼ inch across and is yellow. The flower clusters are produced with extreme freedom when the tree is leafless. A mature tree in full flower is a very beautiful sight, especially when it is backed by dark evergreens. The fleshy, oblong, red fruit is about ⅝ inch long and is rarely produced in this country. There are two varieties with their leaves variegated with yellow and also a dwarf form which is very suitable for small gardens. The Cornelian Cherry is perfectly hardy and is not particular as to soil. Increase is by cuttings.

CORYDALIS NOBILIS (*Papaveraceae*) [PLATE 11]

Although this beautiful herbaceous perennial was introduced into this country in 1780 it has never become familiar in small gardens. This is rather remarkable as it is very attractive, both on account of its elegant ferny foliage, and delicately tinted blossoms. It is a native of Siberia and is perfectly hardy in this country.

It has a tuberous root-stock and erect, unbranched leafy stems from 1 to 2 feet tall, destitute of any scales, common to many other tuberous rooted species with simple stems. The large, handsome, twice-pinnate leaves are composed of numerous wedge-shaped segments which are coarsely toothed or narrowly lobed. The flowers are borne in terminal, rounded racemes or heads up to 2 inches in diameter in vigorous plants and are composed of 20 to 30 closely packed pale yellow blossoms tipped with green and with long incurved, blunt spurs. They measure about an inch in length and usually commence to open in May.

Like several other species of fumitory (as these plants are called), it is rather partial to a half-shady position in a good, friable, well-drained loam and is usually increased by seeds. The most exquisite of all the members of this genus is *Corydalis cashmeriana*, a little tuberous-rooted species which I have only seen in cultivation in the alpine house at Kew. It has glaucous foliage and bright azure blue blossoms, 4 to 8 in number in crowded racemes and is apparently quite hardy.

CORYLOPSIS PAUCIFLORA (*Hamamelidaceae*) [PLATE 11]

It is a somewhat difficult task to decide which of the several species of Corylopsis in cultivation to describe in these pages. All are most desirable subjects for the amateur garden, being mostly dwarf and producing their dainty, delicately tinted flowers in the dull days of winter when the choice of cut flowers from the outdoor garden is very limited. All the species are natives of eastern Asia, ranging from the Himalaya to China and Japan. The species under consideration is a native of Japan and has larger and more brightly tinted blossoms than any of the others but they are far less numerous.

This deciduous shrub normally reaches a height of 3 to 4 feet and is of a spreading, rather sparse habit. The slender brown branches are somewhat thinly clothed with rounded-heart-shaped, pointed leaves, resembling in shape and size those of the hazel; they are deep green and are margined with red when young. Each has a pair of yellowish-brown bracts or scales at the base of its stalk. The delicate primrose-yellow blossoms have orange anthers and are borne in profusion in 2- to 3-flowered racemes, at the nodes of the previous season's growths, when the shrub is leafless. They are about $\frac{3}{4}$ inch across and are produced from February to April. A good light loam and a sheltered position meets this plant's requirements, and it is increased by layers and cuttings.

COTONEASTER SEROTINA (*Rosaceae*) [PLATE 11]

The genus Cotoneaster comprises a comparatively small number of deciduous and evergreen shrubs and small trees, chiefly valued for their attractive foliage and brightly coloured fruits. At least three species of cotoneaster have become completely naturalised in the wild in this country and owe their presence in such situations to the fondness of blackbirds and thrushes for their berries. I have counted more than a dozen different perennials, shrubs and trees with berry-like fruits which have appeared as seedlings around my bird-table over the years. Most of the desirable cotoneasters are natives of the Himalaya and China and several of the species introduced from the latter country have proved to be superior to those we have already in our gardens, amongst which is the species under consideration.

It is an evergreen shrub which will eventually reach a height of 10 feet, but will produce an abundance of fruits when only a third of that height. Its spreading branches are clothed with ovate, dark green, medium-sized leaves. The white, 5-petalled flowers measure about ½ inch in width and possess conspicuous red anthers. They are borne in corymbs 2 to 3 inches across in July. The bright red, egg-shaped fruit measures about a ¼ inch long and is produced in prodigious quantities, remaining on the bushes until April. It is not particular as to soil and is increased by seeds, cuttings and layers.

CROCUS BYZANTINUS (*Iridaceae*) [PLATE 11]

Amateur gardeners unfamiliar with the various members of the genus Crocus, would at first sight probably mistake this remarkable and at the same time beautiful crocus for a dwarf iris when it is fully open and the outer segments are spreading. It is among the most distinct of the crocus species in cultivation and is not difficult to grow under the same conditions as it has in its native Hungary and Transylvania where it is found in deciduous and evergreen woodland, thriving in semi-shade. The rather small bulb produces from 2 to 3 narrow, pointed leaves of the usual crocus type. The flower has a slender tube and ovate-lance-shaped outer segments and much narrower inner ones. The former are about 2 inches long and 1 inch wide and are of a rich purple. The latter are about 1 inch long and are pale purple or nearly white. Russian Asia is the home of several beautiful bulbous plants we cultivate in our gardens, and *Crocus korolkowi* is one of the

PLATE 11

1. *Corydalis nobilis* 2. *Corylopsis pauciflora* 3. *Cotoneaster serotina*
4. *Crocus byzantinus* 5. *Crocus pulchellus*
6. *Cyananthus microphyllus*

PLATE 12

1. *Cyclamen pseudibericum* 2. *Cynoglossum amabile* 3. *Cypripedium reginae*
4. *Cytisus battandieri* 5. *Daboecia azorica* 6. *Daphne retusa*

best of them. It has a large, squat corm, which produces several stiff, pointed, flat leaves with incurved margins. The rich golden yellow flowers almost equal in size those of the common yellow crocus, but their outer segments are rather heavily shaded with brown and purple, rendering the flower most attractive and perhaps unique in its colouring. It flowers in February and March and its corms should be planted 4 inches deep in rich, sandy loam in full sun. Increase is by seeds and offsets.

CROCUS PULCHELLUS [PLATE 11]

Crocus pulchellus thoroughly deserves its specific name for it is without doubt one of the most beautiful of the numerous crocus species in cultivation. Unfortunately where the various crocus species are grown in quantity for commercial purposes and in private gardens they are often near one another; the bees, which diligently seek the honey secreted by the blossoms, also bear the pollen to the stigmas of other species, thus producing hybrids which may be less desirable than their parents. It is no easy matter to obtain from growers the type as collected in the wild and even collected corms frequently produce flowers which vary in their ground-colour and their markings.

Crocus pulchellus has a rather small, somewhat flattened corm, which produces several linear, pointed leaves that are very short when the flowers are open. The beautiful lavender blue or bright bluish-lilac blossoms have an orange throat and ovate, pointed segments $1\frac{1}{2}$ inch long, veined with purple. There is an exquisite white form, also veined with purple. This delightful little species grows in open, bushy places on the shores of the Bosphorus, both in Greece and Turkey, and flowers from September to the end of December. It should be planted at a depth of 3 to 4 inches in deep, sandy loam, in a sheltered, sunny, well-drained position. It is increased by offsets and seeds which should be sown as soon as they are ripe in sandy soil in the open or in pots in a cold frame.

CROCUS TOMASINIANUS

This charming but somewhat variable little Crocus, with regard to the tinting of its blossoms, is perhaps not quite so uncommon as the preceding species, for it is easily grown and increases freely in light soil, but does not appear to be so happy when planted in grass. Even when the blossoms of the typical form are closed, they are very elegant in the silvery dove-colour of their outer segments.

It has a small, flattened corm, which produces 4 to 5, linear, pointed leaves, which like those of all the early flowering species, lengthen very considerably when the flowers have passed. The segments of the blossom measure from $1\frac{1}{2}$ to 2 inches long in the finest forms and vary a great deal in colour. Lavender-blue seems to be the prevailing tint of the type, but forms are available with lilac, rosy mauve, sapphire blue and amethystine-violet flowers. In some forms the colour deepens towards the tips of the segments.

This crocus has been given the pretty name of Cloth of Silver Crocus and is a native of Dalmatia and the Balkans. In mild seasons it commences to flower in January and continues to do so until March. The flowers stand up to rough weather better than those of most early flowering species and are very lasting. The corms should be planted as early as possible in good fibrous loam in a sunny position. Increase is by offsets and seeds, which take four years to produce flowering corms from the time they germinate.

CYANANTHUS MICROPHYLLUS
(*Campanulaceae*) [PLATE 11]

The genus Cyananthus is a small one and consists of a few elegant trailing perennials native in the Himalayas, the mountains of central Asia and western China. Several are very beautiful and should be more frequently seen in small gardens for they are not difficult to grow and will repay any trouble taken to provide them with a suitable position and soil. Their long-tubed flowers and other botanical features separate them from the campanulas to which they are closely related.

Cyananthus microphyllus is of tufted habit with a woody root-stock and several rather slender, reddish, trailing stems. Those bearing the flowers become sub-erect, and are from 9 to 12 inches long. Both are clothed with rather small, alternate, narrowly elliptic or ovate, dark green leaves with recurved margins and very short, winged stalks. The very pretty violet-blue blossoms are solitary on the tips of the branches and branchlets, which become sub-erect at flowering time. The flower has a cylindrical tube about $\frac{3}{4}$ inch long, which expands at its mouth into 5, egg-shaped lobes, forming a blossom $1\frac{1}{2}$ inch in diameter. The flowers are produced in August when the rock garden is usually a dull spot. It is a native of Nepal and is quite hardy, needing a moist, peaty soil mixed with leaf-mould. It thrives in a sunny or semi shady position and is increased by seeds and sometimes by cuttings which are difficult to root.

CYCLAMEN PSEUDIBERICUM (*Primulaceae*) [PLATE 12]

Probably the most beautiful of all the twenty or so species of Cyclamen that can be grown more or less successfully in the open air in this country is *C. libanoticum*, but unfortunately our climate does not seem to suit it.

FOR YOUR GARDEN 49

Like that lovely little Alpine plant *Eritrichium nanum* it is difficult to establish and equally difficult to retain in cultivation in the open here and is a plant for specialists only. In my opinion the cyclamen under consideration almost equals it in beauty and has the great advantage of being perfectly hardy and easy to cultivate. Its origin is uncertain, but it is considered to be a hybrid by most authorities.

It has a large, reddish-brown corm or tuber, which produces several large, deep green leaves, beautifully marbled with silvery white on their upper surface and of a purplish-crimson below. The lovely flowers are very freely produced on crimson stems well above the foliage, from February to the middle of April in normal years. The flowers are of a bright rose colour and measure a full inch in length. Each petal has a bright purple spot at its base. Like most hardy cyclamen it thrives in good, limy soil in a half-shady spot and is increased by seeds.

CYNOGLOSSUM AMABILE (*Boraginaceae*) [PLATE 12]

Unfortunately many of the most desirable species of Hounds-tongue, as these plants are called, are of but biennial duration only, including our two native species *C. officinale* and *C. montanum*. Specimens of the latter can be seen in plenty on the wooded slopes of Norbury Park, Surrey. Neither of these plants although interesting, is of any decorative value.

Cynoglossum amabile is a very beautiful biennial and is one of the most garden-worthy of the cynoglossums. It is a native of China and Tibet and has a rather thick deep-delving root and a stoutish erect stem from 1 to 2 feet tall clothed with long hairs. The lance-shaped-oblong, pointed leaves are rather long on the lower part of the stem but diminish much in length towards its apex. The beautiful flowers vary in colour from azure blue to pink; they are sometimes pure white and these are in my opinion less attractive than the coloured ones. They are borne in numerous terminal and lateral racemes, the latter springing from the upper leaf-axils, the whole inflorescence forming a large, loose panicle which is at its best during July and August. The flower has a rather short broad tube which expands at its mouth into 5, ovate lobes, forming a somewhat bell-shaped corolla nearly $\frac{1}{2}$ inch in diameter. This species is perfectly hardy and does not seem particular with regard to soil or situation but a good, deep loam will produce fine specimens. The seeds should be sown where the plants are to bloom.

CYPRIPEDIUM REGINAE (*Orchidaceae*) [PLATE 12]

It is very difficult to understand why this very beautiful and easily grown

Slipper Orchid is so rarely met with in gardens where conditions are ideal for its cultivation. It is quite catholic in its choice of habitat in the wild, and seems to thrive as well in damp woods of deciduous and coniferous trees as it does in raised ground in swamps and peat bogs. It is a native of eastern U.S.A. and Canada and is of course perfectly hardy in this country.

The Moccasin Flower as this species is called has a thickened root-stock which produces numerous long, fleshy roots. The rather stout, erect stems will reach a height of 3 feet in vigorous specimens and are clothed with rather large oval, pointed, rich green, downy leaves, narrowed below where they clasp the stem. The very beautiful blossoms, from 1 to 4 in number on each stem, are borne on stalks of varying lengths at its apex during May and June.

The flower measures nearly 4 inches in length and the same measurement across the lance-shaped, spreading petals, which together with the tepals or sepals are pure white. The inflated lip is about 2 inches long and is pale pink or pale purple usually marked with a deeper purple. There is also a pure white form which is very lovely. The Moccasin Flower thrives in a half-shady situation in cool, moist, leaf-soil and sand and is increased by division, but has been known to reproduce itself by self-sown seeds in cultivation.

CYTISUS BATTANDIERI (*Leguminosae*) [PLATE 12]

Several trees, shrubs and herbaceous plants native of the Atlas mountains in North Africa have enriched our gardens by their introduction into cultivation; the most noteworthy of which is the Atlas Cedar, which is now more frequently planted than its close relative the Cedar of Lebanon. *Cytisus battandieri* is found in the Azron district of Morocco in the Atlas mountains at an elevation of 6,000 feet in company with the Atlas Cedar.

It is a small, semi-deciduous, sparsely branched tree from 10 to 20 feet high, of loose habit with a tendency to become leggy with age. Its young branchlets are thickly covered with blue-grey down and are sparsely furnished with rather large leaves, densely clothed with soft, silky hairs on both surfaces. The leaves are composed of 3, oval or elliptic leaflets, the centre one being much the largest. The very beautiful rich golden yellow flowers, over $\frac{1}{2}$ inch in length, are borne in very crowded, erect racemes about 6 inches long, during the month of June.

Their fragrance is said to resemble that of a quince, but to me it has a pineapple scent, which is very perceptible when the sun is shining on the plant. It should be planted in a sheltered position in a light, well-drained loam and looks well and does well on a wall facing south. It is a fairly rapid growing shrub and is usually increased by seeds, which should be sown in pots as it resents root disturbance.

DABOECIA AZORICA (*Ericaceae*) [PLATE 12]

Although this very beautiful little shrub is a native of the Azores, where it inhabits the islands of Fayal and Pico, it can be grown with complete success in the open air in this country in a sheltered position where it is not exposed to searing northerly and easterly winds. It has been in cultivation in this country for about 30 years and when not crowded by other plants forms a more or less prostrate little evergreen bush from 3 to 4 inches high of compact, slowly spreading habit.

The slender stems and especially the young shoots are furnished with glandular bristles. The branches and branchlets are closely set with small, dark green, oval leaves, furnished with many glandular hairs, which also appear on their stalks. The under surface of the leaf is clothed with white, felted hairs. The rich, dark red flowers resemble in size and shape those of the well-known *D. cantabrica* and are borne in erect racemes 2 to 3 inches long in May and June. Each raceme is composed of from 4 to 10 nodding blossoms borne on short, glandular stalks. This most desirable little member of the heath family needs a well-drained but moist soil similar to that in which heaths thrive, but it must never be allowed to dry out. It is increased by cuttings of side shoots taken in July.

DAPHNE RETUSA (*Thymelaeaceae*) [PLATE 12]

The majority of the most beautiful daphnes suitable for cultivation in small gardens are difficult to retain in health for any length of time and there do not seem to be any rigid rules in their cultivation that will enable one to grow such gems as *D. blagayana* and *D. cneorum* with complete success. Fortunately we have in *Daphne retusa* a species much more amenable to cultivation and almost equal in beauty to the two above mentioned species.

Daphne retusa is a native of western China and has been available for the past 60 years yet is rarely seen. It forms a compact, dense, evergreen bush of extremely slow growth, taking many years to reach a height of 3 feet. The leathery, oblong-egg-shaped or elliptic-oblong, medium sized leaves are usually notched at the apex and are very dark green above and paler beneath. They are densely arranged towards the tips of the branchlets. The flowers, which are produced in May, are borne in crowded clusters on the apex of the branchlets. They measure about $\frac{3}{4}$ inch in diameter and have a short, broad tube and 4, spreading, pointed lobes. The flowers are pink or rosy purple outside and white tinged with lilac or purple inside and are extremely fragrant. This species will cover itself with flowers when only 12 inches high and is perfectly hardy and flourishes in any peaty mixture. It is increased by cuttings and seeds, the seedlings needing 5 years of growth to produce flowering plants.

DAVIDIA INVOLUCRATA
var. VILMORINIANA (*Cornaceae*) [PLATE 13]

This exceedingly beautiful tree was introduced into this country over sixty years ago and has been given the rather poetic and pleasing name of Dove Tree by the Americans, because the large bracts on their long, slender, flexible stalks, when stirred by a breeze, bear a fanciful resemblance to a flock of white doves fluttering over the tree. It is also known as the Pocket Handkerchief Tree. A well-grown specimen of this beautiful Chinese tree is an unforgettable sight in May and June when covered with numerous snowy bracts.

It is deciduous and flowers when quite small, eventually reaching a height of from 40 to 60 feet and is of upright, sparse habit, with erect or slightly spreading branches. These are clothed with large, handsome, light green ovate leaves, heart-shaped at the base, tapering to a point at the apex and margined with coarse teeth; they are glaucous beneath and somewhat resemble those of a nettle in shape. The inflorescence consists of a rounded mass of red and black anthers on white filaments and is partly enclosed in 2, or very rarely 3, white or cream coloured egg-shaped, pointed, more or less concave, shallowly toothed bracts, the larger being about 6 inches long and 2½ inches wide. The fruit is egg-shaped, berry-like and is green with a purple 'bloom'. This tree is quite hardy, but its bracts are sometimes browned by late frosts. It is not particular as to soil and is propagated by seeds and cuttings.

DECAISNEA FARGESII (*Lardizabalaceae*) [PLATE 13]

This member of the *Lardizabalaceae* rather closely resembles some of the mahonias, especially *M. lomariifolia* but the fruit is very much larger than that of any barberry, and together with the robust handsome foliage forms the chief attraction of this plant, for its flowers have but little decorative value. *Decaisnea fargesii* is a deciduous shrub, which will reach a height of 10 to 12 feet under congenial conditions. The stout rootstock produces several thick, branched stems with pithy centres, the handsome, rather dark green leaves are very large often reaching a length of nearly 3 feet; they are pinnate and are composed of 6 to 12 pairs of large ovate leaflets with an odd leaflet at the apex; they are glaucous beneath, quite entire and are more or less smooth on both surfaces.

The comparatively small yellowish-green flowers are rather like those of the barberry and are borne in slender racemes on the ends of the lateral branches in June; the whole inflorescence forming a large panicle. In some seasons the remarkable fruits set freely; they are cylindrical, up to 4 inches in length and $\frac{3}{4}$ inch in diameter, dull blue in colour and covered with small warts. They are said to be eaten by the inhabitants of western China of which this plant is native. It is quite hardy and thrives in a mellow loam mixed with sharp sand and is increased by seeds and cuttings.

DEINANTHE CAERULEA (*Saxifragaceae*)   [PLATE 13]
The floras of the temperate regions of China and Japan contain the majority of the superlatively beautiful plants now cultivated in our gardens in the open air, the majority of which have been introduced during the past two hundred years. Both the Chinese and Japanese are and have been for many centuries lovers of beautiful flowers. As a matter of fact more than a few of the beautiful Chinese plants in our gardens were originally discovered growing in the gardens of the Mandarins by our plant collectors; several of which have never been found in a wild state.

This very lovely Chinese herbaceous perennial was introduced into this country in the form of seeds about 60 years ago and is very rarely seen in small gardens. It is perfectly hardy and has a thick, horizontal root-stock, from which stout stems spring to a height of about 1 foot, each bearing a whorl-like cluster of 4, opposite leaves at its apex. The leaves are large, broadly ovate or elliptic, pointed, rough on the upper surface, coarsely toothed and of a deep green, with reddish-pink stalks. The charming, nodding flowers are produced in July and August; they measure about $1\frac{1}{2}$ inch in diameter and are borne above the leaves on reddish stems about 2 inches long, bearing from 4 to 7, fertile and sterile lavender-blue blossoms. A cool moist spot in friable loam and leaf-soil meets its requirements. Increase is by seeds.

DELPHINIUM CARDINALE (*Ranunculaceae*)   [PLATE 13]
This brilliantly coloured Delphinium is a favourite of mine and I have grown it on and off for years and find that although it is a true herbaceous perennial, it is better to treat it as an annual, for once its roots are completely frozen it is the end of the plant. Seedlings raised in a greenhouse or frame in March or April will give a grand display of richly coloured blossom in late summer and autumn.

Delphinium cardinale is a native of California and possesses a stout, fleshy root-stock which produces a tuft of large deep green leaves, assuming tints of bronze in hot, sunny summers. They are deeply divided into 5 lobes which are cleft into 2 to 3 linear segments. The uppermost stem leaves are frequently entire. The flowers are borne in long, many-flowered racemes on fairly long stalks, springing from the flower-stem which reaches a height of 2 to 3 feet. The individual flower measures from 1 to $1\frac{1}{4}$ inch wide and is bright scarlet with a metallic shine and the petals are sometimes edged with yellow. The spur is about $1\frac{1}{4}$ inch long and is curved.

This species thrives best in deep, rich, moist soil in full sun and if desired its fleshy roots may be dug up in the autumn and stored in a frost-proof structure in pots of sandy soil which should not be allowed to become bone dry. *Delphinium formosum*, a beautiful perennial with large sky-blue flowers, was once a popular bedding plant in conjunction with scarlet pelargoniums.

DELPHINIUM NUDICAULE [PLATE 13]

In this charming Delphinium we have yet another species from western North America, for it is found in well-drained soils in sunny situations in Oregon and California and should be given the same conditions in cultivation. It dies down to ground-level before the autumn merges into winter, and if not marked in some way, is rather liable to be dug up and consigned to the rubbish heap during the final tidy-up of the garden before winter sets in.

It is a true perennial with thick, fleshy roots and a sparse tuft of elegant, refined, medium-sized, pale green, rather fleshy leaves. They are more or less rounded in outline and are shallowly divided into 3, rounded, coarsely toothed lobes. Those on the stems are usually 3-lobed. Each of the 3 lobes is 2-lobed or toothed laterally or is quite entire. Both the root-leaves and those on the stems have long stalks. The root-stock produces several flower-stems which reach a height of 1 to $1\frac{1}{2}$ foot and are normally pale green, tinted with lilac. Each bears a loose raceme of 5 to 10 bright vermilion blossoms, which are continuously produced from April to July. The flower measures about $\frac{5}{8}$ inch wide and $1\frac{1}{2}$ inch long including the spur, which is curved. There is a form with orange-coloured flowers and one with pale yellow, both are desirable. This delphinium is quite hardy and is usually increased by seeds. It should be grown under conditions similar to those of its native habitat.

DELPHINIUM ZALIL

One usually associates the colour blue with delphiniums and we even have

PLATE 13

1. *Davidia involucrata var. vilmoriniana*   2. *Decaisnea fargesii*
3. *Deinanthe caerulea*   4. *Delphinium cardinale*   5. *Delphinium nudicaule*
6. *Dendromecon rigidum*

PLATE 14

1. *Deutzia longifolia* 2. *Dianthus callizonus* 3. *Dicentra spectabilis*
4. *Dictamnus albus* 5. *Dierama pulcherrimum* 6. *Dipelta floribunda*

a tint called Delphinium Blue but it may be news to many amateur gardeners that a beautiful yellow-flowered species is in cultivation. Of course none of the species can vie with the giant-flowered garden hybrids in decorative value but having grown the three species described in these pages, I can thoroughly recommend them to the attention of amateur gardeners who are interested in beautiful and uncommon plants in which hybridisation plays no part.

Delphinium zalil is an elegant and quite decorative species and is perfectly hardy and easily grown. It is a native of the mountainous districts of Persia and although a herbaceous perennial some authorities consider that it should be treated as a biennial in cultivation. In an open situation it forms a handsome tuft of bright green foliage composed of long-stalked leaves cleft into long, linear, pointed segments. The rather stout erect flower-stem reaches a height of 2 to 3 feet; it is fairly leafy and bears a much-branched inflorescence composed of many stiff racemes of numerous brilliant yellow blossoms, with 5, ovate, spreading sepals about 1 inch across. The spur is rather short and the petals are quite inconspicuous. This species flowers in July and is not particular as to soil but needs a sunny position; it is increased by seeds which frequently take several months to germinate.

DENDROMECON RIGIDUM *(Papaveraceae)* [PLATE 13]

The floras of California, Mexico and Chile contain a number of supremely beautiful plants, that are not quite hardy enough for culture in an exposed position in gardens in the colder parts of this country, but may be grown successfully and their beauty enjoyed for many years if they can be given the protection of a warm wall and a soil which promotes short-jointed, frost-resisting wood. A soil which induces sappy growths is quite unsuitable for such border line plants. Grown under suitable conditions in poor stony soil, *Dendromecon rigidum* has endured twenty degrees of frost and survived unscathed. With all these plants it is the searing north and east winds that cause the most damage.

The Californian Tree Poppy, as this evergreen shrub or semi-shrubby perennial is called, is of loose, open habit, with long, willow-like branches from 6 to 10 feet long. They are sparsely clothed with leathery, lance-shaped, smooth, medium-sized, glaucous, alternate leaves. The lovely fragrant flowers are produced singly on the ends of the current season's shoots and also on the lateral branchlets of the old growths. They measure from 2 to 3 inches across and are composed of 4 egg-shaped, bright yellow petals with a tuft of golden stamens in the centre. They are produced in

July. This beautiful plant should be given a position at the foot of a south wall in stony, sandy soil, and well supplied with water in dry weather. It is increased by cuttings.

DEUTZIA LONGIFOLIA (*Saxifragaceae*) [PLATE 14]
Although the type of this Deutzia has been in cultivation in this country for nearly sixty years, it does not seem to have attracted the attention its merits deserve, for not only is it the finest of all the species of deutzia in cultivation, but is one of the best of the flowering shrubs of moderate size.

It is deciduous and when allowed to develop naturally it forms an elegant bush from 6 to 8 feet tall, with gracefully arching branches, clothed with opposite, rather narrow, ovate-lance-shaped, medium-sized leaves, tapering to a slender point and margined with fine teeth. The upper surface of the leaf is of a rather dark green, below it is clothed with felted hairs. The delicately tinted blossoms are borne in fairly dense corymbose panicles from 2 to 3 inches in length and about the same measurement in width and are at their best in June. Each blossom is composed of 5, oblong or ovate-oblong, spreading petals and measures about 1 inch in diameter when fully expanded. In the type they are purplish-rose when in bud but become somewhat paler when mature. The variety *veitchii* is far superior to the type with regard to the colouring of its flowers for they are of a pure rose pink and are larger.

Both the type and its variety, although quite hardy, need a sunny, sheltered position and thrive best in well-drained sandy loam, with plenty of water in dry weather. Increase is by cuttings taken with a heel and inserted in a sand frame.

DIANTHUS CALLIZONUS (*Caryophyllaceae*) [PLATE 14]
Of the several beautiful alpine pinks in cultivation this species is in my opinion, the most desirable, for its flowers are larger than those of any of the others and are perhaps more strikingly coloured. It forms close cushions of very attractive foliage from 2 to 3 inches high, composed of stiff, linear, pointed, very glaucous leaves, from amongst which numerous erect or spreading, sparsely leafy stems spring to a height of 4 to 6 inches. Each bears a lovely rose-pink flower with a speckled zone of white and purple near its centre and measures fully $1\frac{1}{2}$ inch in diameter. The petals which are wedge-shaped, are truncate and irregularly toothed at the apex. This species is a native of the high mountains of Transylvania and usually flowers in June. It is of course perfectly hardy and is easily cultivated in

light, rich loam, and seems to thrive better in semi-shade than in full sun. It is propagated by seeds and cuttings.

In *Dianthus haematocalyx* we have another unfamiliar dianthus. It is a very desirable and brilliantly coloured species whose fibrous root-stock produces tufts of glaucous, silvery grey leaves and 6 to 12 inches high stems bearing almost scarlet flowers, each measuring $1\frac{1}{2}$ to 2 inches across and springing from a blood-red calyx. It is a native of Greece and is not difficult to grow in light soil in full sun.

DICENTRA SPECTABILIS *(Papaveraceae)* [PLATE 14]

Many years ago, in a former garden, I had a flourishing clump of this most lovely plant in a border of good, deep, friable loam, well-drained, but moist in summer. It was planted in the shade of a bullace tree, but not under the drip of its branches. Here it throve for many years, eventually forming a clump 3 feet across and in most years the stems reached a height of well over 3 feet and when laden with its arching sprays of most exquisite blossoms was a picture of floral perfection. This hardy perennial is found in Siberia, northern China and Japan.

When in a flourishing condition and well established the Bleeding Heart or Lyne-flower produces many, somewhat succulent, leafy stems from $1\frac{1}{2}$ to 3 feet tall, according to the conditions under which it is cultivated. The large, long-stalked, glaucous leaves are divided into many egg-shaped, toothed and cut segments and are very decorative. The exquisite pendant flowers are borne in graceful, arching racemes, composed of 6 to 12 blossoms of a most lovely shade of rose-pink, only to be matched in a few roses. They resemble a pair of bellows in shape. Each measures over an inch in length and is borne on a slender, curving stalk. Normally they are produced from May to July.

It is accounted a difficult plant to establish in some localities but requires a moist, half shady spot, and resents a dry root-run and full exposure to the sun. It is increased by careful division, cuttings and seeds. Its enemies are late spring frosts and slugs.

DICTAMNUS ALBUS *(Rutaceae)* [PLATE 14]

The Burning Bush, Fraxinella or False Dittany as this handsome old fashioned plant was popularly called, graced many a cottage garden in years gone by, but can now be included among the unfamiliar flowers with complete justification. This is a pity for it is very decorative, easily grown and has a most interesting and probably unique characteristic. The whole plant, especially the branches, is sprinkled with pustular glands which secrete a volatile oil, very noticeable on a still, hot day or warm evening. When a lighted match is brought near the plant the inflammable vapour produced by the volatile oil ignites and envelopes the plant in a sheet of flame, which when extinguished, leaves it quite undamaged. It ranges from France and Spain, eastwards through Siberia to Japan and is perfectly hardy.

The Fraxinella emits a pleasant odour when rubbed resembling that of lemon-peel and has stout, almost woody, branching stems, up to 3 feet in height, clothed with large pinnate leaves composed of 9 to 15 leaflets. The flowers measure from $1\frac{1}{2}$ to $2\frac{1}{2}$ inches across and are formed of 5, narrow petals. The upper 4 are erect and the lower one is curved downwards. They vary in colour from white to pink, red and purple and are borne in long terminal racemes in May. A good well-drained loam and a sunny position suits this species admirably. Increase is by seeds as it resents disturbance when once established.

DIERAMA PULCHERRIMUM *(Iridaceae)* [PLATE 14]

Known as the Wand Flower, this exceedingly graceful South African herbaceous perennial is perfectly hardy and should be cultivated in all gardens, large and small. There are several distinct species of Dierama which differ one from the other by slight botanical characteristics of no importance to the gardener. *Dierama leuto-albidum* is one of the most delicately beautiful of the Wand Flowers, and has a pure white bell-shaped perianth up to $1\frac{1}{2}$ inch long. It has a very restricted habitat in Natal, and is apparently not in cultivation in this country. The species described below is the only one readily available, but several attractive garden forms have been raised, with flowers various shades of red and purple.

Dierama pulcherrimum possesses a large corm densely covered with brown fibres. It produces a slender, flexuous but stiff stem up to 6 feet tall, usually gracefully arching towards its tip. It is clothed below with several linear, grass-like, stiff, bright green leaves, about one-third of the length of the stem. The beautiful blood red flowers are borne in clusters of 3 to 6, on thread-like, arching flower-stalks; the whole inflorescence forming a loose, many-flowered, one-sided panicle. The individual flower measures about one inch in length and is bell-shaped with a short tube and 6, oval segments. This species flowers from July to September and is at its best in moist but well-drained rich, light loam and peat in full sun. It is increased by seeds.

DIPELTA FLORIBUNDA *(Caprifoliaceae)* [PLATE 14]

Related to the Weigelas, or Diervillas as they are now termed, and very much resembling them in habit and appearance, this extremely beautiful deciduous shrub certainly deserves to be much more widely grown than it is at present. When in full flower in May and June, with its long, arching branches crowded with fragrant, delicately tinted blossoms, it is indeed a very beautiful sight.

It is perfectly hardy and forms a sparsely branched bush from 10 to 12 feet tall of erect habit, with spreading and arching side branches; they are furnished with medium-sized, rather dull green ovate-lance-shaped, pointed leaves. The elegant flowers resemble those of a diervilla in shape and have an inflated tubular corolla, about $1\frac{1}{2}$ inch long, which expands at its mouth into 5, rounded lobes and measures about 1 inch across when fully expanded. The flowers are of a beautiful pale pink, with a yellow throat and are rose-pink on the outside. They are borne in small clusters in the leaf-axils in such enormous numbers that the slender branches appear to be borne down by their weight. This species is a native of a western and central China and has been in cultivation in this country for about sixty years.

The dipeltas need a half-shady position in a good loamy soil and do not seem to grow well in a stony one; they are not easy to propagate, but cuttings of half-ripened wood taken in June and inserted in a sand-frame with bottom heat may be tried.

DODECATHEON MEADIA (*Primulaceae*) [PLATE 15]

The blossoms of the American Cowslips very much resemble those of the cyclamen, but here the likeness ceases, for whereas the flowers of the cyclamen are solitary on the tips of the stems, those of the dodecatheons are borne in umbels like those of many primulas, which they very much resemble in their likes and dislikes. Why they are not popular to-day is not easy to discover for they are easily accommodated and thrive under the same conditions as the moisture-loving primulas or our native cowslip. A thriving clump of American Cowslips in full flower in late spring is a beautiful and uncommon sight.

It has a stoutish root-stock which produces a tuft of rather long, broadly oval, toothed leaves, pointed at the apex and narrowed to the base. The more or less pendant flowers are borne in umbels of a dozen or more on very long, reddish stalks, springing from the tip of the stout flower-stem which reaches a height of from 12 to 15 inches. The individual flower measures about an inch in length and has a short, broad tube and 5 abruptly reflexed, lance-shaped petals, varying in colour from rose-pink to lilac, purple and white, with a pale V-shaped mark at the base of each petal and a crimson line around the mouth of the tube. The long stigma protrudes from the mouth of the tube conspicuously. It is a native of eastern U.S.A. and thrives in a compost of peat and loam in sun or semi-shade and must be kept very moist when in growth. Increase is by seeds and division.

DOWNINGIA PULCHELLA (*Campanulaceae*) [PLATE 15]

California, like South Africa, is the native country of a number of beautiful hardy and half-hardy annuals, several of which are deservedly popular, very decorative garden plants such as eschscholtzias, nemophilas, phacelias etc. The two little species described below are most elegant hardy annuals and grow in open situations in company with other dwarf plants.

Downingia pulchella is, one must admit, of straggling habit, but is most attractive when well-flowered, producing its lobelia-like blossoms throughout the summer. The slender, spreading, branching stems are clothed with small linear-oblong or egg-shaped leaves. The flowers which are very freely produced, are terminal on the tips of the branches and are of an unusual shape. The corolla has a short tube and is divided upwards into 2 lips. The lower lip is cleft to the middle into 3, egg-shaped lobes, rounded at the apex and narrowed below. Each lobe has a narrow yellow blotch at its base, bordered by a white margin and the throat of the blossom is lined with yellow and violet. The small oblong-lance-shaped diverging lobes of the upper lip are deep blue-violet.

Downingia elegans is even more loose in habit than the above species and has bright blue flowers with a broad white streak at the base. If possible the seeds of both species should be sown under glass and the seedlings planted out in May, or they may be sown where they are to bloom in April and May. Any light soil suits both species.

DRACOCEPHALUM GRANDIFLORUM

(*Labiatae*) [PLATE 15]

Several species of Dragon's Head, as these showy border plants are termed, should certainly be cultivated more frequently than they are. They comprise a small number of perennials and annuals; few of the latter are worth cultivating.

Dracocephalum grandiflorum is a native of Siberia and is at present the most decorative of all the Dragon's Heads in cultivation, although one or two Chinese species nearly equal it in beauty. It produces a crowded tuft or rosette of rather long root-leaves, which are ovate-oblong in outline, escalloped and saw-toothed on their margins, wedge-shaped at the base and long-stalked. The flower-stems reach a height of 6 to 9 inches. They are clothed with smaller, ovate, shorter-stalked leaves and bear an inflorescence consisting of distinct whorls of lovely blue flowers nearly 2 inches long, subtended by oblong bracts with almost entire, revolute margins and ending at the tip in a long, hair-like point.

This very beautiful and desirable plant produces its flowers in succession for a very long time, from June until it is cut down by frost. It should be given a well-drained, sunny position in gritty, rich soil, with moisture below in the summer and drier conditions in the winter. In some gardens where slugs abound it is very difficult to retain this plant in cultivation, in the open, so great is their liking for its young growths. Increase is by seeds and division in spring.

ECCREMOCARPUS SCABER (*Bignoniaceae*) [PLATE 15]
In gardens where the soil is cold and heavy, this Chilean perennial climber rarely survives our winter, although its roots may be protected by a covering of ashes or other protective material. In such districts it is better to treat it as a half-hardy annual and sow the seeds under glass in March or April and plant the seedlings in their permanent quarters when the danger of late frosts has passed. Thus treated the plant will produce an abundance of blossom in late summer and autumn. I have grown specimens of this plant in poor, stony soil for a number of years, in which they have survived several consecutive winters and given me much pleasure with their elegant foliage and queer yet beautiful, inflated blossoms. It is found in southern Chile, festooning shrubs and low trees in open situations.

The rather stout root-stock produces several much branched, 4-sided stems, which may reach a height of 12 feet in a season. They are rather sparsely furnished with pinnate, pale green leaves with irregularly-shaped leaflets, which increase in size towards the base of their stalk. The main stalk ends in a branched tendril. The rich orange-coloured flower measures about 1 inch long and is shaped like a curved bottle with a very narrow base and a restricted mouth, divided into 5, very small lobes. The flowers are borne in upcurved racemes 6 inches long. There are yellow and pale red forms in cultivation.

EDGEWORTHIA PAPYRIFERA (*Thymelaeaceae*) [PLATE 15]
The specific name of *papyrifera* was given to this plant on account of its inner bark being used by the Japanese in the manufacture of high class

paper. It was formerly known as *E. chrysantha* and *E. gardneri* and is apparently the sole member of its genus. It is closely related to the Daphnes and is a most desirable deciduous shrub both on account of its early flowering and its sweetly scented blossoms. In addition to Japan it is also found in China.

When growing naturally it is a compact, rounded bush, from 8 to 12 feet tall and flowers freely when but half that height. The branchlets are furnished with entire, narrowly oval or elliptic medium sized, dark green leaves, hairy on both surfaces and borne on very short stalks. The bright yellow blossoms are borne in dense, rounded heads $1\frac{1}{2}$ to 2 inches in diameter, each composed of 30 to 40 flowers and are produced on the tips of the previous season's shoots, normally in February and March. The flower measures about $\frac{3}{8}$ inch in diameter and has a rather long, almost cylindrical tube, expanding at its mouth into 4, spreading, rounded lobes. This shrub grows fairly rapidly and thrives in a not too rich, lime-free light loam. It should be given a sheltered position where the morning sun does not reach it in the early months of the year. The best method of increase is by layers.

ELAEAGNUS MACROPHYLLA *(Elaeagnaceae)* [PLATE 15]

The genus Elaeagnus is composed of a number of shrubs and small trees, ranging from southern Europe eastwards to China and Japan, most are hardy in this country and are known in southern Europe as Oleasters or Wild Olives. In my opinion the best of the evergreen members of the genus for small gardens is *E. macrophylla*, but where space can be afforded the deciduous *E. multiflora* should be included.

Elaeagnus macrophylla is an oriental species and is chiefly desirable on account of its beautiful foliage and the delightful fragrance of its flowers. It forms a rounded, rather leafy bush, of elegant habit, from 6 to 10 feet tall, according to the soil in which it is growing. The rather slender branches are well-clothed with ovate or broadly oval, medium-sized, rich, shining green leaves, usually with wavy margins. They are completely covered below with a beautiful silvery, metallic sheen, which is very conspicuous when the foliage is stirred by a breeze. A similar sheen covers the young shoots and is very intense on the juvenile foliage. The sparse clusters of small, bell-shaped, 4-lobed flowers are also silvery and possess an extremely agreeable, vanilla-like scent. In favourable seasons the flowers are followed by small, oval, red fruits. It should be given a sheltered position as it is liable to be browned in severe winters if very exposed. It thrives in any well-drained loam and is increased by cuttings and seeds.

PLATE 15

1. *Dodecatheon meadia*   2. *Downingia pulchella*   3. *Dracocephalum grandiflorum*
4. *Eccremocarpus scaber*   5. *Edgeworthia papyrifera*   6. *Elaeagnus macrophylla*

PLATE 16

1. *Enkianthus cernuus var. rubens*
2. *Eomecon chionanthum*
3. *Epimedium pinnatum*
4. *Eremostachys laciniata*
5. *Erica ciliaris var. maweana*
6. *Erythronium grandiflorum*

ENKIANTHUS CERNUUS
var. RUBENS (*Ericaceae*) [PLATE 16]

Unfortunately, several desirable members of the genus Enkianthus are not quite hardy except in the southern and western counties, where flourishing specimens of these graceful shrubs may be seen in the large private gardens occasionally open to the public. Both *E. cernuus* and its variety *rubens* are quite hardy but thrive best in a not too sunny, sheltered position.

The type is a very beautiful deciduous shrub of loose habit, from 5 to 8 feet tall in this country and is furnished with oblong, elliptic or elliptic-ovate, pointed, rather small, darkish green leaves, margined with rounded, blunt teeth. The white, bell-shaped, shallowly lobed flowers measure about ⅜ inch wide and are borne in curving racemes composed of about a dozen blossoms, which are at their best in May.

The variety *rubens* is infinitely more desirable than the type, which it resembles in habit, but not in foliage, nor in the colouring of its flowers. It has slightly hairy, egg-shaped, toothed leaves, which are vividly tinted in the autumn. The bell-shaped flowers are about ½ inch wide and are of a beautiful raspberry-red, which deepens in tint towards the mouth of the bell. They are borne in copious racemes in May. Both are natives of Japan and are easily grown in a lime-free, well-drained compost of light loam, peat and leaf-soil and are a success where rhododendrons thrive. Increase is by cuttings and seeds.

EOMECON CHIONANTHUM (*Papaveraceae*) [PLATE 16]

It has been my practice in this little work to exclude plants with widely creeping root-stocks which throw up growths and invade the space allotted to other plants, except where the plant in question is of outstanding beauty and its habit of spreading can be contained; this applies to the species under consideration.

This Chinese Poppywort is the sole member of its genus and has been named the Cyclamen Poppy, not that its flowers resemble those of a cyclamen, but its leaves certainly do. When growing in soil which meets its requirements, it reaches a height of 1½ to 2 feet. The leaves which all spring from the creeping rhizomes are of a glaucous pale green above and greyish beneath; they are heart-shaped, with scalloped margins and measure up to 6 inches in length and about the same measurement in width and are borne on stalks about 6 inches long. The exquisite poppy-like blossoms are about 2 inches in diameter and are formed of 4, spreading, wax-like petals, with a tuft of numerous yellow stamens in the centre. The flowers are borne on slender stalks springing from reddish stems, each remaining decorative for several days.

It flowers from May to September and thrives best in a reasonably moist loam, leaf-mould, peat and sand, in a sheltered position facing west. In some gardens it is necessary to restrict its root-run to induce it to flower freely. Propagation is effected by division and root cuttings when the plant is at rest.

EPIMEDIUM GRANDIFLORUM (*Berberidaceae*) [PLATE 16]
One does not see these elegant members of the barberry family in cultivation in amateur's gardens as frequently as their elegance and usefulness merit, for they belong to the class of herbaceous perennials, which will thrive under the drip of trees. Such plants of decorative value are none too common. The Epimediums or Barrenworts as these plants are called are quite easily accommodated and are far from difficult to retain. Their foliage is very attractive and their flowers although small and not showy are prettily tinted.

Epimedium grandiflorum is probably the most decorative species, both in leaf and flower. It has a rather long, rhizome-like root-stock, from which several slender stems rise to a height of 9 to 12 inches; each bears a ternate leaf composed of heart-shaped-ovate, pointed, comparatively large leaflets, margined with spiny teeth. The pretty, nodding flowers are borne in racemes, from April to June and vary in colour from white and pale yellow to rich rose and violet in the various forms. It is a native of Japan and is quite hardy.

The Persian *E. pinnatum* is a beautiful species with handsome leaves, composed of 5 to 11, ovate leaflets which assume beautiful tints in the autumn. The bright yellow flowers are borne in loose racemes in May and June. A compost of loam and leaf-soil suits these plants. Increase is by division and seeds.

EREMOSTACHYS LACINIATA (*Labiatae*) [PLATE 16]
From a distance the inflorescence of this old-fashioned hardy perennial reminds one of our handsome Yellow Deadnettle, quite plentiful in half-shady places on our chalk and limestone hills. All the Eremostachys are hardy herbaceous perennials of easy culture, with flowers in whorled spikes. They are natives of Asia Minor and the neighbouring countries, which seem to be the headquarters of several genera of the Labiatae and Boraginaceae containing species of considerable decorative value.

Eremostachys laciniata has been in cultivation in this country for over 230 years and is a native of the western districts of Asia Minor where it is found in dry situations on the mountain. It produces a tuft or loose rosette of fairly long root-leaves, deeply divided into lance-shaped segments, which are again divided into smaller and narrower lobes or slender teeth. The stems, which usually branch from the base, are from 1 to $1\frac{1}{2}$ foot tall and bear large, very decorative, rich yellow flowers of the usual deadnettle shape, in whorls of 10 to 20 blossoms, forming a long inflorescence in which the upper whorls are rather close together. This useful plant produces its flowers in July and August and is not particular as to the composition of the soil in which it is grown, so long as it is well-drained. It should be given a position in full sun and is increased by seeds and division in the spring.

ERICA CILIARIS var. MAWEANA (*Ericaceae*) [PLATE 16]
Our native Dorset Heath, *Erica ciliaris*, is one of the most beautiful of this very extensive genus, the headquarters of which is South Africa, where several hundred different species grow in company with other beautiful shrubs in various habitats. Many years ago the Cape Heaths were extensively cultivated in greenhouses and much care and patience was expended to flower them to perfection. Except for *E. hyemalis* and one or two other species, they have passed out of cultivation except in botanical gardens such as Kew. Personally I consider Maw's variety of the Dorset Heath the most decorative of the hardy heaths and it is an ideal dwarf shrub for sandy soils. It was discovered in Portugal by the late George Maw in 1872.

It has a more compact and upright habit than that of the type and under suitable conditions it will reach a height of 18 inches. The reddish branches and branchlets are densely clothed with soft hairs. They are furnished with small, linear or awl-shaped bright green leaves, fringed with hairs and usually placed on the stems and branches in whorls of 3. The pitcher-shaped, deep rose coloured flowers measure nearly $\frac{1}{2}$ inch in length in good forms and are borne on short, stiff, down-curved stalks in very crowded, pyramidal racemes, up to 5 inches long. It should be given an open sunny position in a sandy, well-drained loam with the addition of a little peat if possible and is increased by layers and cuttings.

ERYTHRONIUM GRANDIFLORUM (*Liliaceae*) [PLATE 16]
The true *Erythronium grandiflorum*, of which several inferior forms are in cultivation, is the most beautiful of all those species possessing yellow blossoms and deserves to be more frequently cultivated in gardens where

bulbous plants are appreciated. It is a native of the mountainous districts of western U.S.A. and is quite hardy. The conical bulb produces 1 to 2, oblong-lance-shaped, rather long leaves of a rich green colour without any mottlings, which are present in those of several other species. The slender flower-stem reaches a height of 6 to 9 inches and bears from 1 to 5 rich, golden yellow flowers, usually in March and April. The perianth measures about 2 inches in diameter and is composed of 6, pointed, recurved segments. The fleshy bulbs should be planted at a depth of 2 inches in loam, leaf-soil and a little sand, in a slightly shady position.

Erythronium revolutum var. johnsonii is perhaps the most beautiful of all the pink-flowered Dog's-tooth Violets and a large clump in full flower is a very beautiful sight. It is a native of California and is quite hardy. The rather long, broadly cylindrical bulb produces 2 to 3, rather long, oblong or oval, yellowish-green, faintly mottled leaves. The flower-stem reaches a height of 9 to 12 inches and bears 1, or occasionally 2 or 3, lovely deep rose coloured blossoms 2 to $2\frac{1}{2}$ inches across. The type has cream-coloured flowers, tinged with purple. Both the type and its variety thrive under the same conditions as the preceding species. Increase is by seeds and offsets.

ESCALLONIA RUBRA (*Saxifragaceae*) [PLATE 17]
As sea-side shrubs and in sheltered inland localities, several species and hybrids of these very attractive South American shrubs have become very popular and are even used as hedge-shrubs in the warmer counties. Having seen practically all the species and hybrids growing together in a large plantation of escallonias I have no hesitation in stating that the above mentioned species is still one of the best, if not the best, of these delightful shrubs for the embellishment of the amateur's garden.

It is elegant in habit and beautiful in flower and produces a wealth of its brilliant blossoms when only 2 feet high. It is a native of Chile and forms a rounded, spreading, evergreen bush, 4 to 6 feet tall when growing in light soils. The rather stiff branches and branchlets are well furnished with very attractive, rich, shining green, rather small, ovate to egg-shaped leaves, finely toothed on their margins. The flowers are borne in racemes from 4 to 6 inches long on the current year's shoots and are of an exceedingly beautiful carmine-crimson with a darker centre; they are composed of 5, egg-shaped, long-clawed petals, rounded at their tips, close-set and forming a flat corolla nearly $\frac{3}{4}$ inch across. The topmost blossom usually has 6 petals and is the largest. This species flowers from July to September and is propagated by seeds, cuttings and layers.

EUCHARIDIUM CONCINNUM *(Onagraceae)* [PLATE 17]

The genus Eucharidium is merged by some botanists into that of Clarkia. In superficial appearance the two genera very much resemble one another. The chief difference between them is that in Clarkia the flowers have 8 stamens and in eucharidium only number 2. If one may judge from illustrations in the several Floras of western North America there is a considerable number of apparently beautiful annuals, native in that region, which are not listed by any seedsmen in this country. Some were introduced many years ago but seem to have passed out of cultivation.

Eucharidium concinnum is a native of California and is a hardy annual of sparse, erect habit. The slender, wiry stem reaches a height of 1 to 2 feet and is either simple or slightly branched. It is rather thinly furnished with small, oblong entire leaves tapering to a stalk. The beautiful rose-coloured flowers are about 1 inch in diameter and very much resemble those of *Clarkia pulchella*, the once popular annual, which now seems to be rarely cultivated in the type form. The flower of *E. concinnum* has a long tube and 4- to 5-lobed petals. In flowers with 5-lobed petals the centre lobe is the longest. This pretty little annual does not seem particular with regard to soil but it should not be dust dry in the summer. The seeds should be sown in a sunny position in April and May.

EUCRYPHIA GLUTINOSA *(Eucryphiaceae)* [PLATE 17]

Formerly better known under the specific name of *E. pinnatifida* this extremely graceful Chilean shrub or small tree is, apart from its great beauty a very desirable subject, for it bears its exquisite flowers in July and August when but few shrubs and trees are in bloom. That it is not so frequently seen in small gardens as it deserves to be is perhaps due to the mistaken idea that it is only suitable for cultivation in gardens situated in the more favoured districts of the British Isles with regard to climate. However, this is not the case since large specimens in eastern Scotland have withstood the hard winters which occur in that part of the British Isles, including that of 1928–29 when much of the gorse was killed to the ground, even south of London.

This eucryphia is of upright, compact habit and reaches a height of 10 to 20 feet. The branches, which are not very numerous, are clothed with large, elegant, rich green, pinnate leaves, composed of from 2 to 4 pairs of ovate, pointed, toothed leaflets and a terminal one. They are deciduous and turn to bronze, orange and scarlet in the autumn. The 4-petaled flowers, which resemble large, white roses are borne in the greatest profusion in the leaf-axils on the young shoots on comparatively short stalks.

This species should be planted in deep, light soil mixed with peat and its roots should be protected from hot sun by a heavy mulch. Propagation is by layers, cuttings and seeds.

EUONYMUS LATIFOLIUS (*Celastraceae*) [PLATE 17]

The only fault that one can find with the various spindle trees is that they take a considerable time to grow to fruiting size, especially if they are raised from seeds. This is rather unfortunate for their decorative value lies in their brilliantly coloured seed-vessels and seeds and not in their flowers which are very small and quite inconspicuous. The Broad-leaved Spindle Tree is a native of southern Europe and is one of the most elegant of these evergreen and deciduous shrubs and trees. When allowed to grow naturally it is a slender, sparsely branched, deciduous tree, up to 20 feet in height. In very poor soil it usually remains a shrub 6 to 8 feet tall.

The graceful, arching branches are rather thinly clothed with rich green opposite, rather large, ovate-oblong or oblong-lance-shaped, pointed, finely serrate leaves which turn to an attractive tint of pale yellow before they fall in the autumn. The very small, pale yellowish-green, 4-petaled flowers are under $\frac{1}{4}$ inch wide, and are borne in loose clusters or cymes on stalks of varying lengths, which arise from the leaf-axils. The cymes are composed of 6 to 12 flowers and are produced in June. The brilliant fruit, which ripens in September is formed of a 3-valved, fleshy, crimson or rose-red capsule, which contains large, orange coloured seeds. This spindle tree is not particular as to soil. Propagation is by seeds and cuttings.

EXOCHORDA RACEMOSA (*Rosaceae*) [PLATE 17]

Formerly better known as *E. grandiflora*, this very beautiful deciduous shrub, although introduced into this country over a hundred years ago, is yet a stranger to most amateurs, despite the fact that it is quite hardy and not difficult to grow. In its native China it is known as the Pearl Bush, a name which it well deserves, for when in a flourishing condition and in full flower in April and May, its branches are actually borne down by the weight of its blossoms.

In an open situation it is a bushy, compact shrub of rounded habit, from 10 to 12 feet high, with slender branches furnished with smooth, narrowly egg-shaped, oval or oblong, pointed, medium-sized leaves, either entire or toothed above the middle. The very lovely snowy white blossoms sometimes measure as much as 2 inches in diameter; they are composed of 5, rounded petals abruptly narrowed into a claw at the base. The tuft of yellow stamens in the centre of each blossom much enhances their beauty.

PLATE 17

1. *Escallonia rubra* 2. *Eucharidium concinnum* 3. *Eucryphia glutinosa*
4. *Euonymus latifolius* 5. *Exochorda racemosa* 6. *Feijoa sellowiana*

PLATE 18

1. *Felicia bergeriana*   2. *Fendlera rupicola*   3. *Fothergilla monticola*
4. *Fremontia californica*   5. *Fritillaria pallidiflora*   6. *Galanthus byzantinus*

FOR YOUR GARDEN   69

They are borne in more or less erect racemes, composed of about half a dozen flowers and remain decorative for a considerable time.

The exochordas are not particular as to soil but must have a well-drained sunny position. They resent disturbance when established and must therefore be planted in their permanent position when quite small. In my experience cuttings do not root very readily, so to increase this lovely shrub layers and seeds must be resorted to.

FEIJOA SELLOWIANA (*Myrtaceae*)   [PLATE 17]
One usually assumes that Brazil is an essentially tropical country and that none of its native plants could be grown successfully in the open air in this country. This is not quite correct as several lovely plants from the extreme south-east corner of this vast country have proved sufficiently hardy to enable them to be cultivated in the warmer counties quite successfully unprotected from the inclemency of our climate and even on a warm wall in cold districts.

In addition to Brazil *Feijoa sellowiana* is also a native of Uruguay. In an open position it forms a large, evergreen bush from 6 to 12 feet high. Its slender branches are furnished with leathery, medium-sized, oval leaves of a dark green on their upper surface and clothed with thick, white felted hairs on the lower one. The young shoots and also the flower stalks are clothed in a similar manner. The very handsome blossoms are borne singly in the axils of the lower leaves in September and measure about $1\frac{1}{2}$ inch across and are composed of 4, large recurving petals which are deep red on the upper surface, fading to white on their margins; their under surface is clothed with white, felted hairs. The fruit is egg-shaped, about 2 inches long and is edible, and has the flavour of an over ripe strawberry. It requires a light soil in a sunny spot and is increased by cuttings rooted in heat.

FELICIA BERGERIANA (*Compositae*)   [PLATE 18]
In this beautiful little South African annual we have a member of the daisy family with really pure blue flowers without any tinge of purple or lilac. It has been given the popular name of Kingfisher Daisy, a most appropriate name as its flowers are pure cobalt or kingfisher-blue.

When not over-crowded it forms a neat little miniature bush up to 4 inches high; the slender branches are more or less erect and are furnished with small, oblong or lance-shaped, pointed leaves of a rich green colour. The slender flower-stems are carried erect and rise to a height of about 6 inches above the foliage, terminating each branch and branchlet. The beautiful flowers are borne singly on the naked flower-stems and are composed of 20 to 25 narrow, spreading, strap-shaped florets, forming a flower about 1 inch in diameter.

With regard to its time of flowering, this of course is governed by the date on which the seeds are sown. Seeds of this half-hardy annual sown in the open in May normally produce plants which are in full flower in August, but if they are sown under glass at the end of March and the seedlings are planted out when the danger of frost has passed much earlier flowers may be had. The once popular greenhouse species *Felicia amelloides*, the Blue Marguerite, is a beautiful perennial with sky-blue flowers.

FENDLERA RUPICOLA (*Saxifragaceae*) [PLATE 18]
Although this beautiful deciduous shrub is found wild in hot, dry, desert localities, it will pass through severe winters with periods of zero temperature unscathed. Nevertheless it needs the hottest position in the garden and is at its best at the base of a south wall where the sun will ripen its wood, which is so necessary for the production of flowers. It is a native of southern U.S.A. and is confined to Texas and New Mexico.

It covers itself with a wealth of elegant flowers when quite small but will eventually reach a height of 6 to 8 feet, forming a densely branched bush, well clothed with sub-sessile, greyish-green, oblong, rather small, entire leaves with prominent mid-ribs and hairy blades. Each branchlet usually terminates in a solitary 4-petaled flower, nearly $1\frac{1}{2}$ inch across; their petals have an oval, toothed, pointed blade, gradually tapering from above the middle to the base; they are white, tinted down the centre of the back with pink. The flower buds are of a beautiful rose-pink and the whole flower is occasionally tinted with the same colour and is then very lovely.

It flowers during the months of April and May and is not particular with regard to soil, but a sandy, well-drained loam will promote the necessary short-jointed growths for free-flowering. Propagation is by seeds and cuttings.

FOTHERGILLA MONTICOLA (*Hamamelidaceae*) [PLATE 18]
There are four species of Fothergilla in cultivation, all of which are well worth growing on account of their fragrant, feathery flowers and the brilliant tints their foliage assumes in the autumn. Undoubtedly the best species for the decoration of small gardens is *Fothergilla monticola*, for it is floriferous, and possesses the most vivid autumn tints. It is a native of North Carolina and is perfectly hardy and easily grown in soils in which

rhododendrons flourish; it does best in a shady or semi-shady position, but is not fastidious.

It is a slow-growing deciduous shrub, rarely reaching a height of more than 4 to 5 feet, but flowers profusely when less than half that height. It is of open, rather sparse habit and is somewhat thinly clothed with handsome, rather large, pale green leaves, much resembling those of the hazel or witch hazel, both in size and shape. The inflorescence, which is produced in March and April on the naked twigs, is composed of numerous, long, closely packed, creamy white stamens, borne in oblong or rounded spikes from 1½ to 3 inches long, on the tips of the branchlets and is very fragrant. The leaves turn to brilliant tints of orange and scarlet in the autumn, remaining decorative until the first stiff frost clears them from the branches. Fothergillas, like several other deciduous shrubs, are very difficult to increase by means of cuttings for they rarely produce roots. Seeds offer the most satisfactory method of propagation.

FREMONTIA CALIFORNICA (*Sterculiaceae*) [PLATE 18]

The beauty of the flowers of this californian plant lies not in their petals, for they have none, but in their large, rich orange sepals, which are persistent for a considerable period. Unfortunately this beautiful evergreen shrub or small tree is not hardy in bleak, exposed districts except when trained to a sheltered wall. In the more favoured districts with regard to climate it thrives in the open and specimens 20 to 30 feet tall have been recorded in Devon and Cornwall.

It is usually of erect habit and sparsely branched, with its branches and twigs densely clothed with down. The leaves are of medium size, shortly stalked and irregularly or 3 to 7 lobed; they are dull green above and clothed with pale brown, felted hairs beneath. The flower consists of 5, rounded sepals which are densely hairy on their backs. The flowers are borne singly on short stalks which spring from the twigs opposite the leaf-joints; they measure from 2 to nearly 3 inches in diameter and are produced from early May to late autumn in normal years.

It needs a compost composed of sandy loam, with a little peat and leaf-mould, and a sunny well-drained position, with plenty of moisture in dry weather. It is usually increased by layers and also by seeds.

FRITILLARIA PALLIDIFLORA (*Liliaceae*) [PLATE 18]

Although the flowers of this rather robust fritillary are not brightly coloured, they are very elegant in shape and delicate in tint. Like a number of our cherished border plants, it is a native of Siberia and is of course quite hardy. The rather large, scaly bulb produces a stout, erect stem from 1 to 2 feet tall. It is clothed with numerous oblong or lance-shaped, alternate, medium-sized, pointed, glaucous leaves. The elegant, creamy white, green-tinged, bell-shaped blossoms measure about $1\frac{1}{2}$ inch in length and slightly less in width and are dotted inside with minute, reddish-purple spots. The nectary is in the form of a raised, yellowish-green spot at the base of each of the outer segments. This species may be grown in an open position in deep, rich, light loam, well supplied with water when the plant is in growth. Increase is by offsets and seeds.

Fritillaria pyrenaica is another desirable species. It has a small, scaly bulb and an erect stem from 1 to $1\frac{1}{2}$ foot high, furnished with rather long, scattered, linear, glaucous leaves. The flower measures from $1\frac{1}{4}$ to nearly 2 inches long and is remarkable in its coloration, which is somewhat variable. The outside of the blossom is normally claret coloured, spotted with dull red and the inside is shining green, checkered with maroon. Some forms are green outside, flushed with reddish-purple and glossy yellow within. This fritillary flowers in June and should be planted 4 inches deep in good, friable loam in sun or shade.

GALANTHUS BYZANTINUS (*Amaryllidaceae*) [PLATE 18]

There are three or four very desirable, robust, large-flowered snowdrops obtainable such as *G. elwesii*, *G. fosteri* and *G. plicatus*, but the species under consideration is considered by most enthusiastic gardeners who make a speciality of snowdrops to be more beautiful than any other species or variety in cultivation. It is a rather rare snowdrop and its bulbs are expensive.

The bulb is large for that of a snowdrop and the leaves are plicate when young but as they mature, flatten out into a long, broad blade which changes from a rich green to blue-green when fully developed. The magnificent flower frequently measures $1\frac{1}{2}$ inch in length and 2 inches in width. The outer segments are white and the inner have green markings at the base and apex or are occasionally bright green almost to the base.

Some snowdrop specialists maintain that this galanthus is a hybrid between *G. plicatus* and *G. elwesii*. This may be so as both the above mentioned species inhabit practically the same tract of country in Asia Minor. In mild seasons it produces its flowers from January to March, and although quite uncommon in gardens it is easily grown in any light, well-drained soil in a position where the bulbs are thoroughly ripened. Increase is by offsets. *G. plicatus* almost equals *G. byzantinus* in beauty, and is less expensive to purchase. It may be distinguished from other snowdrops by its leaves, which remain folded at the margins after they are quite mature.

GALTONIA CANDICANS *(Liliaceae)* [PLATE 19]

In the maritime counties of southern and western England this majestic South African bulbous plant may be successfully grown in an open position in the border or in the front of the shrubbery without protection. In the London district I find it necessary to plant it at the foot of a wall facing south or west, at a depth where the top of the bulb is at least 6 inches below the surface of the soil. Under such conditions and in good soil my plants have produced stout stems, some reaching a height of 6 feet and bearing 30 or more blossoms to a stem.

The large globose, brown-coated bulb may produce 2 flower-stems, which are normally 3 to 4 feet high. The leaves, about half a dozen in number, are long, strap-shaped, erect and recurved and are of a bright slightly glaucous green. The funnel-shaped or bell-shaped, white or creamy white flower measures from $1\frac{1}{2}$ to 2 inches long and is erect when in the bud and pendulous on a down-curved stalk when mature. The flower has a very broad tube, which expands at its mouth into 6 ovate-lance-shaped, pointed segments. The flowering period is from June to August. The bulbs may be planted in the autumn or early spring in clumps of about half a dozen and left undisturbed for years. Each bulb should be surrounded by a layer of sand, and a good mulch of leaf-soil in the autumn will help to protect them from severe frost. Increase is by seeds and offsets.

GAULTHERIA TRICHOPHYLLA *(Ericaceae)* [PLATE 19]

There are many dwarf members of the heath family which bear attractively coloured fruits, but none can surpass in this respect those of this most desirable little member of the genus Gaultheria. It is a native of the mountainous districts of south-western China and also the Himalaya, where it reaches an elevation of 12,000 feet above sea-level and is perfectly hardy.

This species is a very dwarf evergreen shrub, rarely up to 6 inches in height, but is usually not more than half that height. The root-system consists of a number of underground shortly creeping stolons, from which numerous thin, wiry stems spring; they are clothed with fine bristles and are furnished with numerous small, oblong-lance-shaped, rich green leaves, minutely saw-toothed on their margins and covered with fine hairs. The pink, urn-shaped flowers, measure just under a $\frac{1}{4}$ inch long; they are borne singly in the leaf-axils in June and are followed by exquisite pale blue, oval or rounded fruits, nearly ½ inch long, which remain decorative for several months after ripening. Like most members of the heath family it is a lime-hater and thrives in a half-shady position in a compost of cool, moist loam, peat and sharp sand. It is increased by seeds and layers.

GENISTA AETHNENSIS *(Leguminosae)* [PLATE 19]

According to some gardeners the only fault of this graceful shrub is that after a few years of growth it becomes leggy and untidy in habit. To me this is a part of its charm, for its crooked stem, sparse branches and canopy of long, slender, drooping, green branchlets, each ending in a pendant raceme of golden yellow blossoms, render it one of the most beautiful of flowering shrubs. It is known as the Mount Etna Broom and is said to grow nearer the rim of the crater than any other plant. In cultivation it may reach a height of 15 to 20 feet.

Its slender, thong-like, pendant branches and branchlets are very sparsely furnished with small, linear, rather pale green, alternate, inconspicuous leaves, clothed with short, silky hairs. The golden yellow flowers, which measure about ½ inch in length, are at their best in July, but continue to be produced until the autumn. Its sparse habit and graceful mode of growth renders it eminently suitable for planting as a solitary specimen in a circular bed, with the ground beneath its branches planted with a dwarf blue-flowered plant, requiring the same cultural conditions and of course flowering at the same period of the year as the broom. *Genista cinerea* is another beautiful and very floriferous broom of rather drooping habit, up to 10 feet in height, with terminal, leafy racemes of rich yellow flowers, produced in July. Both brooms flower best in poor, stony soil in full sun and are increased by seeds.

GENISTA LYDIA

The genus Genista contains a considerable number of shrubs, many of which are of value for the decoration of the garden or greenhouse. Most of them inhabit countries with a low rain-fall, growing in rocky or sandy soils. All are lovers of sunshine. The species under consideration is a native of eastern and south-eastern Europe and also western Asia Minor and is also sometimes known under the synonym of *G. spathulata*.

In an open sunny position in poor, stony soil it is a low deciduous bush, taking many years to reach 2 to 3 feet in height and the same measurement in width. The slender, rush-like, rather rigid, arching branches are furnished with numerous, rather short lateral branchlets which are spread out horizontally giving the bush a distinctive appearance. The whole plant is spineless except the flowering branches which are tipped with a sharp spine. The leaves are few in number and are very small. They vary from elliptic-linear to narrowly egg-shaped and are usually pointed.

It flowers in May and June and is then one of the most conspicuous of dwarf shrubs, for every little branchlet becomes a sub-terminal, spine-tipped raceme laden with brilliant, deep golden yellow blossoms, each about ¾ inch in length, the whole plant being smothered in richly tinted flowers. This genista is quite hardy and is usually increased by imported seeds.

GENTIANA VEITCHIORUM *(Gentianaceae)* [PLATE 19]

Of the several Alpine gentians introduced into this country during the present century from China, at least three are of outstanding merit for furnishing the alpine garden. Two—*G. farreri* and *G. sino-ornata*—are deservedly popular, but the third—*G. veitchiorum*—is almost unknown to amateur gardeners. This is a pity as it is easily cultivated and its deeply tinted blossoms are very attractive. It is found on the mountains of western China and is perfectly hardy.

The root-stock produces a compact central rosette of medium-sized linear-oblong leaves, and numerous, short, almost prostrate flower-stems clothed with smaller, pointed leaves. The flowers are borne singly on the tips of the stems and usually make their appearance in August. The corolla measures about 2½ inches in length and is widely funnel-shaped, with broadly triangular lobes. In colour it varies from purplish-blue to a deep royal blue and is furnished with broad bands of white or greenish-yellow within. The trailing stems do not root at the nodes, therefore the best method of increase is by seeds. It seems to thrive best in a gritty, limy soil in full sun.

It appears that the gentian that we have long grown under the name of *G. septemfida* is but a loose-growing, more robust form of *G. lagodechiana*, both are natives of the Caucasus and are equally desirable from a decorative point of view. The latter forms a prostrate mass of stems bearing terminal clusters of large, soft blue blossoms in early autumn and thrives in moist peat and loam in full sun.

GERANIUM FARRERI *(Geraniaceae)* [PLATE 19]

The greater number of the Geranium species are, in my opinion, only suitable for cultivation where space is a matter of no importance. Many are excellent subjects for the wild garden. On the other hand a few are among the most charming of alpine plants and should find a home in every garden where alpines are cultivated.

Geranium farreri is a tufted perennial and possesses a short rhizome, well furnished with cylindrical roots, like those of the well-known *G. sanguineum*. The slender, more or less decumbent stems measure up to 6 inches in length and are clothed with small, bright green leaves, cleft into 3 to 5, egg-shaped or wedge-shaped, coarsely toothed or lobed segments. The lower leaves are long-stalked. The lovely flower, which measures about $1\frac{1}{2}$ inch in diameter and is of the usual geranium shape, varies in colour from pale rose to lilac and has black anthers, which are most conspicuous. The flowers are borne on stalks 1 to $1\frac{1}{2}$ inch long, on flower-stems 2 to 4 inches in length, usually in pairs, and start to open in June. It is a native of the Alps of western China and is quite hardy, needing a gritty, rather moist soil in full sun and is increased by seeds and division.

Geranium argenteum, a native of the Alps of Italy, is a very beautiful species. It produces carpets of silvery leaves and very lovely pink flowers with crimson veins. It flowers in June and July and needs a stony, limy soil in full sun.

GEUM × BORISII (*Rosaceae*) [PLATE 19]

The status of this brilliant flowered Geum as a species seems to be somewhat doubtful. It was apparently discovered on Mount Rilo in Bulgaria a considerable time ago and was considered by its discoverer to be a hybrid between *G. reptans* and *G. bulgaricum* but there seems to be no record of it having been collected since it was first discovered. Hybrid or species, it is a most valuable plant for the herbaceous border or spacious rock garden, as it seems to be never out of flower from early spring to late autumn.

To obtain the full advantage of its glowing blossoms, it is advisable to plant it in groups of about half a dozen, in an open sunny position, in full sun, in good, loamy soil. It is perfectly hardy and forms large but neat tufts of dark green, evergreen leaves, very similar in shape but perhaps larger than the popular forms of *G. chiloense*, commonly grown under the name of *G. coccineum*. The branching stems reach a height of from 9 to 12 inches and bear several blossoms of a symmetrical, rounded form, nearly 2 inches in diameter of a glowing orange-red or orange-scarlet.

Several other geums are worthy of cultivation on account of their attractively coloured flowers, amongst which is *Geum × heldreichii splendens* and *G. montanum*. The former has rich orange flowers almost of a tangerine tint and the latter is an alpine of dense, tufted habit, with large golden yellow, almost stemless flowers, which are produced in early spring.

PLATE 19

1. *Galtonia candicans* 2. *Gaultheria trichophylla* 3. *Genista aethnensis*
4. *Gentiana veitchiorum* 5. *Geranium farreri* 6. *Geum × borisii*

PLATE 20

1. *Glaucidium palmatum* 2. *Gypsophila oldhamiana* 3. *Halesia carolina*
4. *Halimium lasianthum formosum*
5. *Hamamelis mollis* 6. *Hedysarum coronarium*

GLAUCIDIUM PALMATUM (*Ranunculaceae*) [PLATE 20]

Like several members of the Buttercup Family this very choice perennial herbaceous plant has but very rudimentary petals. The showy part of the blossom consists of coloured sepals and it has aptly been likened to that of a tuberous-rooted begonia. *Glaucidium palmatum* is a native of Japan and appears to be rare in its native habitat, which is said to be restricted.

It is quite hardy and has a short, stout cylindrical, rhizome-like rootstock which emits numerous creeping roots. The fairly stout, cylindrical stem bears 2 very large palmate leaves which are heart-shaped at the base and cleft above the middle into 5 to 7, ovate-diamond-shaped, sharply toothed lobes, with a long, slender point. The middle lobe is again cleft towards the apex into 3, toothed segments. When the plant is growing under congenial conditions the leaves frequently measure a foot across the lobes. The lovely flowers are composed of 4, broadly egg-shaped sepals of a pale mauve or pale purple tint. Each sepal measures $1\frac{1}{2}$ inch wide and the 4 sepals form a blossom 3 inches in diameter with a large tuft of yellow stamens in the centre. The flowers are produced in April and May and last some time in perfection.

It is certainly rare in cultivation but any trouble incurred in obtaining a specimen will be well repaid when the plant is in bloom. This very desirable herbaceous plant thrives in good fibrous loam mixed with plenty of humus and is increased by offsets.

GYPSOPHILA OLDHAMIANA (*Caryophyllaceae*) [PLATE 20]

It has long been the ambition of those who admire *G. paniculata* to possess a species or hybrid of similar habit with really pink flowers. This wish has now been fulfilled for the charming flowers of *Gypsophila oldhamiana* are, in the best form, a delightful shade of deep pink and to add to its attractiveness the flowers have the fragrance of some of the pink family. It is a native of north-eastern Asia and is a perfectly hardy perennial.

When fully grown it forms very symmetrical dome-shaped bushes from 2 to 3 feet high. The numerous panicled branches and branchlets, which spring from the thong-like root-stock are furnished with narrowly oblong to oblong-lance-shaped, rather leathery leaves of medium size. They are produced in opposite, alternate pairs and are bright olive green on both surfaces. The flowers are borne in many-flowered panicles in August and September. The individual flower measures from $\frac{1}{4}$ to $\frac{1}{3}$ inch in diameter and is almost white in the bud stage but when it opens it gradually assumes the deep pink tint mentioned above and usually has a white eye. All it needs is a good light soil in full sun and should not be cut down in the autumn. Propagation is effected by division in the spring and by seeds. *Gypsophila repens var. rosea* is a charming little perennial about 6 inches high with pale pink flowers. It is very suitable for furnishing a sunny bank in friable loam or for embellishing a dry wall.

HALESIA CAROLINA (*Styracaceae*) [PLATE 20]

The Snowdrop tree or Silver-bell tree is one of the most beautiful hardy trees yet introduced into this country but although it has been in cultivation in England for over two hundred years, one very rarely sees it in small gardens.

Formerly known as *H. tetraptera* and a native of eastern North America where it is a deciduous tree up to 100 feet high with a trunk diameter of 3 feet. In cultivation here it never reaches those dimensions and is frequently a spreading bush 15 or more feet high and the same measurement across. The slender branches are clothed with oval leaves, rounded at the base and pointed at the apex, from 3 to 4 inches long and are bright green above, paler and clothed with greyish hairs below. The pure white, bell-shaped flowers are borne in clusters of 3 to 5 on slender pendulous stalks springing from the leaf-axils the whole length of the slender, arching branches. The blossoms measure about $\frac{3}{4}$ inch long and consist of 5, egg-shaped petals rounded at the tips and narrowed below and a tuft of yellow stamens which much enhance their beauty. The flowers are at their best during the months of April and May and are usually followed by woody, 4-winged seed vessels of a rich brown tint, which remain on the branches long after the leaves have fallen and frequently throughout the winter. It was introduced in 1756.

H. monticola is very closely allied to the preceding species and was formerly considered to be one of its varieties. In its native habitat in central U.S.A. it is an erect tree up to 100 feet in height, clothed with oblong-ovate or elliptic leaves with long slender points. The white, bell-shaped flowers are borne in the leaf-axils in May and are slightly larger than those of *E. carolina*. The var. *rosea* has pale pink flowers and is very lovely. The halesias flourish in any good well-drained loamy soil and are usually increased by imported seeds.

HALIMIUM LASIANTHUM FORMOSUM

(*Cistaceae*) [PLATE 20]

Formerly known as *Helianthemum formosum* this rather dwarf evergreen shrub is by far the best of the yellow-flowered sun roses. I have a specimen of this delightful sun rose in my garden which I purchased about ten years ago when it was not more than 6 inches high, being pot-grown and in full flower.

It is planted at the base of a south wall and flowers profusely every year and frequently sets a goodly crop of seeds. In such a situation it is a spreading, much-branched shrub rarely reaching more than 3 feet in height but is frequently much more in width. The branchlets are clothed with grey down mingled with whitish hairs. The leaves which are clothed in a similar manner to the branchlets when young become green with age, having lost the grey-green of the juvenile foliage; they are rather small, varying from oblong to egg-shape and have 3, prominent nerves. The richly tinted blossoms, which measure up to $1\frac{1}{2}$ inch across, are very freely produced on the short branchlets of the current season's growths and are at their best during May and June. In the best form they are bright yellow with a large crimson blotch at the base of each petal. In some specimens the blotch is crimson-brown.

This desirable shrub is a native of Portugal and although it has been in cultivation since 1780 it is very rarely seen in small gardens. It needs a well-drained light soil in full sun and is increased by seeds, cuttings, layers and division.

HAMAMELIS MOLLIS (*Hamamelidaceae*) [PLATE 20]

The best of the Witch Hazels, as these deciduous shrubs or small trees are termed, are natives of China and Japan and the most desirable of the Chinese and Japanese species is undoubtedly *Hamamelis mollis*, a native of China. It has been in cultivation for a considerable number of years but is not so frequently seen in small gardens as it deserves to be, for it flowers very early in the year and is most decorative when smothered with its starry golden yellow flowers when it is quite leafless.

It is a slow grower but flowers freely when but 2 feet high. When fully mature it forms a large bush or small tree up to 30 feet in height. The slender, diverging, dark brown branches are rather sparsely clothed with handsome, rather large, dark green leaves, shaped like those of the hazel, with deeply sunk veins and saw-toothed margins. The flowers are borne in almost stemless clusters composed of from 2 to 6 flowers with 4, very narrow strap-shaped, curving and twisted petals about 1 inch long, springing from a cup-shaped, bright purplish-red calyx; they are at their best in December and January in normal seasons and last well as cut flowers. This species is perfectly hardy and is not particular as to soil; it is increased by seeds and by grafts on *H. virginiana*.

HEDYSARUM CORONARIUM (*Leguminosae*) [PLATE 20]
The popular name of French Honeysuckle, by which this rather robust herbaceous perennial is known, was probably given to it on account of the faint resemblance of the scent of its flowers to that of the honeysuckle. In the middle of the last century it was a popular forage plant in France and many parts of southern Europe. Like many other members of the Leguminosae it can be grown in very poor, stony soils unfit for the cultivation of any other fodder plant and should make good silage.

The French Honeysuckle is perfectly hardy and is a very showy plant when in full flower, possessing much to recommend it for garden decoration but is rarely seen. It is a leafy perennial or sometimes biennial from 3 to 4 feet high of bushy habit, with rather spreading, branching stems, furnished with deep green pinnate leaves composed of from 3 to 5 pairs of elliptic or rounded, comparatively small leaflets. The very handsome deep red flowers are produced in densely packed ovoid clusters, from 2 to 4 inches long and are produced in June and July. To secure the best results this species should be given a sunny position and a rich loamy soil. It is increased by seeds and root-cuttings.

HELICHRYSUM BELLIDIOIDES (*Compositae*) [PLATE 21]
Of the two species of these charming little shrubs or sub-shrubs stocked by nurserymen who specialise in rock and alpine plants, the above-mentioned is probably the best for the amateur's garden. Although it is a native of the mountains of Southern Island, New Zealand, it is more amenable to cultivation in this country than *H. frigidum* which grows on the higher mountains of Corsica and is a very difficult subject to retain out of doors in our winters of alternating frost and thaw.

Helichrysum bellidioides is a prostrate evergreen shrublet rarely more than 3 to 4 inches high, forming a close mat of long, slender, silky branches and branchlets, well furnished with very small spoon-shaped or egg-shaped deep green leaves with cobweb-like hairs beneath. In July and August the whole plant is a sheet of snowy white everlasting flowers, composed mostly of solitary, terminal heads of scaly bracts and very numerous florets. Each head measures about $\frac{1}{2}$ inch across. This species is hardier than the majority of the perennial helichrysums and providing it is planted in gritty, perfectly drained soil in full sun or semi-shade it will survive most winters and thrive for years. It is increased by seeds and division.

H. frigidum very much resembles the preceding species and is also mat-forming, with its small leaves and stems densely clothed with hairs or down. Its flower-heads are rather larger and are solitary and sessile on the tips of the branchlets.

HELONIAS BULLATA (Liliaceae) [PLATE 21]
The genus Helonias apparently contains but few species. All are natives of North America and need a moist soil and a shady position for their well-being. The only available species seems to be *H. bullata* as the others do not appear to to be in cultivation here. It is a native of eastern North America and is perfectly hardy.

The short, stout, tuberous root-stock emits a number of rather thick, cylindrical roots after the manner of most of the moisture-loving plants. The rather stout, hollow flower-stem is furnished with a few bracts upwards and reaches a height of 1 to 2 feet. It is clothed at its base with long, broad, grass-like, pointed, rather thin, deep green, shining leaves, narrowed at the base and shortly stalked. The pink or purplish-pink flowers are borne in dense spikes 2 to 4 inches long. They commence to open in early April and continue to do so until early June. The individual blossom has a short tube which expands at its mouth into 6, lance-shaped, pointed segments, forming a flower about ½ inch wide. The very conspicuous bright blue stamens add much to the decorative value of the blossoms which are frequently rather pale in tint.

This desirable herbaceous plant should be given a cool, shady position in fibrous loam and peat, kept moist when it is in growth. Increase is by seeds and careful division in the spring. *H. latifolia* is a broad-leaved variety of the type and not a synonym.

HELONIOPSIS JAPONICA (Liliaceae) [PLATE 21]
The genus Heloniopsis as at present constituted numbers four species of bog or marsh evergreen perennial plants with pretty flowers, rather resembling those of a lily in miniature. This desirable plant is a native of Korea and Japan and is perfectly hardy. It is also known as *H. breviscapa* and has long, whitish, cylindrical roots springing from a small, stout root-stock.

The leaves, which number 20 or more, spring from the crown of the root-stock, forming a rosette or tuft 4 to 5 inches in diameter. They are fairly long, oblong-lance-shaped, gradually taper towards the base and are pointed at the tip; they have the almost unique habit of thrusting their tips into the soil and eventually producing tiny plants on their points, under favourable conditions. Their colour is a rich green, frequently tinted with purple or dull crimson when the plant is growing in a sunny position. The stout flower-stem springs from the centre of the rosette to a height of 4 to 6 inches and is furnished below the middle with from 1 to 3 narrow bracts. The stem is usually curved in the upper half and bears a raceme of 4 to 10 nodding flowers on down-curved stalks. The individual flower measures up to 1 inch in diameter and is of a pale or deep rose colour with purple anthers and a much elongated style. It thrives best on the banks of a pond or in the bog-garden, but can also be successfully grown in a low, moist position in the border.

HIPPEASTRUM PRATENSE (*Amaryllidaceae*)   [PLATE 21]
The South American continent is the native country of many very beautiful bulbous plants only a few of which thrive in the open air in this country, although they may inhabit elevated districts in the temperate regions of that continent. The brilliantly beautiful member of the amaryllis family described below is one of the exceptions for it is quite hardy in all but the bleak districts where periods of prolonged frost are normal. In the southern and western counties of Great Britain it needs no protection whatever.

It is a native of Chile and has a large, more or less globose, rather long necked bulb, which produces several dark green, rather long, linear leaves and a stout, erect flower-stem from 1 to $1\frac{1}{2}$ foot tall, bearing 3 to 4 bright scarlet flowers 2 to 3 inches across, with lance-shaped segments occasionally feathered with yellow. It flowers in the open air in July and August and has been in cultivation in this country for one hundred and twenty years, but one does not meet with it frequently even in mild districts although it is not difficult to cultivate. To obtain the best results the bulbs should be planted at the foot of a wall facing south, about 9 inches deep in good friable loam and left to establish themselves. The foliage will withstand fifteen degrees of frost and remain undamaged. It is also known as *Habranthus pratensis* and is subject to the ravages of the Merodon Fly, a serious pest to all growers of daffodils for commercial purposes.

HOUSTONIA CAERULEA (*Rubiaceae*)   [PLATE 21]
In its native Virginia this pretty little herbaceous plant is known by the name of Bluets, obviously on account of its flowers being normally blue. It is one of the many dwarf herbaceous plants suitable for carpeting the ground beneath sparsely branched deciduous shrubs, which flower at the same time of year and flourish under the same conditions as the carpeting plant. Some very pleasing colour combinations can be obtained in this manner. *Houstonia caerulea* is a small, tufted perennial reaching a maximum

PLATE 21

1. *Helichrysum bellidioides*   2. *Helichrysum frigidum*   3. *Heloniopsis japonica*
4. *Helonias bullata var. latifolia*
5. *Hippeastrum pratense*   6. *Houstonia caerulea*

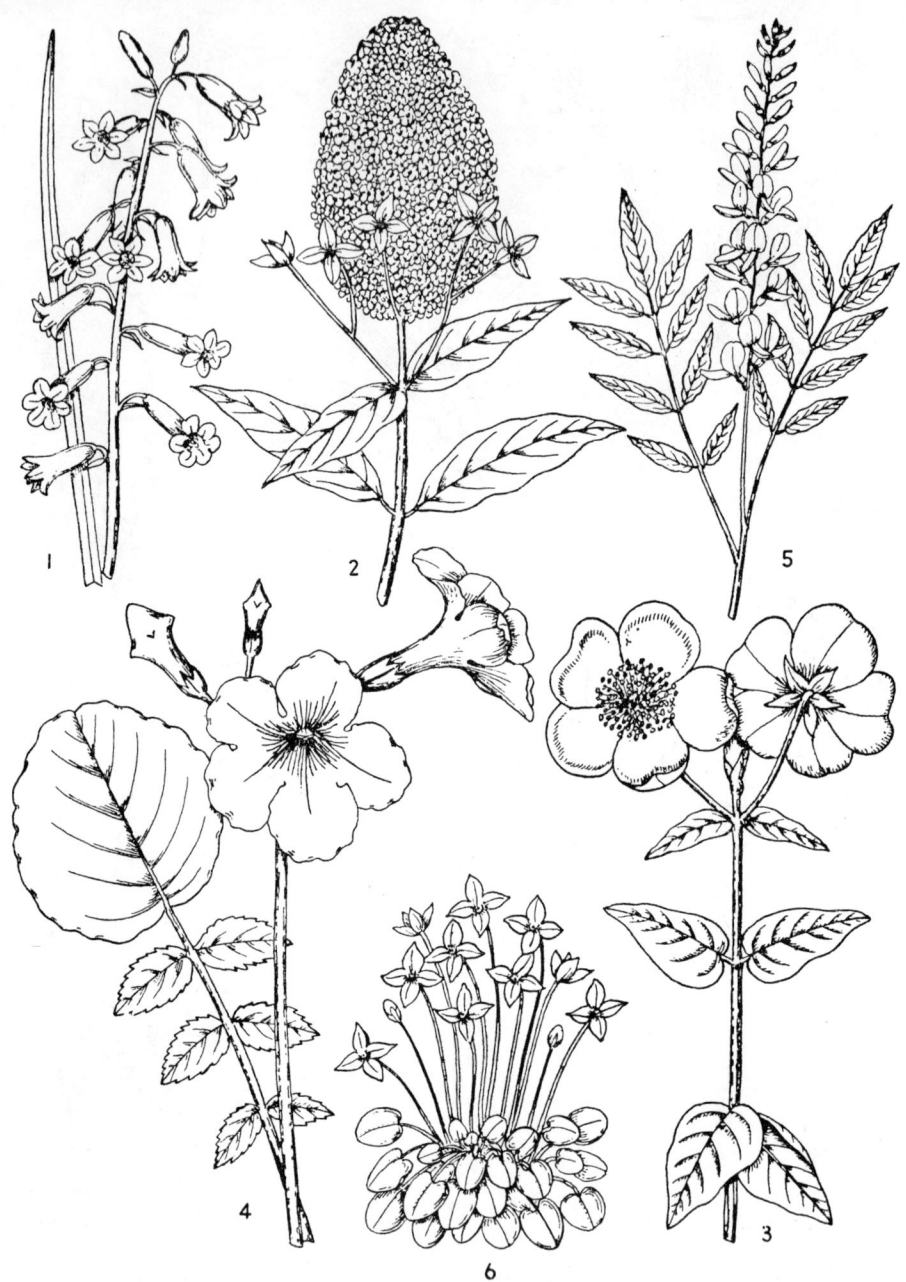

PLATE 22

1. *Hyacinthus amethystinus*
2. *Hydrangea paniculata var. grandiflora*
3. *Hypericum patulum var. forrestii*
4. *Incarvillea grandiflora var. brevipes*
5. *Indigofera gerardiana*
6. *Ionopsidium acaule*

height of 6 inches. The root-leaves are spoon-shaped and hairy; those on the stems are small, ovate-lance-shaped and narrowed to the base. The dainty flowers are solitary on the tips of the slender flower-stems and are saucer-shaped, about ½ inch in diameter and are normally of a bright azure blue, with a yellow eye. In some specimens the blue is sometimes tinged with pink. There is a white-flowered, yellow-eyed form which is not so striking as the blue type.

This little plant flowers during the summer and autumn months and is quite hardy. It does not seem to be over particular with regard to soil, for it will thrive equally well in leaf-soil and sand, peat and sand and moderately rich loam, but it must be lime-free and well supplied with underground moisture in summer. The position in which it is planted should be one shaded from the mid-day sun. Increase is by seeds and division.

HYACINTHUS AMETHYSTINUS (*Liliaceae*) [PLATE 22]
The general opinion amongst those who know this little bulbous plant—including myself—is that it is by far the most beautiful of the hyacinth species in cultivation. It has been in cultivation in this country for over two hundred years and is yet very rarely seen in small gardens where it should be as popular as the well-known roman hyacinth. It is known as the Spanish Hyacinth and is found on the thinly wooded slopes of the Pyrenees.

It has a smallish ovoid bulb which produces up to 8, fairly long, narrow-linear, rich green leaves. The flower-stem is from 4 to 12 inches long and bears a loose raceme of from 6 to 15 lovely bright blue blossoms. Each is about ⅝ inch long and is subtended by a linear, pointed bract. The flower has a narrow, cylindrical tube which widens upwards and is cleft into 6, ovate, tooth-like lobes at its mouth. The flowers usually start to open at the beginning of May and continue to do so until the end of June. Like all the hyacinth species it has a pure white form. It should be given a semi-shady position in good friable loam and leaf-soil and is increased by offsets and seeds.

Hyacinthus azureus is a very charming little species found on the mountains of Asia Minor. It has dense, conical spikes of sky-blue, bell-shaped flowers, which are more open than those of the muscari to which it has been referred. It thrives in a light, loamy compost in a sunny position and flowers from February to April.

HYDRANGEA PANICULATA
                   var. **GRANDIFLORA** (*Saxifragaceae*) [PLATE 22]
Although one does occasionally see a specimen of the type of this Chinese

and Japanese deciduous shrub in suburban gardens, it is very much less frequently cultivated than the popular *H. hortensis*, which is only truly hardy in the southern and western districts of the British Isles. The type of *H. paniculata* is usually a small bush in this country, kept in shape by judicious pruning, but in the wild it frequently reaches tree-like dimensions.

It is sparsely branched and its branchlets are rather thinly furnished with large, oval or ovate, pointed, toothed leaves. The inflorescence is an erect panicle, pyramidal in shape, from 6 to 18 inches long, borne on the tips of the branchlets. It is composed of fertile and sterile flowers. The sterile flowers measure up to $1\frac{1}{4}$ inch across and are pure white at first, later turning to pink and finally to green. The fertile flowers are small, closely packed and of a yellowish white. The type flowers from July to October and the variety *grandiflora* about a month earlier. In the variety all the flowers are sterile and its panicle is longer, sometimes reaching a length of 2 feet. The type and its variety should be planted in good loam and leaf-soil in an open, sunny position and the previous season's branches should be cut back to within 2 or 3 buds of the base as this shrub flowers on the young growths. It is easily increased by layers and also by cuttings.

HYPERICUM PATULUM
var. FORRESTII (*Hypericaceae*) [PLATE 22]

The type of this most beautiful of the hardy, shrubby St Johnsworts is a native of the Himalaya and western China and is quite frequently seen in suburban front gardens, but is much less desirable from a decorative point of view than its two varieties *henryi* and *forrestii*. Of the two varieties *forrestii* is the better for its flowers are larger and of greater substance.

In an open situation where it is not crowded by other shrubs it forms a spreading bush from 2 to 4 feet tall, with arching branches which are purplish when they are young. The deciduous ovate or ovate-lance-shaped leaves are of medium size and are a rich red when they develop in the spring, gradually changing to a soft, fairly light green as spring passes into summer, when the under surface of the leaf assumes its normal silvery colour. In the autumn they change to delightful tints of gold and crimson before they fall. The golden yellow flowers measure from 2 to nearly 3 inches in diameter and have rounded, overlapping petals and numerous yellow stamens arranged in bundles of 5.

This variety of *H. patulum* produces its blossoms from July to October and is a native of China. It is not exacting as to soil and any light medium is suitable, but it should have a sunny position to ensure the ripening of the side shoots which will bear next year's flowers. Propagation is by cuttings and also by seeds, the seedlings taking 4 years to form flowering plants under normal conditions.

INCARVILLEA GRANDIFLORA
var. BREVIPES (*Bignoniaceae*) [PLATE 22]

Of the several hardy species of Incarvillea in cultivation *I. grandiflora* is without doubt one of the most beautiful. It was discovered in stony, alpine meadows on the Lichiang mountains in north-western Yunnan, western China and has been in cultivation here for over fifty years. It is a hardy perennial, and dies down to below the ground level in the autumn.

The long, thick, rather woody root-stock produces a sparse tuft of long-stalked, rich green pinnate leaves, composed of 7 to 9 leaflets or segments. The lateral ones are ovate, pointed and coarsely toothed. The terminal one is very much larger than the lateral segments and is rounded and bluntly toothed. The lovely flowers resemble those of a gloxinia and measure about 3 inches across. The variety is much to be preferred to the species since the colour of the flowers is very much more brilliant. They are of a rich crimson throughout except the throat which is orange streaked with white and are borne on short stalks springing from the apex of the stout, erect flower-stem, which reaches a height of about $1\frac{1}{2}$ foot. They are at their best during August and September.

This handsome plant does best in a position shaded from the mid-day sun in good, deep, sandy loam, which should be well-drained but moist when the plant is in growth. Such pests as wire-worm and other root-eating grubs seem to have a special liking for the roots of incarvilleas and many a plant's demise may have been caused by these pests. Propagation is by hand-fertilised seeds.

INDIGOFERA GERARDIANA (*Leguminosae*) [PLATE 22]

The reason why this graceful pea-flowered shrub is not more frequently seen is perhaps because of its liability to be killed to ground level by severe frost, and it is only in mild localities that it attains its full development. This may be true, but as the flowers are borne on the current year's growths it is of no moment, for the plant invariably sends up fresh shoots, 3 to 5 feet high which usually bear larger inflorescences than those that have survived the winter. The species under consideration is a native of the Himalaya and seems to be used as a fodder plant by some of the inhabitants of these elevated regions. It is deciduous and when not cut down by frost may reach a height of 8 to 10 feet.

The slender, branching stems are moderately well clothed with pinnate, fresh green leaves, composed of 6 to 10 pairs of ovate- lance-shaped leaflets and an odd terminal one. The dainty pink flowers, which measure about $\frac{1}{2}$ inch long, are borne in many-flowered racemes springing from the leaf-axils and are produced from June to September. If space can be afforded the two following very desirable species should certainly be grown. They are *I. atropurpurea* with beautiful rosy maroon flowers and *I. deilsiana* with bright rosy pink ones. Both are natives of China. The indigoferas are not particular as to soil but should be given a sunny, sheltered position. Increase is by seeds and cuttings.

IONOPSIDIUM ACAULE (*Cruciferae*) [PLATE 22]
The Violet Cress, as this charming little annual is termed, is a native of Portugal, Spain and Morocco and is now relegated to the genus Cochlearia under the name of *C. acaulis*, but I have purposely retained the name by which it has been known for many years and under which it may usually be traced in seedsmen's catalogues. It is a most useful little plant to sow beneath sparsely-leafy trees, soon forming a carpet of verdure and lovely little flowers. In following this advice care should be taken to sow the seeds around trees and shrubs which thrive under the same conditions and flower at the same time as the Violet Cress.

The plant forms tufts of small, spoon-shaped or almost circular, rich green leaves but 2 to 3 inches high, either entire or sometimes 3-lobed. The 4-petaled flowers measure about $\frac{3}{8}$ inch in diameter under good cultivation and are lilac with a violet tinge, or almost pure white, when they are not in the least attractive. They are borne on long stalks and are produced very freely from June to November, almost hiding the foliage and have a sweet, honey-like scent. The seeds should be sown out of doors in April, in almost any soil which is not hot, dry and sandy, for this little plant needs cool conditions and moisture at the root to give of its best. As a rule it is only necessary to make one sowing as it maintains itself by self-sown seeds. Seeds sown in April will produce flowering plants in June.

IPHEION UNIFLORUM (*Liliaceae*) [PLATE 23]
In the light gravelly soil of my garden which is situated in the London district, this delightful little bulbous plant has become a weed, but a very charming one. I have had it in cultivation for over forty years and over that period we have of course experienced some very severe winters, but it has always come through unscathed despite the fact that its leaves appear

during the month of November. It has acquired the very apt name of Spring Star-flower and blossoms from March to May.

The root-stock is an oblong or irregularly shaped, tuber-like, white bulb. It produces 2 or sometimes more, linear, rather long, pale but bright green leaves, which are usually curved sideways and lie more or less upon the surface of the soil. The leafless flower-stem is from 4 to 6 inches long and bears a membranous bract below the solitary flower, which is composed of 6, oblong, pointed or blunt segments, spreading in a star-shaped manner, forming a blossom about $1\frac{1}{2}$ inch across. They are fragrant and vary in tint from pale porcelain blue to pure white and there appears to be a rose-coloured form which does not seem to be in cultivation.

This species is a native of the Argentine and appears to be common in sandy localities around Buenos Aires and was introduced in 1832. It naturalises itself by seeds and thrives in any light, well-drained soil in full sun. The leaves and stems emit a strong odour of garlic when bruised. It is also known as *Milla uniflora* and *Triteleia uniflora*.

IRIS CRISTATA *(Iridaceae)* [PLATE 23]

Although the flowers of the four species of Iris described in the following pages have not the value for garden decoration possessed by the popular varieties of the flag or bearded iris, their construction and the exquisite colouring of their flowers should appeal to all flower-lovers who value them for their intrinsic loveliness, apart from their size and decorative value.

Iris cristata is a native of eastern North America and produces tufts of narrow, grass-like, rather short, blue-green leaves. The charming, amethyst-blue flowers have yellow, crested, beautifully fringed falls and are very freely produced on stems about 6 inches high, normally in April but in some mild seasons may be gathered in early March. This species should be grown in light, friable loam and leaf-soil, in semi-shade. It is advisable to plant this iris on the surface of the soil and secure it with pieces of stone until it has rooted.

Iris danfordiae is a little gem. It has a long, narrow bulb and grass-like leaves which are extremely short at flowering time. The flower-stem is from 2 to 4 inches high and bears a solitary flower with yellow or orange falls, spotted with brown or green and has bristle-like standards. This species is a native of Asia Minor and flowers in February and March. It should be given a position where the early morning sun does not reach it in rich, sandy loam. A pane of glass should be placed over it when the leaves die down to ripen the bulbs.

IRIS GRACILIPES [PLATE 23]

The flowers of this delightful little Iris are of an unusual shape, the standards being small and oblong and the falls large and almost violin-shaped. It is a native of central Japan and is quite hardy in this country. Unlike that of the preceding species the root-stock of this iris is a slender rhizome

It produces dense tufts of usually glaucous, fairly long, linear or narrowly sword-shaped, pointed leaves. The slender flower-stems are produced beside the tufts and reach a height of about 9 inches. Each bears 2 to 3 blossoms on fairly long stalks, subtended by a long, slender, pointed bract or sheath. The lower part of the flower-stem is clothed with a few glaucous, reduced leaves. The flowers are produced in April and May and have pale purple or lilac standards and falls which are striped with deep purple and have yellow crests. This species thrives in moist loam and leaf-soil in semi-shade and is increased by seeds and division.

In my opinion the most beautiful species of iris in cultivation is *I. wattii*. It too is a native of Japan and has a root-stock which produces tubers and tufts of dark green leaves very similar to those of *Iris germanica*. The exquisite bluish-mauve, elegantly frilled blossoms have orange crests and are borne in racemes during May and June. It needs a sheltered, well-drained position in gritty soil and a hand-light placed over it in the winter to protect its young growths from frost in the spring. Increase is by division of the tubers.

ITEA VIRGINICA *(Saxifragaceae)* [PLATE 23]

This attractive deciduous shrub is well suited for growing in small gardens but although it was introduced into this country well over two hundred years ago it is but rarely seen. It is quite hardy and is of compact and neat habit.

Its more or less erect stems reach a height of from 3 to 5 feet and are well clothed with attractive, rather large narrow oval or lance-shaped leaves, narrowed below and tapering to a point at the apex; they are borne on very short stalks and the margins of the leaves are very finely serrated. The sweetly scented flowers are borne in erect, dense racemes 3 to 6 inches long, which are more or less cylindrical. They are freely produced during July and August when the majority of flowering shrubs have passed out of flower. The individual flower measures nearly $\frac{3}{4}$ inch in diameter and is composed of 5, narrow white petals, with a tuft of pale yellow stamens in its centre.

It is a member of the saxifrage family and is a native of eastern North America ranging from New Jersey to Florida, inhabiting woods where the

PLATE 23

1. *Ipheion uniflorum* 2. *Iris cristata* 3. *Iris wattii*
4. *Itea virginica* 5. *Ixiolirion montanum* 6. *Jasminum revolutum*

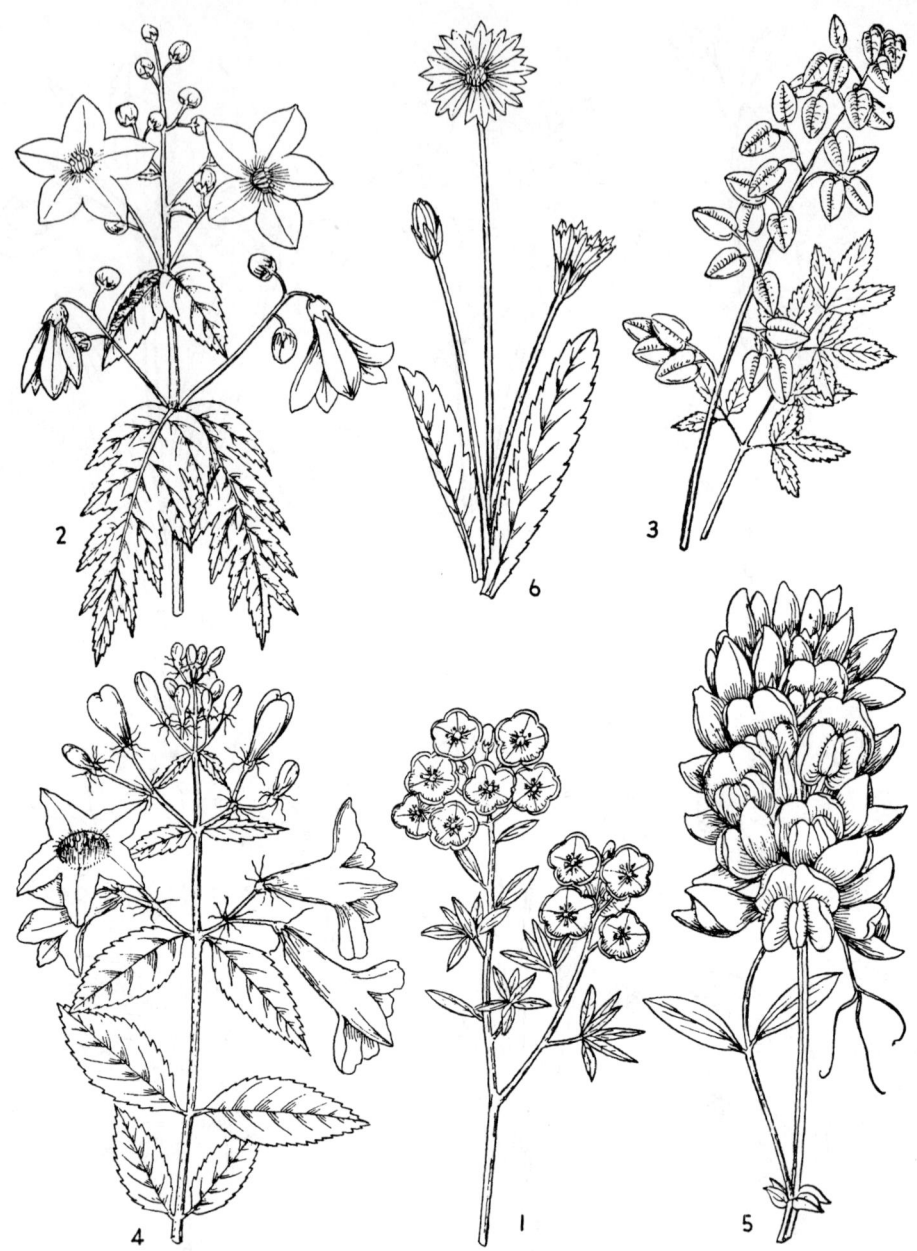

PLATE 24

1. *Kalmia polifolia var. microphylla*
2. *Kirengeshoma palmata*
3. *Koelreuteria paniculata*
4. *Kolkwitzia amabilis*
5. *Lathyrus pubescens*
6. *Layia elegans*

soil is moist but not swampy. It is easily grown in good, deep, friable loam or in peaty soils in a position where it is not exposed to full sunshine, with plenty of water in dry weather. Propagation is by seeds and also by suckers.

IXIOLIRION MONTANUM (*Amaryllidaceae*) [PLATE 23]
In my old much valued copy of Cassell's *Dictionary of Gardening* published at the beginning of this century, under the heading of Ixiolirion the following statement occurs: 'Syrian bulbous-rooted plants which, though introduced in 1844, have not become very common. They are perfectly hardy, and produce such charming flowers that they are worthy of inclusion in every garden.' The above statement is thoroughly applicable at the present day and *Ixiolirion montanum* may definitely be considered an unfamiliar flower.

It possesses a fairly large globose-ovoid bulb which produces several, rather long, broadly linear leaves tapering to a point. The erect flower stem reaches a height of from $1\frac{1}{2}$ to 2 feet and bears a panicle of beautiful flowers varying from sky blue to purple, each with 6, oblong or ovate, spreading and recurved segments forming a somewhat starry blossom quite 2 inches in diameter. They are produced in June and are very useful as cut flowers. This species is a native of central Asia, the native country of a number of beautiful bulbous plants including the finest of all the tulips, *Tulipa fosteriana*.

The bulbs of this ixiolirion should be planted in light, sandy soil in a position fully exposed to the sun at a depth of 2 to 3 inches. It is better to plant them in the autumn than in the spring. In counties with a low sunshine record they should be lifted and baked in a sunny greenhouse or window and are increased by offsets and seeds.

JASMINUM REVOLUTUM (*Oleaceae*) [PLATE 23]
One occasionally sees an old bush of this very attractive evergreen shrub in old gardens, but considering its sterling merits, it is difficult to understand why it is not more frequently cultivated. This may be because in open, bleak situations it is apt to be severely damaged in hard winters but given the shelter of a south or west wall it will thrive and unfailingly produce a wealth of its rich, golden-yellow, very fragrant blossoms in June and July. This jasmine is sometimes termed the Italian Jasmine although it is a native of Afghanistan and is considered by some authorities to be a robust form of *Jasminum humile*.

It is of a somewhat dense, lax habit, with slender, arching, green branches, furnished with pinnate rich green leaves from 2 to 4 inches long, with 5 to 9, ovate-lance-shaped, pointed leaflets, the terminal one being much the largest. The lovely flowers measure about 1 inch in diameter and are borne in loose clusters of about a dozen on slender, branched stalks, springing from the top of the flower-stem, in the leaf-axils. In warm sunny seasons the flowers are followed by a crop of oval, black berries. This jasmine thrives in a sunny position in any light soil however poor and is increased by layers, cuttings and seeds. The unripened autumnal growths are at times killed by frost, but as the flowers are borne on the current year's shoots this is of no consequence.

KALMIA POLIFOLIA (*Ericaceae*) [PLATE 24]

Where a choice dwarf shrub is needed to keep the low-growing daphnes company, especially in gardens of limited extent this beautiful Kalmia should be chosen, for it rarely exceeds two feet in height and is very floriferous. This kalmia is often listed as *K. glauca*. It is an evergreen shrub and takes a number of years to reach the above mentioned height and flowers freely when but a foot tall.

The numerous slender branches are furnished with rather small, oblong to lance-shaped, rich green leaves, tapering at both ends. They are glaucous or nearly white beneath. The very beautiful blossoms vary from rose-lilac to bright rose-purple, each measuring up to $\frac{3}{4}$ inch in diameter. They are borne very profusely in terminal umbels about 2 inches wide in April and May, and frequently again in the autumn. This species is a native of U.S.A. and Canada. All the kalmias are slow in growth but this is no drawback as they flower when quite small.

The variety *microphylla* is an extremely beautiful diffuse, evergreen shrub, always under a foot in height, with oval or egg-shaped leaves and flowers of a rosy lilac tint, very freely produced. It is a native of north-western America from California to Yukon and has been in cultivation here for nearly sixty years. All the kalmias thrive in peat, loam and leaf-soil and are lime-haters. Propagation is by seeds and cuttings.

KIRENGESHOMA PALMATA (*Saxifragaceae*) [PLATE 24]

Japan possesses a more interesting and beautiful flora than any other country in the temperate regions of similar area. The plant under consideration is among the most desirable of the Japanese plants which grace our gardens. It is rarely cultivated by amateur gardeners and deserves to be more widely known on account of its handsome foliage, graceful habit and the beauty of its interesting flowers. In Japan it is found on the moist, shady sides of low hills and is perfectly hardy in this country.

Kirengeshoma palmata is herbaceous and a sound perennial with slender, branching, purple or almost ebony coloured stems which reach a height of 3 to 4 feet when the plant is in flower. They are well clothed with large, handsome, long-stalked sycamore-like, thin, hairy, deep green leaves, divided for one-third of their length into from 5 to 9 triangular, sharply pointed coarsely toothed lobes. The shining, creamy or straw-coloured flowers are borne in clusters of usually 3, on long curving stalks, springing from the axils of reduced leaves or bracts on the upper part of the stems, the whole forming a large, loose, spreading inflorescence. The flower is composed of 5, ovate-oblong, rather fleshy petals forming a bell-shaped flower $1\frac{1}{2}$ inch wide; they are produced from August until October and last well as cut flowers. This plant needs a moist shady position in a slightly acid soil but not under the drip of trees and is increased by division in spring.

KOELREUTERIA PANICULATA (*Sapindaceae*) [PLATE 24]
It must be admitted that this extremely handsome deciduous tree is perhaps too robust in habit when fully developed to be afforded a place in gardens of limited area. Nevertheless, I would advise any of my readers who have, say, an unwanted sycamore or one of our native forest trees in their garden, to have it removed and replaced by a specimen of this tree which is completely hardy and very decorative in foliage, flower and fruit. There is a fine old specimen of this tree at Hampton Court which is a beautiful sight in July and August when laden with great panicles of bright yellow flowers.

It is a native of north-eastern Asia and when mature is a round-headed tree from 30 to 40 feet high, with a stout, short trunk and thick, spreading branches. The large bright green, pinnate leaves are composed of from 9 to 15, ovate, coarsely toothed leaflets which gradually turn to a bright yellow in the autumn. The bright yellow flowers are borne in huge panicles on the ends of the branchlets all over the tree. Each individual flower is composed of a bell-shaped, toothed calyx and 3 or rarely 4 narrowly oblong, blunt petals, spread out fan-wise, each about $\frac{5}{8}$ inch long, with 2 red glands at the base. The fruit is a membraneous capsule about 2 inches long, containing several large black seeds. A well-drained soil in an open, sunny position meets its requirements. Increase is by seeds and cuttings.

KOLKWITZIA AMABILIS (*Caprifoliaceae*) [PLATE 24]
I do not know how this very elegant shrub acquired its popular name of Beauty Bush, possibly on account of its specific name. A more appropriate

one it would be difficult to find. This most desirable shrub is a stranger to the majority of non-professional gardeners and certainly deserves to be as widely cultivated as are the well-known weigelas and other members of the honeysuckle family, to which this deciduous shrub belongs. In early summer when smothered with its delicately tinted blossoms it is a perfect picture of floral beauty, but to ensure an abundant display of flowers this shrub must be given a sunny position in poor stony soil with restriction of its root-run. A rich soil produces much foliage and but few flowers. It is a native of north-western China and has been in cultivation in this country for sixty years, and is perfectly hardy.

Under favourable conditions it forms a rounded, many-branched bush from 6 to 10 feet high. The slender branches are clothed with opposite, medium-sized, broadly ovate, pointed, bright green leaves, toothed and ciliate on their margins. The lovely pale pink, yellow or orange-throated blossoms have a broadly funnel-shaped tube expanded upwards into 5, spreading lobes and are about 1 inch across. They are borne in corymbs 2 to 3 inches long, composed of a dozen or so blossoms. Increase is by seeds and cuttings.

LATHYRUS PUBESCENS (*Leguminosae*) [PLATE 24]
It must be admitted that this beautiful climbing herbaceous or semi-evergreen perennial will not survive a hard winter in exposed districts, but I grew it with complete success in a narrow border along the base of a south wall a few miles south of London with only a little protection to its roots and growths. I raised my plants from seed which is still procurable and I would like to advise my readers to purchase a packet of seeds and make an attempt to grow and flower this very desirable plant.

When growing under congenial conditions it will reach a height of 8 feet or more. The brittle, branching, winged, hairy stems are rather thinly clothed with pale green leaves, composed of a pair of rather large oblong-lance-shaped leaflets margined with fine hairs. They are borne on a long stalk with a 3-branched tendril at its apex and a pair of conspicuous stipules at its base. The lovely flowers are borne in dense racemes 3 or more inches long, carried on long, grooved, hairy stems. The raceme is composed of at least 20 blossoms of the usual pea-flower shape, each measuring about 1 inch long and the same measurement in width. It has a violet-blue standard, lilac wings and a white keel with a red tip. This species is a native of southern Brazil, Uruguay, Argentina and Chile. It is not a long-lived plant and needs a good, light, well-drained loam and a sheltered position.

LAYIA ELEGANS (*Compositae*) [PLATE 24]
In its native country of western North America this very attractive member of the daisy family is known as Tidy Tips. This name is probably given to the plant on account of the tips of the ray florets being white and the remaining portion coloured. In an open sunny position where it is not encroached upon by other plants, it forms a much-branched little bush about 12 inches high. The slender, reddish-brown stems and branches are furnished with attractive, bright green, medium-sized, pinnate, cut and lobed leaves below and narrowly lance-shaped, entire, almost stem-clasping leaves towards the flower-heads.

In well-grown plants the numerous flower-heads almost hide the foliage and it is then that the plant well deserves its specific name. Each flower-head measures from $1\frac{1}{2}$ to 2 inches in diameter and is composed of 10 to 12 strap-shaped or oblong, densely arranged ray florets, each with 3 teeth at its truncate apex. They are normally bright yellow, tipped with white, but there is a pure white form which is not so attractive. The disc florets are tubular and are of a deep yellow tint, which adds to the beauty of the flowers. Unlike those of most of the daisy family they are sweetly scented, and are very excellent as cut flowers. *Layia elegans* thrives in any light soil and seeds may be sown under glass in March or April or in the garden where they are to bloom in May.

LESPEDEZA THUNBERGII (*Leguminosae*) [PLATE 25]
Flowering as it does in October and November, this graceful member of the pea-flowered family is a very desirable subject for garden decoration in the last months of the year when there are only a few shrubby plants in flower. The lespedezas comprise a number of annual, perennial herbaceous plants and shrubs, collectively known as Bush Clovers, only a few of which are worth growing where space is limited. *Lespedeza thunbergii* has also been known as *L. bicolor* and *Desmodium penduliflorum* and is a semi-woody or shrubby perennial with stems which are persistent in mild winters like those of the hardy fuchsias.

The stems are produced annually and reach a height of from 4 to 8 feet. They are furnished with stalked, trifoliate bright green leaves with medium-sized, ovate-lance-shaped leaflets, which are clothed with grey down beneath. The middle leaflet has a rather long stalk. The pretty flowers are borne in many-flowered racemes from 3 to 6 inches long in the upper leaf-axils, the whole inflorescence forming a loose panicle up to 2 feet in length. The rosy purple flowers measure from $\frac{1}{2}$ to $\frac{3}{4}$ inch long and are usually followed by small, ovate, scaly pods. It is a native of northern China and Japan and is quite hardy. In the cultivation of this shrub the best results are obtained if the previous season's growths are cut down almost to the ground level in early spring. Propagation is usually by seeds.

LEUCOJUM VERNUM
var. VAGNERI (*Amaryllidaceae*) [PLATE 25]

The variety of the Spring Snowflake known as *vagneri* and formerly as *carpathicum* is a native of Hungary and is much superior to the type from a decorative point of view, although it must be admitted that the type of the Spring Snowflake is a very elegant plant and is perhaps more graceful than the variety.

The variety has a rather large globose bulb, covered with a tough skin. It produces up to half a dozen long, broad, strap-shaped, rich green leaves. The flowers, which are often fully open before the leaves have reached their full dimensions, are usually borne in pairs, on down-curved stalks, subtended by a large bract-like sheath on the apex of the stem, which reaches a height of 9 to 15 inches. The flower is similar to that of the type but frequently measures an inch in diameter when fully open. In the type the coloured spot at the tips of the segments is always green. In the variety it is usually yellow, but specimens may occur in which the spot is yellowish-green. Normally it flowers in January and February, but in mild seasons it may flower a month earlier.

It is easily cultivated in rich loam and requires a certain amount of moisture at the roots when growth is active. It seems to thrive best when planted amongst sparsely-leaved shrubs, and the bulbs are covered with about 4 inches of soil and left undisturbed to establish themselves. Increase is by offsets and seeds.

LEWISIA HECKNERI (*Portulacaceae*) [PLATE 25]

All the species of Lewisia in cultivation are worthy of a place in our gardens; some have flowers of almost unique tints, rarely seen in the other occupants of the rock garden. The various species of which there is no great number, are found on the mountains of western North America, growing in crevices in rocks in sunny places, and to cultivate them successfully in our comparatively dull climate it is necessary to imitate as far as possible the conditions under which they thrive in the wild.

Lewisia heckneri is certainly one of the most beautiful of these charming, somewhat succulent perennials. It has a fleshy root-stock which produces a rosette of fairly long, dark green, egg-shaped or spoon-shaped, slightly

PLATE 25

1. *Lespedeza thunbergii* 2. *Leucojum vernum var. vagneri*
3. *Lewisia heckneri* 4. *Liatris pycnostachya* 5. *Lilium amabile*
6. *Lilium × testaceum*

PLATE 26

1. *Limnanthes douglasii* 2. *Linaria alpina* 3. *Linum arboreum*
4. *Liriope graminifolia* 5. *Lithospermum rosmarinifolium*
6. *Lonicera tragophylla*

toothed, somewhat crinkled leaves, margined with stiff hairs. Several flower-stems are produced, which curve outwards and reach a height of about 6 inches. Each bears from 10 to 12 very beautiful flowers of a pure pink with oblong, blunt petals, forming blossoms about 1 inch diameter. This species is a native of California and flowers from May to July.

Lewisia tweedyi is an exceedingly beautiful species with a large rosette of big, fleshy, ovate or egg-shaped, shining, rich green leaves and several stout flower-stems, each bearing 1 to 2 blossoms of a pale straw-colour, shading to pink on the tips and margins of their petals. Each flower is composed of 6 to 8 petals and measures 2 to $3\frac{1}{2}$ inches across. A compost of gritty loam and peat suits both species. Increase is by seeds.

LIATRIS PYCNOSTACHYA *(Compositae)* [PLATE 25]

All the species of Liatris, of which some twenty have been described, are natives of North America and grow in open situations among grasses and thin vegetation. In addition to their unquestionable decorative value, they are of considerable importance for furnishing poor, dry soil in sun-baked positions.

Liatris pycnostachya is known in its native habitat as Button Snake-root and Blazing Star. It is perhaps more frequently grown than any other species, but is not so common in gardens on hungry soils as its merits deserve. Like all the members of its genus, it has a corm-like root-stock, which produces offsets from which several erect, stiff stems arise to a height of from 4 to 6 feet. They are unbranched and are rather densely clothed above with narrow, sessile, pointed leaves and with longer lance-shaped ones below. The upper 12 inches of the stem are occupied by a cylindrical spike of very densely crowded purplish flower-heads, surrounded by scaly bracts of the same colour. The flower consists of a number of linear ray-florets, each about $\frac{1}{2}$ inch long, with the usual tubular disc florets in the centre. The flower heads are at their best in August.

Liatris elegans is another desirable species, which is considered by some hardy plant specialists to be superior to the preceding. Its leafy stems terminate in spikes 12 to 20 inches long of purplish flower-heads. Both species are increased by offsets and seeds.

LILIUM AMABILE *(Liliaceae)* [PLATE 25]

Apart from such well-known lilies as *candidum, croceum, regale, tigrinum* and *umbellatum,* one does not see the many other easily cultivated species in cultivation in suburban gardens. The six lilies described below are amongst the most easily grown of these beautiful plants and are very showy and decorative. Unfortunately most of the lily species require special treatment, and many are plants for the specialist only, being decidedly difficult to grow.

Lilium amabile is a handsome species, introduced from Korea about fifty years ago. The stem is more or less naked below and reaches a height of 3 to 4 feet. It is clothed with scattered, narrowly lance-shaped leaves, covered with minute hairs. The showy flowers are borne in racemes, composed of 3 to 6 nodding blossoms of a grenadine red, spotted with black and are produced in July. It should be planted in a position where its roots and stem are shaded by other plants—this applies to all lilies—in good, friable loam. This species is a stem-rooting lily, which should be mulched with rich soil as soon as the roots appear at the base of the stem.

Lilium chalcedonicum is a remarkably showy species. It is a native of Greece and has an erect stem 2 to 4 feet high, furnished with lance-shaped leaves. The brilliant, sealing-wax scarlet blossoms are borne in racemes of up to 6, in July. They are nodding and have much recurved segments. This species needs the same cultural treatment as the preceding.

LILIUM DAVIDII

A considerable number of very desirable lilies have been introduced into this country from China and Japan during the present century, amongst which *Lilium davidii* is one of the most easily grown and decorative. It is a native of China and is one of the stem-rooting lilies which produces stolons with small bulbs at their tips. The stiff, erect, slightly hairy stem is furnished with numerous, fairly long, lance-shaped leaves with their margins curved under. The showy orange-red or scarlet flowers are spotted with black and have recurved segments. They are borne in spreading panicles of up to 20 blossoms in July and August. This species thrives under the same cultural conditions as *Lilium amabile*.

In *Lilium hansonii* we have yet another of the showy eastern species of easy culture. It is a native of Siberia and Korea and has been in cultivation in this country for nearly a hundred years. It is elegant in habit and has a smooth, slender stem from 3 to 4 feet tall, clothed with several whorls of fairly long lance-shaped, pointed leaves. The nodding flowers are borne in loose racemes or rather crowded umbels in June and July. The rather fleshy flower has lance-shaped, recurved segments of an orange yellow colour, spotted with brown. This is also one of the stem-rooting lilies, and although it is not particular as to soil, thrives best in a good, friable loam and should be well supplied with moisture when in active growth.

LILIUM SUPERBUM [PLATE 25]

Several very handsome lilies are very suitable for planting on the banks of a stream or pond and *Lilium superbum* is one of the best of them and well deserves its specific name for it is a magnificent plant. Its stout, erect stem reaches a height of from 4 to 8 feet and is furnished with whorls of narrowly linear- lance-shaped, pointed leaves. The brilliant flowers are borne in large panicles composed of 20 to 30 flowers with recurved petals 3 to 4 inches long, ranging in colour from orange to crimson, and thickly spotted with maroon. It flowers in July and August and is a native of eastern North America. This species thrives best in a moist, peaty soil, similar to that suitable for rhododendrons.

Lilium × *testaceum* is one of the most elegant lilies in cultivation and is a garden hybrid between *L. candidum* and *L. chalcedonicum*. It partakes of the habits of both its parents and has a slender, grooved stem, from 4 to 6 feet tall, clothed with very many, scattered, linear leaves. The flowers are nankeen or pale apricot yellow, and are borne in racemes composed of 6 to 12 blossoms in July and August. It thrives under the same conditions as the Madonna Lily. If possible all lily bulbs should be obtained as soon as their stems die down and planted immediately at a depth of 3 to 10 inches according to the size of the bulb which should be surrounded by sharp sand. Propagation is by seeds, offsets, bulbils and scales. Seedlings rarely take less than five years to form flowering bulbs.

LIMNANTHES DOUGLASII (*Limnanthaceae*) [PLATE 26]

In this species we have yet another delightful Californian annual which is occasionally seen in amateurs' gardens, especially if they are bee-keepers, for together with *Phacelia tanacetifolia* it was rather extensively grown in the past as bees are very fond of it, but it is far less commonly cultivated to-day. Six or seven species of Limnanthes have been described by botanists, all of which are natives of the coastal states of western U.S.A. The species described below is probably the best of these hardy annuals from a decorative point of view.

Limnanthes douglasii produces several ascending stems from its root-stock which reach a length of 6 to 9 inches. These are clothed with rather fleshy, yellowish-green leaves, deeply divided into from 3 to 9, toothed segments. The dainty flowers are borne on slender stalks from 3 to 9 inches long, in the greatest profusion in the summer or autumn, according to the period of the year in which the seeds are sown. The flower is formed of 5, rounded petals and measures from 1 to $1\frac{1}{4}$ inch across. It is normally white with a very conspicuous golden yellow centre. There is a form which lacks the yellow centre of the type. This delightful annual will prosper in almost any soil, but delights in a warm, sunny position. The seeds should be sown in September to produce spring-flowering plants and in March or April for summer flowers. It is advisable not to sow the seeds in the autumn before September.

LINARIA ALPINA (*Scrophulariaceae*) [PLATE 26]
Habit, form and colour render the Alpine Toad-flax the most beautiful of all the dwarf species of this extensive genus for the embellishment of the rock garden and alpine house. Unfortunately although said to be a perennial it is usually short-lived, but when growing under congenial conditions, will reproduce itself by means of self-sown seeds and it is such a delectable little plant that one cannot have too much of it.

Despite its delicate and somewhat succulent habit it is quite hardy and is a tufted little plant up to 6 inches in height, but in poor, stony soil in which it is more perennial, it is less than half the above height. The comparatively short, grey-green leaves clothe the stems in whorls of 4. They vary in shape from linear to linear-lance-shaped. The exquisite blossoms are borne in terminal, head-like racemes from May to autumn in plants that have survived the winter. The flower measures about $\frac{3}{4}$ inch long including the spur which is more or less straight. In the type it is of a bluish-violet colour with a golden yellow area on the lower lip but the colour of the corolla varies and there is a lovely white form with a yellow palate. The true plant is not frequently met with and a less beautiful plant under the name of *hybrida* is frequently mistaken for it. The Alpine Toad-flax is a native of the European Alps and is not a lime-hating plant. It is usually increased by seeds and sometimes by cuttings.

LINUM ARBOREUM (*Linaceae*) [PLATE 26]
This desirable little evergreen shrub is a native of the Mediterranean region and is an ideal plant for a snug sunny alcove in the amateur's garden, preferably backed by a south or west wall. It is a lovely sight when in full flower, but unfortunately is not a long-lived shrub and is liable to collapse in a year or two after reaching maturity, especially after it has set seeds abundantly.

It was introduced into this country in 1788 and forms a neat, rounded, compact bush, rarely more than 2 feet high, but mostly a foot or under. The rather stout branches and branchlets are furnished nearly to the base with rather small almost steely blue, spoon-shaped or lance-shaped, pointed leaves gradually tapering to the base. The bright golden yellow flowers are borne in the greatest profusion from May to August. Like those of most of the flax family they are rather fugacious but are produced so abundantly in the manner of the familiar Crimson Flax that this habit is of no importance. The flower is composed of 5, egg-shaped, rounded petals, forming a blossom 1½ inch across. This beautiful flax needs a light, well-drained, gritty loam. An occasional dressing of bone-meal will help to prolong its life. It is propagated by seeds and also by cuttings, which root readily. The seedlings should be planted in their permanent quarters when they are quite small.

LIRIOPE GRAMINIFOLIA *(Liliaceae)* [PLATE 26]

Formally known as *Liriope spicata*, this pretty perennial herb is usually treated as a cool greenhouse plant in this country, but it can be grown successfully in the open air in the warmer counties and also in the less favoured districts if given the protection of a hand-light in very frosty weather. It is well worth a trial as its spikes of beautifully tinted flowers are very welcome in late autumn and early winter when but few herbaceous plants are normally in flower, also the flower spikes when cut and placed in water remain decorative for a long time.

This species is a native of eastern Asia ranging from Cochin China northwards, through eastern China to Japan. The thick roots produce dense tufts of grass-like, deep green leaves from 6 to 12 inches long and about ½ inch wide. The stiffly erect flower-stem is from 1½ to 2 feet long; it bears a dense, cylindrical spike of deep violet-blue flowers from 6 to 12 inches long from October to November and December, somewhat resembling an elongated spike of a Grape Hyacinth. The individual flower measures about ⅜ inch across and is composed of 6, oval, concave segments with a tuft of yellow stamens in the centre. It thrives in any friable, fertile soil in a sunny position and is usually increased by division in spring.

LITHOSPERMUM ROSMARINIFOLIUM

(Boraginaceae) [PLATE 26]

After the popular Lithospermum Heavenly Blue the above species is probably the best of the blue-flowered shrubby kinds. Sheltered from cutting winds it is frequently in flower during the whole of the winter months in mild localities and although it is a native of southern Italy, where it grows on limestone rocks, it passes through periods of severe frost unscathed in cultivation.

In an open, sunny situation it forms a neat, evergreen little bush, rarely more than 9 inches high. Its slender stems are clothed with rather small deep green leaves, almost exactly resembling those of the rosemary and have the same incurved margins. The deep blue flowers are borne on the ends of leafy shoots, in short spikes and are at their best in June and July. The individual flowers frequently measure over $\frac{3}{4}$ inch in diameter and have a fairly long tube, which expands at its mouth into 5, spreading lobes, each of which has a white stripe down its centre. Unlike many of the flowers of the Boraginaceae the throat of the flower is quite free from hairs.

This beautiful species needs a very sunny position and in my experience thrives best in a poor, well-drained stony soil to which some lime has been added. It may be increased by layers and internodal cuttings, which usually take a considerable time to root.

LONICERA TRAGOPHYLLA (*Caprifoliaceae*) [PLATE 26]
This exceedingly handsome Chinese Honeysuckle has but one fault: its blossoms are devoid of scent. In other respects it is probably the most desirable of the climbing species hardy enough for out door cultivation throughout the British Isles. Despite its robustness it should be grown in all gardens large and small. In good, well-drained friable loam it reaches a height of 20 feet or more and is eminently suitable for clothing a low tree or a pergola and is very effective when trained on a trellis on a house wall.

It is a deciduous climber, with many slender branches, furnished with rather large, oblong or oval, entire, rich green leaves, the uppermost pair being united at the base as in our perfoliate honeysuckle (*Lonicera caprifolium*). The golden yellow flowers are borne in huge terminal clusters, formed of 10 to 20 blossoms, which are produced with the greatest freedom and are usually at their best during July and August. The corolla has a tapering tube $2\frac{1}{2}$ to 4 inches long, which expands at its mouth into a 2-lobed limb or segment 1 to $1\frac{1}{2}$ inch wide. The fruit is formed of several globose red berries. It is not particular as to soil but seems to appreciate a little shade and is increased by cuttings which root easily. If a fragrant honeysuckle is desired *Lonicera splendida* is one of the best. Its yellow and red flowers are not so large as those of *L. tragophylla* but they are extremely fragrant. It is an evergreen and is a native of Spain.

LYCHNIS CHALCEDONICA (*Caryophyllaceae*) [PLATE 27]
The reason why this extremely showy hardy perennial is called Jerusalem Cross is apparently on account of the legend that it was so named by the Crusaders. It was a popular plant years ago, but now seems to have gone

out of fashion and is not frequently met with in small gardens. This is rather unfortunate as it is most easily cultivated and is very decorative and in addition its flowers last a long time in perfection. When given an open sunny position in rich soil, it will frequently reach a height of 3 feet and bear proportionally large heads of brilliant flowers.

It has erect, hairy stems from $1\frac{1}{2}$ to 3 feet tall, furnished with dark green, medium-sized, ovate leaves, heart-shaped at the base and pointed at the apex. The brilliant scarlet flowers are borne in dense many-flowered corymbs from 3 to 5 inches wide from June to August. The flower measures about $1\frac{1}{2}$ inch in diameter and its broadly wedge-shaped petals are 2-cleft. There is a double form, also a pink one and one with pure white flowers, both double and single. It is increased by division, cuttings and seeds. The supposed hybrid *L. haageana* is an extremely showy perennial with oblong or ovate leaves and large corymbs of orange-scarlet, crimson and salmon coloured blossoms, each 2 inches wide. In deep, rich loam it will reach a height of 4 feet. It is easily increased by seeds and division.

LYSICHITUM AMERICANUM (*Araceae*) [PLATE 27]

This robust member of the arum family is a very handsome plant when it is growing under congenial conditions. It is found in bogs and marshes in eastern Siberia, Japan and north-western America, where it is known as Skunk Cabbage, a not inappropriate name, for its flowers are very foetid, and its huge foliage could be mistaken for a gigantic cabbage or lettuce. It is hardy in most districts in this country but some protection should be given to its roots in very severe weather.

It has a stout, horizontally creeping root-stock, which produces tufts of rich, bright green, ovate or lance-shaped leaves from 1 to 5 feet in length, according to the richness of the soil in which it is growing. The lemon-yellow spathe is boat-shaped and is pointed at the tip; it measures from 4 to 9 inches in length and is borne on a stout stalk up to 1 foot long. The spadix is more or less conical, $1\frac{1}{2}$ to $2\frac{1}{2}$ inches long and is dark green in colour. The fruit is berry-like, about $\frac{1}{2}$ inch in diameter and of a bright scarlet colour. The fruits are borne in a similar manner to those of our wild arum which they very much resemble. The 'flowers' are produced in May and June and the roots need a rich soil and a perpetually moist position in full sun. Propagation is by division and seeds. There is a pure white form known as *L. camtschatcense*.

MAGNOLIA DENUDATA (*Magnoliaceae*) [PLATE 27]

I would like to advise my readers who have sufficient space in their gardens to allow it to develop to complete maturity, to purchase a specimen of the true *Magnolia denudata*—preferably grown from seed or a layer and not a graft. They should plant it in an open position, but where the sun does not reach it until noon in early spring when they will have the satisfaction, if all goes well, of seeing it grow over the years into a fine specimen of the most beautiful hardy tree in cultivation. Fortunately magnolias are not particular as to soil, but seem to thrive best in a deep, light loam. In heavy retentive soils they are apt to 'die back'. Magnolias like most other trees and shrubs need plenty of water in dry weather. They may be successfully transplanted in autumn or spring, even when as much as 10 feet in height if they are purchased from reputable nurserymen.

The earliest specific name of the magnolia under consideration is apparently *M. heptapeta*, but it is listed under the name of *M. denudata*, so this name has been retained. In an open situation it forms a rounded, deciduous tree from 30 to 40 feet high, with horizontally spreading branches almost reaching to the ground. The branchlets are furnished with rich green, egg-shaped or oblong-egg-shaped, abruptly pointed leaves. The pure white, bell-shaped blossoms are borne on the almost naked branchlets in March and April. They are composed of 9, egg-shaped, concave segments, forming a flower 6 to 7 inches across. This species is a native of central China.

MAGNOLIA × SOULANGEANA LENNEI [PLATE 27]

The origin of this very beautiful magnolia appears to be uncertain. It was said to be a hybrid between *M. denudata* and *M. liliflora*, or *M. denudata* and *M. obuata* but is now usually considered to be one of the several forms of *M. soulangeana*. However, it is one of the most beautiful of the magnolias in its finest form and is very suitable for small gardens.

It flowers freely when quite small and is usually not much over 15 feet in height when aged, and is of rather sparse habit. Its greyish branches are clothed with rather large yellowish-green, lance-shaped or oblong-egg-shaped, pointed leaves which are contemporary with the flowers. The blossom is cup-shaped and measures from 4 to 5 inches across. It is composed of 6, egg-shaped, concave segments of a beautiful carmine rose colour outside and either white or pale rose inside. The flowers are borne towards the end of May and so escape serious damage by frost.

The variety of *Magnolia stellata* known as *rosea* is a most desirable subject for small gardens, for it is compact and slow in growth. Unfortunately it is now rather rare and is difficult to procure. It forms a compact, deciduous bush from 4 to 10 feet high, similar in every respect to the type except that

PLATE 27

1. *Lychnis chalcedonica*   2. *Lysichitum americanum*   3. *Magnolia denudata*
4. *Magnolia stellata*   5. *Mahonia japonica var. hyemalis*
6. *Malus toringoides*

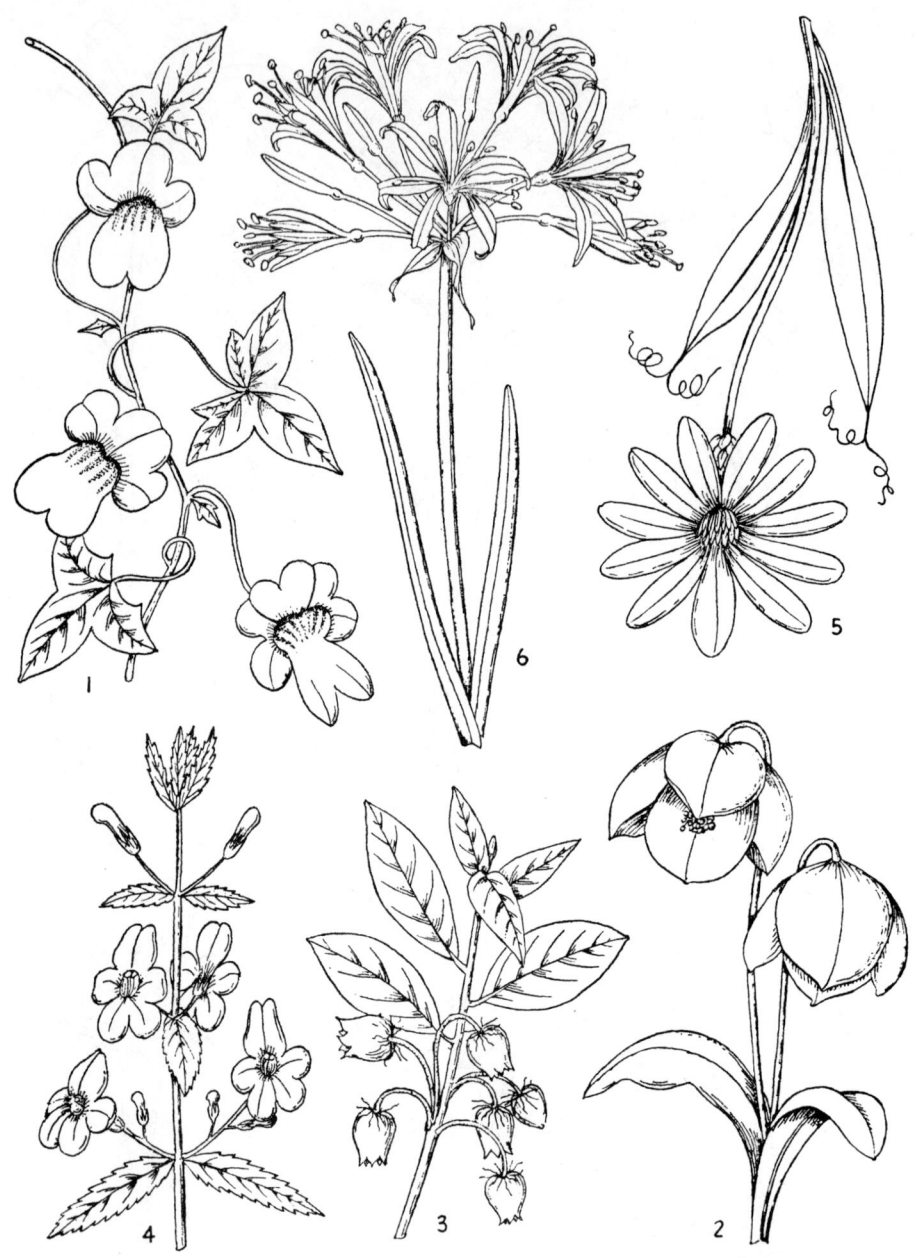

PLATE 28

1. *Maurandia barclaiana* 2. *Meconopsis quintuplinervia*
3. *Menziesia ciliicalyx* 4. *Mimulus cardinalis* 5. *Mutisia decurrens*
6. *Nerine bowdenii*

its flowers are of an attractive shade of rose colour when they first open which deepens with age. The flowers are produced in March and April. A fine specimen of this variety can be seen in the magnolia collection at Kew.

MAHONIA JAPONICA (*Berberidaceae*) [PLATE 27]

This very valuable member of the barberry family is one of the best of our winter-flowering shrubs and never fails to produce its very fragrant blossoms throughout the winter from December to March and is perfectly hardy. The typical form is a stiff, erect, evergreen shrub rarely more than 6 feet tall. The unbranched stems are clothed with very handsome leathery, glossy, deep green, pinnate leaves as much as 15 inches in length; they are composed of from five to nine pairs of large, fairly widely separated narrowly ovate, pointed leaflets with escalloped, spiny margins. The solitary terminal leaflet is but little larger than the others. The bright yellow flowers are shaped like those of the barberry, each measures about $\frac{3}{8}$ inch in diameter when fully open. The inflorescence is composed of numerous densely flowered racemes 4 to 8 inches long. The fruit is a black berry about $\frac{1}{3}$ inch long, covered with a whitish 'bloom'.

The variety *hyemalis* is a more handsome plant than the type and when mature is slightly taller; its leaves are 18 inches long and the racemes are much longer than those of the type, also the flowers are more widely spaced and of a deeper colour. This mahonia is a native of China but was first introduced into this country from Japan. All the mahonias seem to thrive best in a heavy loamy soil, either in full sun or shade and are propagated by layers and also by seeds which take a long time to germinate.

MALUS TORINGOIDES (*Rosaceae*) [PLATE 27]

In my opinion this species is the most beautiful of all the white-flowered crab-apples in cultivation in this country. It is also known as *Pyrus toringoides* and is more suitable for small gardens than either *M. floribunda* or *M. spectabilis*, both of which can reach a height of 30 feet. It is a picture of beauty when smothered in its exquisite blossoms in the spring and loaded with its brilliant fruit in the autumn. It flowers and fruits abundantly when 5 to 8 feet high, and will eventually reach a height of 25 feet, but requires a number of years to do so.

It is deciduous and in cultivation is a graceful, loosely branched tree with slender, drooping, spreading and erect branches, furnished with medium-sized ovate or lance-shaped, rich green leaves which are either entire or lobed. In some specimens the leaves almost resemble those of a hawthorn. The creamy white flowers bear some likeness to the blossoms of a cherry. They measure from ⅜ to 1 inch in diameter and are borne on long, slender stalks in corymbs or clusters of 6 to 9 on the ends of the branchlets in May. The fruit, which sets with the greatest freedom, is globose, ovoid or squat top-shaped, about ½ inch in diameter and is of a rich and beautiful yellow when ripe in September and October, with a bright scarlet flush on the side exposed to the sun. It is a native of China and is perfectly hardy; it is not exacting with regard to soil but needs a sunny position. Increase is by seeds and cuttings.

MAURANDIA BARCLAIANA *(Scrophulariaceae)*   [PLATE 28]

In this beautiful climbing perennial we have yet another introduction from Mexico, where so many desirable herbaceous plants and shrubs are native. Unfortunately only a comparatively small number will survive one of our occasional severe winters and are best treated as half-hardy annuals where this method of cultivation is effective, although most of the members of this delightful genus will frequently produce new growths from the base in the spring after a mild winter, like the Chilean climber *Eccremocarpus scaber*. Even so, it is more satisfactory to treat them as half-hardy annuals and sow the seeds under glass in March, in heat if possible, and plant them out at the end of May in light, rich soil in full sun, in a fairly moist position.

Maurandia barclaiana has slender, branching stems which climb to a height of 5 or more feet, according to the quality of the soil in which the plant is growing. They are clothed with medium-sized, long-stalked, heart-shaped, pointed, leaves of a most attractive shade of green. The very beautiful flowers are borne in the leaf-axils on very long stalks and vary in colour from violet and purple to rose and white. They are freely produced during the months of July and August if the seeds are sown under glass in March. The corolla has a funnel-shaped tube up to 3 inches long, expanding at its mouth into 5, rounded lobes.

MECONOPSIS QUINTUPLINERVIA

(Papaveraceae) [PLATE 28]

As a rule most of the members of the genus Meconopsis are not long-lived in cultivation even if they are perennials in their native country. Most after ripening their seeds perish. The species under consideration is an exception to this rule, for if given the right conditions it is a very vigorous and somewhat invasive perennial. It is known as the Harebell Poppy and is a native of northern Tibet and Kansu in northern China and is perfectly hardy.

It spreads fairly rapidly by underground runners or stolons which produce from their nodes numerous rosettes or tufts of long egg-shaped or lance-shaped leaves, densely clothed with straw-coloured or rust-coloured hairs. The charming flowers are usually solitary or occasionally in two's and three's, borne on slender unbranched stems from 12 to 18 inches high. The bell-shaped or goblet-shaped blossom measures nearly 3 inches in diameter and is normally composed of 4 or occasionally 6 rounded petals of a beautiful lavender blue in the best form, which has silvery stamens. The flowers are produced from late May to October in normal seasons.

This desirable species thrives in a fairly rich soil and is at its best in friable loam and leaf-mould in a cool, moist half-shady position and should be lifted and replanted every second year. One of the most beautiful of the yellow-flowered perennial species is *Meconopsis villosa*, until recently known as *Cathcartia villosa*. It is a native of the Himalaya. It produces a tuft of handsome, cleft and lobed leaves and 12 to 18 inch stems, bearing solitary golden-yellow flowers about 2 inches in diameter in June and needs a rich soil and a sheltered, sunny position.

MENZIESIA CILIICALYX (*Ericaceae*) [PLATE 28]

There is a portrait of this little Japanese deciduous shrub in a Japanese book entitled *A Pocket Atlas of the Alpine Plants of Japan*, showing the corolla as white from its base to the middle, and from there to the tip, including the lobes of the blossom, bright scarlet. If this very striking coloration is correct, this form does not seem to be in cultivation in this country, for the flowers of all the specimens I have seen were pinkish-purple towards the mouth of the blossom and white above. Nevertheless, it is an interesting little shrub and well worth including in small gardens as it is slow growing and does not occupy much room. Also, its habit of growth allows the planting of suitable carpeting plants beneath its branches.

It is perfectly hardy and is found on the mountains of the central provinces of the main island of Japan at an elevation of nearly 7,500 feet above sea-level. In cultivation it forms a compact, somewhat sparsely branched bush, from $1\frac{1}{2}$ to 3 feet tall, with spreading, brown branches, furnished towards their tips with rich green, medium-sized, alternate, oval or egg-shaped leaves, tapering at both ends. The urn-shaped flowers measure from $\frac{1}{2}$ to $\frac{3}{4}$ inch in length and are cleft at the mouth into 4 to 5, small, ovate, pointed lobes. They are borne in clusters of 3 to 6 on down-curved stalks of varying lengths. It flowers in May and June and thrives in any light, lime-free soil and is increased by layers and seeds.

MIMULUS CARDINALIS (*Scrophulariaceae*) [PLATE 28]

One does not see this fine old Monkey Flower so frequently in gardens as in years gone by. This is a pity as it is very decorative and is easily cultivated, given the conditions it needs. Its only fault is that normally the foliage is too ample in comparison to the size of its flowers. This fault can be mitigated to some extent by planting it in a not too-rich soil. Nevertheless, the combination of the delicate green of its foliage and the almost pure scarlet of its blossoms, never fails to attract the attention of those who meet the plant for the first time.

It is perfectly hardy and most persistent in the production of its flowers, often commencing to blossom in June and continuing to do so until cut down by late autumn frosts. It is a herbaceous perennial from 1 to 3 feet high, with branching stems, clothed with rather large, ovate or egg-shaped, deeply veined, pointed, coarsely toothed, sessile, bright yellow-green leaves; the vividly tinted flowers are of the usual Mimulus shape but are rather narrow and are from $1\frac{1}{4}$ to $1\frac{1}{2}$ inch long.

Mimulus lewisii somewhat resembles the preceding species in shape, but is not so leafy. It reaches a height of $1\frac{1}{4}$ to 2 feet and has oblong or lance-shaped, toothed leaves and usually beautiful pink flowers and like the preceding species is a native of north-western America. Both species need to be planted in a damp but sunny place in friable loam and peat and are easily increased by division and seeds.

MIMULUS PRIMULOIDES

Despite its fragile appearance this little herbaceous perennial will survive a zero temperature quite undamaged when at rest. It is found in damp, open situations on the mountains of California. In a sunny, moist position it forms mounds of pale green foliage from 1 to 3 inches high, composed of slender, creeping stems and numerous sparse rosettes of elliptic, toothed, hairy leaves of medium size.

The dainty, bright yellow flowers measure about $\frac{3}{4}$ inch wide and have a funnel-shaped tube and 5, spreading, egg-shaped lobes, rounded and indented at the apex. They usually have a few brownish spots in the throat and are solitary, borne on very slender stalks up to 4 inches long, springing from the upper leaf-axils. The flowers are very freely produced during the summer months and together with the delicate green foliage form a charming picture. It is propagated by seeds and division, the seedlings frequently flower within four months of the sowing of the seeds.

The hardy annual species *Mimulus brevipes* is a most delightful plant with golden yellow flowers 2 inches across and 2 inches long, borne in the leaf-axils of the unbranched stems, which are usually not more than 9 inches high. Like most of the members of the genus it needs moisture at the root but does not seem particular as to soil for I have grown it with complete success in a very light one in full sun.

MUTISIA DECURRENS (*Compositae*) [PLATE 28]
The mutisias have the reputation of being difficult to cultivate in the open air in this country and under the best of conditions are not usually long-lived plants. They also have the unfortunate habit, like several other desirable climbing plants, of collapsing suddenly when apparently in the best health and in full flower. Several of the climbing species are such very beautiful plants that any trouble taken to meet their requirements is well worth while. Like those of the clematis, their slender stems must be adequately protected from strong sunshine and in a hot, dry position, in which the blossoms revel, it is very necessary to cover the roots with a thick mulch of decayed leaves or peat, for strong sunshine on the roots in a dry soil is fatal.

Mutisia decurrens is one of the best if not the best of the climbing species. It has slender, sparsely branched stems which will reach a height of at least 10 feet. These are furnished with rather large, evergreen, narrowly oblong, stalkless leaves, with their lower margins prolonged down the stems in the form of wings. The mid-vein of the blade is extended beyond the tip of the blade in the form of a long, branched tendril. The daisy-shaped flower-heads measure from 3 to 5 inches across and are composed of 12 to 15, broad ray-florets varying in colour from rich orange to vermilion and are borne on slender stalks from June to September. It should be given the shelter of a west wall in a compost of loam and leaf-soil. Increase is by seeds.

NERINE BOWDENII (*Amaryllidaceae*) [PLATE 28]
Planted at the base of a warm wall and well supplied with moisture when in full growth this very beautiful South African bulbous plant can be grown successfully even in bleak, cold districts. In the more favoured counties with regard to climate it needs no shelter and can be safely planted in the open border. In some localities in this country it is apparently ever-green, its leaves being able to withstand quite severe frost unscathed but in my experience the flowers have appeared in late autumn after the leaves have withered and died away.

The rather large globose or ovoid, long-necked bulb produces a few, fairly long, broadly linear or narrowly strap-shaped, glossy bright green leaves which are usually blunt at the apex. The very elegant rose-pink blossoms are borne in 6- to 12-flowered umbels on slender stalks, springing from the apex of the rather stout flower-stem which reaches a height of 1 to 2 feet, according to the richness of the soil in which the plant is growing. The blossoms are up to 3 inches in diameter and have 6, broad, strap-shaped, recurving, slightly wavy segments, each with a crimson line down the centre. The chocolate coloured anthers enhance the beauty of the flowers. The bulbs should be planted at a depth of at least 6 inches in light, rich, well-drained soil, in as sunny a position as possible. Increase is by offsets and also by seeds.

NIEREMBERGIA CAERULEA (*Solanaceae*) [PLATE 29]

The genus Nierembergia is a small one and consists of hardy and half hardy annuals and perennials, several of which are sufficiently hardy to withstand our winters with little or no protection. The annual species are sometimes grown as pot plants but are rarely seen. All are natives of South America and are found in open situations of that continent, mostly in the temperate regions.

Nierembergia caerulea was formerly known in gardens as *N. hippomanica* and is a perennial herbaceous plant, native in Argentina. It has a fibrous root-stock, which produces cushions of dull green foliage and several slender, much-branched stems, from 6 to 12 inches high, held stiffly erect. They are rather thinly clothed with short, narrow-linear leaves, acute or blunt at the apex. The flowers are termed rotate or wheel-shaped by botanists and rather resemble those of a potato in shape. They measure from 1 to $1\frac{1}{2}$ inch wide and vary in colour from a delicate lavender blue to deep blue-violet, with darker lines and a yellow throat. They are borne on very short stalks towards the ends of the slender branchlets from May to September and are very numerous. It needs a sunny position in good, well-drained friable loam and is increased by seeds and division. In severe winters it is advisable to place a hand-light over the plant to protect it from drying winds combined with hard frost.

OENOTHERA FRUTICOSA (*Onagraceae*) [PLATE 29]

The variety *youngii* of this North American Oenothera is the most desirable of all the Evening Primroses whose blossoms remain open and in perfection during the whole of the day. It is a garden form of the type and should be afforded a place in every garden however small, for it is neat in foliage and very beautiful in flower. A remarkable trait in this oenothera is that, as soon as the flowers have faded and folded up they drop off and thus do not remain in a withered state on the plant and so disfigure it.

The slowly extending root-stock produces neat tufts of fairly large oblong or lance-shaped, pointed, remotely toothed, deep green, crimson-tinted leaves, which form a close carpet of evergreen foliage. Each tuft produces a stiff, erect, crimson-tinted stem which dies away as winter approaches; it rises to a height of 2 to 3 feet and is rather sparsely clothed with leaves similar to those of the tufts but smaller. The rich, golden yellow, fragrant blossoms are borne in terminal and lateral clusters towards the upper parts of the stems continuously from May to September; they measure 2 inches wide, lasting well as cut flowers. A sunny position in good, moist soil meets its requirements. It is propagated mainly by seeds.

OENOTHERA MISSOURIENSIS

This Evening Primrose is also known under the name of *O. macrocarpa* and is a native of the U.S.A. as its name implies. It is a perfectly hardy herbaceous perennial species and is in my opinion without a fault, yet one rarely sees it in suburban gardens. A plant in my garden has been in the same position for the past fifteen years and is growing in a raised bed of light, loamy soil in full sun. It comes up year after year in May and bears its lovely flowers continuously from early July to the end of October, without any attention whatever.

Oenothera missouriensis possesses thick thong-like roots, which produce about half a dozen prostrate crimson stems, which curve upwards at their tips and then become erect, reaching a height of 9 to 12 inches. They are rather sparsely furnished with elegant, lance-shaped, pointed, rich olive-green, fairly long leaves tapering below into distinct, crimson stalks. The delicate primrose-yellow blossoms measure fully 3 inches in diameter and are solitary in the leaf-axils. They open in the evening and remain decorative for several days. The fruit is an oblong, broadly, 4-winged capsule about 2 inches long, containing many seeds, which offer the best means of increase.

Oenothera rosea has fairly large flowers of a beautiful shade of pink in its best form, and is very invasive but its creeping roots can be confined in the same manner as those of *Convulvulus elegantissimus*.

OMPHALODES CAPPADOCICA (*Boraginaceae*)   [PLATE 29]

The most beautiful of all the perennial Navelworts, as these Forget-me-not-like plants are called, is *Omphalodes luciliae* but it is a plant for the specialist and not for the amateur. Like *Eritrichium nanum*, another lovely member of the borage family, it is very difficult to cultivate with any measure of success. *O. cappadocica* usually presents no difficulties in this respect and is almost equally as beautiful as *O. luciliae*.

The species under consideration is a native of Asia Minor and is found in the mountainous provinces of Lazistan and Cappadocica and is perfectly hardy. It has a slowly creeping rhizome which produces rather sparse tufts of comparatively large leaves with ovate blades, heart-shaped at the base and borne on a long stalk. They are dark green on the upper surface and glaucous grey-green beneath. The numerous flower-stems, which are rarely more than 6 inches high, are sparsely clothed with leaves similar in shape to those of the tufts but much smaller. The very beautiful azure blue flowers, which resemble very large forget-me-nots, measure about $\frac{1}{2}$ inch in diameter and are borne in loose, graceful racemes from May to October.

This beautiful plant succeeds best in rich, moist friable loam in semi-shade, and does well in thin woodlands of deciduous trees. Slugs are very fond of the members of this genus. Increase is usually by cuttings but seeds are sometimes offered.

ONONIS CENISIA (*Leguminosae*) [PLATE 29]

The genus Ononis is a rather large one and contains annual and biennial species as well as perennial herbs and dwarf shrubs. Several of the perennial herbs and dwarf shrubs are well worth cultivating if space allows, especially in gardens where the soil is none too rich. The species under consideration is a perennial and bears some resemblance to our native Rest-harrow, but has larger and more brightly coloured flowers. A clump of the variety of our native plant known as *spinosa*, planted in the alpine garden is not to be despised, for its flowers are of a beautiful tint of pink and its habit of growth is attractive.

Ononis cenisia produces numerous glandular-pubescent stems from 2 to 9 inches high, according to the quality of the soil in which it is growing. The branches and branchlets are crowded with small, shortly-stalked, tri-foliate leaves of a rather deep green. They are similar in shape to those of our native species and are deeply toothed towards the tip only. The flowers, which measure about $\frac{5}{8}$ inch in length, are solitary, on short stalks in the leaf-axils and are bright purplish-pink in colour, with darker lines on the standards. This species is found on most of the high mountains of south-western Europe and north Africa and flowers in June and July. It is not particular as to soil but prefers a deep, well-drained one in full sun and usually does well on a dry bank, and is increased by seeds, cuttings and division in the spring.

ONOSMA STELLULATUM (*Boraginaceae*) [PLATE 29]

As a rule the onosmas are not long-lived plants and it is advisable to propa-

PLATE 29

1. *Nierembergia caerulea* 2. *Oenothera fruticosa* 3. *Omphalodes cappadocica*
4. *Ononis cenisia* 5. *Onosma stellulatum* 6. *Orchis maderensis*

PLATE 30

1. *Orontium aquaticum* 2. *Ostrowskia magnifica* 3. *Oxalis enneaphylla*
4. *Oxalis valdiviensis* 5. *Paeonia cambessedesii* 6. *Paeonia peregrina*

gate them frequently, if not annually. In their native countries the winters are severe and they spend many months under a blanket of snow. Here our winters with their alternating periods of frost and thaw do not suit them and they have a tendency to rot during this sunless period, mainly on account of the moisture retained on the hairs on their stems and leaves. A pane of glass placed overhead in the autumn certainly does help to prolong their lives. The onosmas are among the most desirable of rock garden plants and range as natives from central and eastern Europe to Asia Minor and eastwards to the Himalaya where the lovely, scarlet-flowered O. pyramidalis is found.

Onosma stellulatum is probably the most desirable of the Golden Drops, as the yellow-flowered species are called, for it normally survives our winters unprotected. It is a native of south-eastern Europe and Asia Minor and has an almost woody root-stock and is of branching habit, reaching a height of but little over 6 inches. The lower parts of the stems are clothed with oblong or sub-spoon-shaped, rather long leaves. Those on the upper parts are lance-shaped. The pendant primrose-yellow flowers are borne in racemes in May. The corolla is tubular, 5-lobed at its mouth and about an inch long. A deep, well-drained loam in full sun suits this vigorous-rooting species. Propagation is by seeds and cuttings.

ORCHIS MADERENSIS (*Orchidaceae*) [PLATE 29]

This orchid is the most handsome member of a large genus, many of which are very beautiful hardy plants and not very difficult to establish in the outdoor garden when once their needs are understood. Although *Orchis mederensis* is a native of Madeira, it thrives in this country in the open air in a position facing west, where it will not be exposed to the morning sunshine after a late frost, and will also have protection from northerly and easterly winds. Another important factor in its cultivation is that the soil in which it is grown should always be moist when it is in growth and drier when it is at rest.

Orchis maderensis is found in a state of nature in marshy places and on the banks of streams. It has a palmately lobed tuber of considerable size, which produces a very stout stem up to 3 feet tall, clothed with long, oval-oblong, shining green leaves, which are sheathing below and become smaller towards the top of the stem. The very handsome flowers are borne in a dense, cylindrical spike from 5 to 9 inches long and as much as $3\frac{1}{2}$ inches in diameter. The individual flower measures about an inch long and has lance-shaped petals, concave sepals and a 3-lobed lip. It varies in colour from lilac to rich crimson-purple in the best form and is occasionally pure white. This species flowers in July and August and thrives best in a rich soil composed of friable loam and cow manure. It is increased by offsets and seeds, which sometimes germinate around the plant.

ORONTIUM AQUATICUM (*Araceae*) [PLATE 30]
The Golden Club is one of the most beautiful and distinct of the hardy aquatic plants in cultivation in this country, and should be more widely grown in small gardens where its cultural requirements can be satisfied. It is a native of eastern U.S.A. and Canada, where it inhabits swamps, pools and open water. A well-grown specimen in full flower with as many as fifty inflorescences produced in succession, is an attractive and uncommon sight. It has a branched rhizome, which is usually buried to the depth of at least a foot in the soil at the bottom of the water it inhabits, and it is necessary to plant it at a similar depth in cultivation.

The very dull dark green or sometimes glaucous leaves vary in shape from oblong-elliptic to oblong and are borne on long, spreading stalks. The plant is a true aquatic with its leaves floating on the surface of the water, but in shallow pools they are inclined to become ascending. The flowers are bright yellow and are composed of 4 petals and 4 stamens. They are perfect and are crowded on a rather slender spadix 1 to 2 inches long, and are produced from April to June. The spathe, which is pure white is placed at a little distance below the spadix. The inflorescence is borne on a flattened stalk $\frac{1}{2}$ to 2 feet long. The rhizome should be procured in the spring and planted in rich loam, cow manure and sand.

OSTROWSKIA MAGNIFICA (*Campanulaceae*) [PLATE 30]
This noble member of the bell-flower family richly deserves its specific name, for it is indeed a magnificent plant. It is a hardy herbaceous perennial and is a native of western Bokhara. It was introduced into this country in 1887, but is rarely cultivated. This is a pity as it is a grand plant and is worthy of any amount of trouble incurred to cultivate it successfully. Its one fault is that its flowers are fugacious, but as they are produced in considerable numbers in succession over a fairly long period, this fault is amply atoned for.

When fully developed it has a brittle, carrot-like root, frequently 2 feet in length. Two to three comparatively slender, but stiff, erect stems, from 6 to 8 feet tall are produced from the crown of the root-stock. These are furnished rather thinly, with large, deep green, ovate or ovate-lance-shaped, remotely toothed leaves. Each stem bears towards its apex so many as six campanulate, 6- or 7-lobed blossoms, from 5 to 6 inches in diameter. They are of a delicate greyish-mauve or pale lilac tint and are borne on long, slender stalks, springing from the upper leaf-axils, in July and August. This grand bell-flower needs a deeply worked rich, friable loam, mixed with humus and lime rubble and shade from the morning sun. Propagation is by seeds as it is extremely difficult to dig up a mature root undamaged. Seedlings take from 3 to 4 years to form flowering plants.

OXALIS ENNEAPHYLLA (Oxalidaceae) [PLATE 30]

The species under consideration is a beautiful wood-sorrel, which is perfectly hardy and easily cultivated. Equally as beautiful are O. *lobata* and O. *adenophylla*, but these are decidedly capricious, and really only plants for specialists.

Oxalis enneaphylla is a native of the Falkland Islands and the adjacent mainland. The root-stock is composed of several irregular, knotted rhizomes, which increase in number every year when the plant is in a thriving condition. The rhizomes produce tufts of very handsome, silvery leaves composed of from 7 to 20, crinkly, wedge-shaped leaflets, deeply cleft at the apex. They are borne on long, slender, red-tinted stalks. The exquisite, fragrant flower measures about $1\frac{1}{2}$ inch in diameter and is funnel-shaped, with 5, spreading, egg-shaped lobes which are slightly cleft at the apex. Typically the flower is snowy white with a crimson eye but there are some lovely rose coloured forms in cultivation.

This oxalis flowers in May and June and although it is found in open situations in its native land, seems to thrive better in partial shade in cultivation. It needs a moist, gritty loam but appears to have been successfully grown in a compost composed of loam, leaf-soil and sand. The soil in which it is growing should never be allowed to dry out. Increase is by division of the rhizomes.

OXALIS LASIANDRA [PLATE 30]

This Mexican wood-sorrel was introduced into this country in 1840 and is more robust in habit than the preceding species, and although not so beautiful is a desirable plant, possessing attractive foliage and brightly tinted flowers. Its tuber-like root-stock produces a rather sparse tuft of bright green leaves. These are composed of 5 to 9, narrowly oblong leaflets, narrowed towards the base, rounded and shallowly cleft at the apex. The rather stout flower-stem springs directly from the root-stock to a height of 9 to 18 inches, bearing at its apex about a dozen blossoms, each 1 to $1\frac{1}{2}$ inch in width, with spreading, broadly oblong or egg-shaped, bright magenta-rose petals shading to greenish-yellow at the base. They are produced in June and July. This species needs a sunny position in light loam and is increased by seeds and division.

Another bright little Oxalis I have had in my garden for years is *Oxalis valdiviensis*, native in Chile and introduced in 1862. Although occasionally perennial it usually seeds itself to death in its first year, surviving by means of self-sown seeds and kept in check by sparrows which seem to have a strong liking for its unripe capsules. It has a rather thick, fleshy root-stock which branches into several crowns upwards. Each crown produces a tuft of yellow-green, trifoliate leaves and several forked flower-stems bearing many-flowered racemes of bright yellow flowers, each ⅝ inch across.

PAEONIA CAMBESSEDESII *(Paeoniaceae)* [PLATE 30]

It may be safely stated without fear of contradiction that all the wild peonies are worth cultivation where space is available. As peonies occupy a considerable area of ground when fully developed and their flowering period is not a long one, only the very best can be recommended for cultivation in small gardens. The three species described below are, in my opinion, the cream of the wild peonies and should be cultivated in all gardens, large and small. Peonies in general give of their best in a deep, rich loam, which must be well-drained, but reasonably moist in the summer. A moderate quantity of dry cow manure should be included in the compost as it not only enriches the soil but helps it to retain moisture.

Paeonia cambessedesii is a native of Corsica and the Balearic Isles and is without an equal in the genus with regard to the exquisitely delicate tinting of its blossoms. The smooth, stout stems reach a height of 18 inches or more and are clothed with large ternate leaves, divided into many ovate- lance-shaped or oblong, pointed, entire segments, which are deep green above and purplish beneath. The flower, which measures up to 4 inches in width, is composed of from 5 to 10, broadly egg-shaped, wavy-edged petals of a most exquisite shade of deep rose. The yellow anthers are borne on red filaments. The reddish-purple seed-vessels contain jet black seeds. The flowers are produced in April and May. Increase is by seeds and division.

PAEONIA MLOKOSEWITSCHII [PLATE 30]

This magnificent peony is the finest of all the yellow flowered species in cultivation. The crimson, violet and bronze tints of the young growths as they thrust up from the soil in the spring, renders them very decorative. It is a native of the Caucasus and was introduced into this country in 1907.

It is a robust species with the usual tuberous root system and several, stout, erect stems up to 2 feet in height, furnished with twice-ternate, very handsome leaves, with broadly oblong to almost elliptic leaflets: the lateral ones being somewhat oblique. They are dark bluish-green above and are margined and veined with red. The under surface is glaucous. The exquisite flowers are terminal. Each is composed of about 8 broadly egg-shaped petals, forming a flower 4 to 5 inches in diameter, of a beautiful yellow tint. This species is quite hardy and flowers in April.

Paeonia peregrina is the best of the red-flowered species. It is a robust species with erect stems up to 3 feet in height. They are clothed with twice-ternate leaves, much divided into lobed and coarsely toothed segments, of a bright shining green above and glaucous green below. The lovely rich crimson, cup-shaped blossoms measure from $2\frac{1}{2}$ to $3\frac{1}{2}$ inches in diameter and have egg-shaped, strongly concave petals. Peonies usually produce seeds freely, but unless they are sown as soon as they are ripe they take a long time to germinate. Seedlings take several years to form flowering plants.

PANCRATIUM ILLYRICUM (*Amaryllidaceae*) [PLATE 31]

Although this desirable bulbous plant has been in cultivation in this country for nearly four hundred and fifty years one very rarely sees it, even in southern and western England, where it is quite hardy. That this should be is rather strange, considering the beauty of its blossoms and their delicious fragrance. The large pear-shaped bulb produces several long, wide, rather thick, strap-shaped leaves of an attractive greyish-green tint. The elegant star-shaped blossoms are borne on short stalks in an umbel, composed of 6 to 12 flowers, on the apex of a stout flower-stem from 9 to 15 inches long. The flower is dull white and is composed of a more or less cylindrical tube of a greenish colour, expanding at its mouth into 6, narrow, pointed segments about $1\frac{1}{2}$ inch long and nearly 1 inch wide. The slender pale filaments are united at the mouth of the tube into a remarkable cup-shaped structure, the purpose of which is not apparent. The anthers are yellow.

This species of Pancratium is indigenous to southern Europe and is common in Corsica, Spain, Sicily and Sardinia. In cold districts where the soil is liable to be frozen to a depth of a foot or more, the bulbs should be adequately protected. The foot of a south wall, in well-drained fertile soil suits this plant admirably, with a plentiful supply of water during dry periods. The bulbs should be planted 6 inches deep and covered with ashes or dry litter during their first winter. Offsets are freely produced.

PARADISEA LILIASTRUM (*Liliaceae*) [PLATE 31]
The St Bruno's Lily, as this elegant herbaceous perennial is called, was formerly included in the genus Anthericum with the St Bernard's Lily previously described. It is superior to the type of the above-mentioned species from a decorative point of view, for its lily-like flowers are larger and its racemes are longer.

The St Bruno's Lily has a short, branched root-stock and fleshy roots. Each crown produces up to 9 grass-like, recurving, pointed leaves but little shorter than the flower-stem, which is rather stout and reaches a height of from 1 to 3 feet, according to the quality of the soil and the conditions under which the plant is growing. The delicate white flowers are almost transparent and are borne in loose spikes, often over 2 feet in length. The perianth measures about 2 inches in diameter and is bell-shaped, with 6, lance-shaped, spreading-recurved segments, each with a pleasing green spot at its tip. Like the St Bernard's Lily, this plant has a fine form termed *major* in which the flower-stems normally reach a height of 5 feet, with larger flowers than those of the type.

Both the type and its form are quite hardy and are natives of southern Europe. They flourish in a deep, rich, well-drained loam adequately supplied with water in their vegetative period for they are moisture lovers. Propagation is by division of the roots in spring or autumn and also by seeds sown in pans and placed in a cold frame.

PAROCHETUS COMMUNIS (*Leguminosae*) [PLATE 31]
The Shamrock Pea, as this delightful little pea-flowered plant is termed, is remarkable not only on account of its beauty but also for its very wide distribution as a wild plant, for it is spread over a vast tract of temperate and tropical Asia in the mountains, ranging from the Himalaya to parts of southern India, Burma, Java, Ceylon and also East Africa. Yet it is sufficiently hardy to survive a normal winter in this country without protection, but in case one of the old fashioned winters should occur, with long periods of severe frost, it is advisable to secure rooted pieces of the stems or cuttings in the autumn and place them in a frame from which frost is excluded.

The root-stock is slender, and when the plant is in a flourishing condition, creeps about in all directions soon occupying a considerable area. Buds form on the creeping root-stock, from which numerous clover-like leaves arise on stalks about 3 inches long, soon making an attractive carpet of bright green foliage. The very pretty flowers are rich violet or bluish-purple when mature and prussian blue in the bud. They are borne in ones and twos on long stalks rising well above the leaves, in July. If this little plant is given too rich a soil it will be all leaves and no flowers. Therefore, it is advisable to plant in poor, gritty loam in full sun, and it has been known to thrive with its roots in water.

PAULOWNIA TOMENTOSA (*Scrophulariaceae*) [PLATE 31]
In my opinion the two finest flowering trees in cultivation in this country are *Magnolia campbellii* and *Paulownia tomentosa*, on account of the exquisite tints of their superb flowers. Both have but one fault, that is, they have the unfortunate habit of forming their flower buds in late autumn and in winters in which periods of frost and thaw alternate they are liable to be destroyed before they can open in the spring. Therefore, the position in which it is proposed to plant this glorious tree must be chosen with care.

It is a native of China and when mature forms an open-habited deciduous tree from 30 to 50 feet tall, with a rounded or pyramidal head of stout sepia-brown branches and branchlets clothed with handsome, alternate, very large, rich green leaves, more or less triangular, 2- or 4-lobed, very pointed at the apex and slightly heart-shaped at the base. The lovely blossoms are borne in many-flowered panicles, frequently more than a foot in length and are produced in May and June. The flower is from $1\frac{1}{2}$ to 2 inches long and very much resembles that of a foxglove in shape and is usually of a lovely blue-mauve tint. The seeds are produced in large, globose, strongly-beaked capsules and probably offer the best means of increase. It is not particular as to soil but thrives best in a good, friable loam in a warm position, with complete shelter from north and east winds. This species is also known as *P. imperialis*.

PENSTEMON CORDIFOLIUS (*Scrophulariaceae*) [PLATE 31]
There are two very beautiful species of Penstemon that are of more or less climbing or ascending habit, both of which should find favour with amateur gardeners who can give them the shelter of a warm wall or close fence, preferably facing west. The penstemons are purely New World plants, most of them being found in U.S.A. and Mexico, some at considerable elevation above sea level. They range from dwarf cushion-forming, high mountain species to ascending or climbing plants reaching a height of 6 or 8 feet and festooning low shrubs with their slender, leafy stems and lovely brilliant flowers.

Penstemon cordifolius is an ascending shrubby species with a rather woody base and branching stems reaching a height of about 6 feet, clothed with numerous, comparatively small rich green ovate leaves, toothed on their margins and frequently heart-shaped at the base. The brilliant scarlet blossoms are produced in clusters from the leaf-axils towards the ends of the shoots in succession as the shoots lengthen, forming loose racemes, and are produced in June and July. The flower, which measures about 1 inch long, has a broad tube which expands upwards at the mouth into 5, rather small, broadly ovate lobes and measures about $\frac{1}{2}$ inch in diameter. This penstemon is a native of southern California and has been in cultivation in this country for well over a hundred years. It flourishes in good, friable loam and is increased by layers and cuttings.

PENSTEMON ISOPHYLLUS

Although this Penstemon is closely related to the preceding species it is somewhat different in appearance and is considered by some gardeners to be the more decorative of the two, and although it is found much further south than the Californian plant, it is practically hardy in most districts in this country if it is grown under suitable conditions. It is a native of Mexico, and like many of the beautiful shrubs and perennials introduced from that country which now embellish our gardens, will thrive in most districts in this country if it is given a little care and attention. A healthy plant draping a low wall with its elegant foliage and brilliant flowers is a sight that will repay any trouble taken to induce it to thrive.

Like the preceding species it is a shrubby perennial with slender deep purple or almost black, branching stems that will reach a height of 5 to 6 feet on a wall. The branches are rather densely furnished with medium-sized dark green, rather leathery elliptic or lance-shaped, entire leaves. The deep crimson-scarlet flowers are whitish in the throat with deep crimson lines; they are borne in loose, terminal racemes 6 to 8 inches long, from August to October. The individual flower measures up to $2\frac{1}{2}$ inches in length and very much resembles that of the preceding species in shape, and is about 1 inch across. This penstemon should be planted in poor, well-drained soil to induce free-flowering and is increased by layers and cuttings.

PETROCOPTIS LAGASCAE (Caryophyllaceae)   [PLATE 31]

This little alpine garden perennial is frequently listed in nurserymen's catalogues under its former name of Lychnis lagascae, and a well-grown specimen of the carmine-flowered form in full bloom is a very charming sight. It is found on the Spanish side of the Pyrenees and is perfectly hardy.

It has a woody root-stock and forms a rather loose tuft of blue-grey foliage about 3 inches high, from which the flower-stems rise to a height

PLATE 31

1. *Pancratium illyricum* 2. *Paradisea liliastrum* 3. *Parochetus communis*
4. *Paulownia tomentosa* 5. *Penstemon cordifolius* 6. *Petrocoptis lagascae*

PLATE 32

1. *Phlox adsurgens*   2. *Phygelius capensis var. coccineus*
3. *Phyllodoce nipponica*   4. *Physostegia virginiana*   5. *Pieris floribunda*
6. *Platycodon grandiflorum var. mariesii*

of about 6 inches. The rather small, somewhat leathery, oblong leaves have pointed tips. The delicate flowers are very freely produced from May to August and vary in colour from whitish-pink to a beautiful carmine-rose tint; the latter being of course the most desirable form. The individual flower measures about ¾ inch across and has overlapping petals which are cleft at the apex. Like *Lychnis chalcedonica*, this plant responds to a rich soil in a well-drained position. It seems to like being wedged between two large rocks and is increased by seeds and cuttings.

Our rare native *Lychnis alpina* is not to be despised as an alpine garden plant, as it is quite easily grown and when flourishing, produces a profusion of pink flowers over a mat of rich green foliage. It is a native of the Alps of Europe and is found wild in north-western England. This lychnis should be given a cool, moist position in gritty soil and is increased by seeds.

PHLOX ADSURGENS (*Polemoniaceae*) [PLATE 32]
The genus Phlox is a rather large one and includes many species of very considerable decorative value, both for the herbaceous border and alpine garden. The taller growing florists' varieties of *P. paniculata maculata* known as *decussata* are deservedly popular and amongst the dwarfer species *P. subulata* in its various forms is one of the most valuable carpeting plants we have. Their only fault is the shortness of their decorative period, a fault shared by several other alpine species. The flowers of *Phlox adsurgens* are without doubt more beautiful than those of any alpine species in cultivation and although it has been known to horticulturists for a considerable number of years, it is very rarely seen in small gardens. It is a native of north-western North America, ranging from Oregon to California.

The fibrous root-stock produces numerous leafy, creeping stems, forming mats of dark green foliage, composed of rather small, ovate or elliptic, pointed leaves. The sparsely leafy, ascending stems, which bear the flowers, reach a height of from 9 to 12 inches and terminate in a loose, few-flowered corymb of lovely salmon-pink or pure rose-pink flowers, without any suggestion of magenta. Each measures about an inch in width and in May and June the foliage is almost hidden by the wealth of blossom. It needs a semi-shady position in light loam and leaf-soil, with shelter from cutting winds.

PHYGELIUS CAPENSIS
     var. **COCCINEUS** (*Scrophulariaceae*) [PLATE 32]
Known as Cape Figwort, this South African hardy plant was treated as a

greenhouse subject for many years, before it was discovered that it could be grown with complete success in the open air in this country, yet one sees it but rarely except in public gardens. It may be treated as a herbaceous plant, and grown in a border, where it will die down to the ground level each winter and will push up new growths in the spring, which will produce flowers later in the year. It is a true shrub and not a herbaceous plant and if trained on a south or west wall will reach a height of 10 to 12 feet and flower from June to late autumn.

It has rather stout branches, furnished with medium-sized ovate or ovate-lance-shaped leaves which are of an attractive shade of green. The flowers are borne in very large, spreading panicles, from 1 to 2 feet long, on the ends of the branches. The corolla is tubular, about 2 inches long and is narrowed around the ovary. It is dull brick-red in the type and far less conspicuous than that of the variety *coccineus* in which the blossom is vermilion-scarlet or pure vermilion. The Cape Figwort and its variety thrive best in a deep, rich loam in a sunny position, but are really not particular as to soil. It is propagated by seeds, but perhaps more readily by shoots, which spring up around the roots of healthy plants.

PHYLLODOCE NIPPONICA *(Ericaceae)* [PLATE 32]

Phyllodoce nipponica is probably the most beautiful of all these charming plants yet introduced into this country. It is a native of Japan as its specific name implies and like all the members of this genus, is quite hardy and certainly deserves to be widely cultivated in gardens where rhododendrons thrive.

When fully mature it forms a neat, evergreen bush 6 to 9 inches high of more or less erect, branching habit. The slender, curving stems and branches are clothed with linear or narrowly-lance-shaped, small, pointed leaves of a rather deep green. The white, pink-tinted, bell-shaped blossoms are borne singly in the axils of the uppermost leaves on long, curving stems, during the month of May. The flower is divided at its mouth into 5, small, ovate, spreading lobes and measures about $\frac{1}{2}$ inch wide. A compost mainly composed of peat, mixed with a little, light loam meets its needs with regard to soil. It should be given a cool, moist, but not shady position and is increased by seeds, cuttings and layers.

Phyllodoce breweri sometimes known as *Bryanthus breweri* is also a very attractive species. It bears terminal racemes, 2 to 3 inches long, of purplish-rose, broadly bell-shaped flowers about $\frac{5}{8}$ inch wide in May and is a native of California.

PHYSOSTEGIA VIRGINIANA *(Labiatae)* [PLATE 32]
The type of this desirable hardy perennial herbaceous plant can hardly be termed unfamiliar as it may be seen in many a herbaceous border in most of the public gardens maintained by local authorities, especially in the coastal towns. It is a very decorative and floriferous plant and has several very attractive varieties which are much superior to the type and should be seen much more frequently in small gardens than they are at present. *Physostegia virginiana* is known as the False Dragon's Head and Obedient Plant. The latter name has been given to it on account of the probably unique construction of its flower-stalks or pedicels which are swivel-jointed, so that when the flowers are pushed over to right or left they remain in either position for some time. Unfortunately the plant has creeping roots which render it rather invasive. It should if necessary be dug up every two or three years and replanted in fresh soil to curb this objectionable habit.

The erect stems reach a height of 3 to 4 feet and are furnished with rather large, lance-shaped, dark green leaves, saw-toothed on their margins. The flowers vary in tint from pinkish-lilac to rich purplish-rose and are borne in simple or compound spikes from July to October and are like those of our White Deadnettle in size and shape. The varieties *speciosa* and Vivid are much superior to the type which is a native of U.S.A. An open position and a moist, rich soil suits these plants admirably.

PIERIS FLORIBUNDA *(Ericaceae)* [PLATE 32]
I purchased a specimen of this North American Pieris about twenty years ago when it was but a foot high. After all that time it is now only 3 feet high, probably owing to having been planted in poor, stony soil. It flowers profusely year after year and sometimes produces numerous capsules of viable seed from which it is easily raised. In richer soil than mine it would probably reach a height of 6 feet or more. It is a native of south-eastern U.S.A. and is apparently more common in Georgia than elsewhere.

In an open position it forms a rounded evergreen bush of densely leafy habit. Its many branches are clothed with medium-sized, leathery, elliptic-oblong or oblong, pointed, entire leaves of a fairly light green. The urn-shaped, shallowly lobed pure white flowers measure about a $\frac{1}{4}$ inch long and are borne in erect, terminal panicles with stiff, spreading branches. The flowers are very numerous and are all inclined in the same direction, and commence to open at the end of March. This species is perfectly hardy and forms its flower buds in the autumn. These pass through the most severe winter quite unscathed.

Pieris taiwanensis, a native of Formosa, is probably the best of the more recently introduced species. It is an evergreen with spreading branches 3 to 8 feet high and large arching axillary panicles of white, urn-shaped blossoms and like all these shrubs it is a lime-hater, being at its best in peat and leaf-soil. Its chief attraction is the red tint of its young foliage.

PLATYCODON GRANDIFLORUM
var. MARIESII (*Campanulaceae*) [PLATE 32]

The Balloon Flower or Chinese Bell-Flower, as this very near relative of the campanulas is named, is a hardy, herbaceous perennial and is a striking plant for border decoration and does not occupy a lot of space. The type, which is sometimes known as *Campanula grandiflora*, has fleshy, brittle roots, which produce several more or less erect, rather slender stems, which may reach a height of 2½ feet in rich soil, but in ordinary garden mould are usually less than half that height; they are clothed with fairly long ovate-lance-shaped, bright green, toothed leaves, which are arranged in whorls on the lower part of the stems and are scattered towards the flowers.

The beautiful flowers are very large taking into consideration the height of the plant, and are either solitary on the tips of the branches or in twos or threes or occasionally in few-flowered corymbs. The corolla is broadly bell-shaped 1½ to 2 inches wide, margined with 5 broad lobes. The remarkable buds are like miniature balloons, hence the name Balloon Flower. In colour the flowers vary from pale blue to white and they have a satin-like sheen. The type and its varieties range from Siberia, through northern China to Japan and flower in July and August. The variety *mariesii* is about half the height of the type, but it has flowers nearly 3 inches in diameter. The Balloon Flowers thrive in a sheltered position in deep, moist, sandy loam and are increased by seeds and root-cuttings.

POLYGALA CHAMAEBUXUS (*Polygalaceae*) [PLATE 33]

Personally I consider this little member of the milkwort family one of the most beautiful dwarf shrubs, suitable for the embellishment of the rock garden or the front of the herbaceous or shrub border, for it is neat in habit and its charming perky flowers seem about to take wing from the slender stems that bear them. In addition to its other attractions it is rarely out of flower the whole year through.

It has a fibrous root-system and slender, branched, ascending stems, clothed with rather small, alternate, Box-like, evergreen leaves of a deep, rich green. The quaint, but very pretty blossoms are borne towards the ends of the branchlets, opposite the leaves and usually number from 4 to 6 to each branchlet. They measure from ¾ to 1 inch in length and bear some resemblance to those of the pea family in shape but do not possess a standard-like petal, only wings and a keel which is curiously fringed on the front margin. It is quite hardy and inhabits thin woodlands on the Alps of Switzerland and Austria. The outstanding variety is *purpurea*, brilliant carmine and yellow. The type and its variety need a lime-free soil in a moist, shady position and are increased by layers and cuttings.

PONCIRUS TRIFOLIATA (*Rutaceae*) [Plate 33]

This very remarkable and beautiful chinese shrub is very rarely seen outside botanical gardens and large private gardens, where flowering shrubs and trees are a speciality. Only once have I seen it outside such establishments and that was in a large suburban front garden, within twelve miles of Charing Cross. It has much to commend it to the notice of amateurs, but I would not care to plant it where children at play could come in contact with it, as the needle-sharp, stiletto-like, 3-inch spines with which its branches are beset, could inflict terrible injury.

In cultivation it is an erect, deciduous shrub, from 10 to 15 feet high, with smooth, green, angular, somewhat flattened, crooked branches and twigs, growing at all angles. The rich glossy green, trifoliate leaves are of medium size with flattened stalks and turn to a rich yellow before they fall in the autumn. The lovely snowy white, very fragrant blossoms measure about 2 inches across and are composed of from 4 to 5 egg-shaped or spoon-shaped curving petals; they are borne in the axils of the spines in May when the shrub is leafless. The fruit is greenish-yellow and resembles a small orange; it is very astringent and quite inedible. This shrub is quite hardy and thrives in any good loam and is increased by seeds. It is also known as *Citrus trifoliata* and *Aegle sepiaria*.

PRIMULA AURICULA (*Primulaceae*) [Plate 33]

The genus Primula is a large one and has been greatly augmented during the present century by the discovery and introduction in the form of seeds, of many most desirable species from the mountainous districts of south-western China and Tibet. Nevertheless, many species native in other parts of the world, which have been in cultivation in this country for very many years, equal the Chinese and Tibetan species in beauty and the type of our garden auricula is not the least desirable of them, for in its best form it is one of the most beautiful of all.

It is a native of the Alps of central Europe and has a fairly stout root-stock and a rosette of stalkless, ovate or wedge-shaped, medium-sized, bright green leaves, frequently coated with white meal on both surfaces. Their margins are edged with a transparent membrane and are either entire or furnished with rounded teeth upwards. The mealy flower-stem reaches a height of 4 to 8 inches and bears an umbel of about two dozen, beautiful yellow blossoms, each ¾ inch across. This primula flowers in April and seems to thrive best in a rather heavy soil in a position facing north.

The Himalayan *Primula capitata* has always been a favourite of mine ever since I purchased a packet of seeds over fifty years ago. It forms tufts of primrose-like, mealy leaves, from the centre of which a slender, mealy stem rises to a height of 6 to 9 inches, bearing a flattened crowded head of violet-purple flowers. It is a moisture-loving species and needs a retentive soil.

PRIMULA MARGINATA

This charming Primula is one of the best of the alpine species and is not difficult to grow. It is a native of the Maritime Alps, where it is usually found in crevices in limestone cliffs. It has a woody root-stock and stem, which, when aged is clothed with the dried remains of previous seasons' foliage. The tufts of comparatively small, grey-green, ovate or ovate-lance-shaped, strongly toothed leaves have conspicuous white or golden mealy margins. The under surface is normally covered with golden meal. The mealy flower-stalk reaches a height of 2 to 5 inches and bears an umbel of up to 20 blossoms of a clear lilac-blue. The corolla measures about an inch in diameter in good forms. Several forms are in cultivation such as *caerulea*, *grandiflora* and *major*. This primula flowers from April to July and is easily grown in peat, loam and limestone chippings in full sun. Increase is by seeds and cuttings. *Primula secundiflora* is one of the most beautiful of the moisture-loving species and is quite hardy. It is found in damp, mountain meadows in western China and has a stoutish root-stock, which produces a tuft of rather long, lance-shaped or oblong, finely toothed, bright green leaves, coated with yellow meal beneath. The slender, red-tinted stem rises to a height of 9 to 18 inches and bears 1 to 3 superimposed umbels of rich crimson, bell-shaped, pendant blossoms each about one inch long. This species flowers in June and July and needs an open position in good loam and peat kept constantly moist in summer.

PULMONARIA ANGUSTIFOLIA
var. AZUREA (*Boraginaceae*) [PLATE 33]

Several of the lungworts, as these herbaceous perennials are called, are very decorative and should be given a place in every garden large or small. If but one lungwort is required the choice should be the above-mentioned variety of *P. angustifolia*, which is common in various parts of Europe, and is also occasionally found in Hampshire and Dorset.

The creeping root-stock produces tufts of unspotted linear lance-shaped or elliptic-linear, coarsely hairy leaves narrowed to a stalk. Each tuft produces several flower stems, from 6 to 15 inches tall, clothed with small, narrow, alternate leaves. The lovely flowers are borne in forked cymes composed of 6 or more blossoms. The corolla is a pure azure blue without any tinge of pink or purple, normal in the type. It has a straight tube which expands at the mouth into 5, rounded lobes and measures from $\frac{1}{2}$ to $\frac{3}{4}$ inch in diameter. The buds are deep azure or almost prussian blue. In mild winters this variety flowers from November to April, and should be given a sheltered, half-shady position and is not particular as to soil. Increase is by division.

Pulmonaria rubra is a very beautiful Transylvanian lungwort with very large leaves, and stems about 12 inches high, bearing cymes of ruby red or cinnabar red flowers without any tinge of purple as they age, each measuring about $\frac{1}{2}$ inch across. This species is quite hardy.

PULSATILLA ALPINA
var. SULPHUREA (*Ranunculaceae*) [PLATE 33]

The members of the genus Pulsatilla have been included with the anemones but are now considered sufficiently distinct to form a separate genus. *Pulsatilla vulgaris*, formerly known as *Anemone pulsatilla* is found wild in a few localities in England in counties where limestone and chalk formations occur but is usually very dwarf, rising but 2 or 3 inches above the surface of the soil. The pink form of the Pasque-flower, as our native species is termed, is very lovely, with its ferny foliage and nodding blossoms.

Pulsatilla alpina and its varieties range from northern Spain throughout the Alps to the mountains of eastern Europe and the Caucasus. It has a rather stout black root-stock and a tuft of long-stalked much divided leaves, with numerous, narrow, deeply toothed segments. The rather stout flower-stem is from 6 to 15 inches long and bears at its apex a solitary white flower which is shaded with violet or red outside in some forms. The flower-stem is furnished with an involucre of 3 much-divided leaves, 2 to 3 inches below the flower, which measures about $2\frac{1}{2}$ inches wide and is produced in April. The variety *sulphurea* is one of the most beautiful of hardy plants. It has bright sulphur-yellow, more or less cup-shaped flowers 3 inches in diameter with golden yellow stamens. The type and its variety should be planted in good limy loam in an open position and are increased by seeds and careful division.

PUNICA GRANATUM var. NANA (*Punicaceae*) [PLATE 33]
It is perhaps not generally known that the pomegranate is sufficiently hardy in the south of England to thrive and occasionally bear large quantities of fruit in the open air. Unfortunately they only ripen in exceptionally hot summers. A specimen trained on a wall at Hampton Court frequently bears a number of its familiar fruits. The variety *nana* is similar to the type in all its parts, but is very much smaller and is eminently suitable for small gardens. Moreover it flowers freely when quite small and is sometimes grown as a pot plant in a greenhouse, when it is very beautiful.

It is a deciduous shrub from 5 to 6 feet tall, of erect, densely branched habit. Its brown, angular, spiny branches are densely clothed with comparatively small egg-shaped or oblong, pointed, glaucous green leaves, which frequently turn to an attractive clear yellow before they fall in the autumn. The brilliant vermilion coloured flowers have somewhat crumpled petals and measure about $1\frac{1}{2}$ inch long and 1 inch wide. The copious tuft of yellow stamens adds to the beauty of the blossoms, which are either solitary or in twos or threes in the upper leaf-axils and are produced from June to September. The yellowish-red globose fruit is about $1\frac{1}{2}$ inch in diameter. The variety is quite hardy but should be trained on a south wall in order to obtain an abundance of flowers. It flowers on the old wood and thrives in good friable loam. Increase is by layers, cuttings and imported seeds.

RANUNCULUS CALANDRINIOIDES
(*Ranunculaceae*) [PLATE 34]
The buttercup family is one of considerable extent and ranges over the greater part of the temperate regions of the world. The genus contains both annual and perennial species, some of which are the most pestilent of weeds, especially on heavy, wet soils. On the other hand a few are amongst the most beautiful of herbaceous plants in cultivation, especially those which are natives of New Zealand. These unfortunately are very difficult to establish in the open air in this country and are plants for the specialist only.

Ranunculus calandrinioides is a native of north Africa and is found at considerable elevation above sea level, growing in poor rocky, retentive soil on the Atlas mountains and is certainly one of the most beautiful of the alpine crowfoots. It is quite hardy and possesses a stout, cylindrical

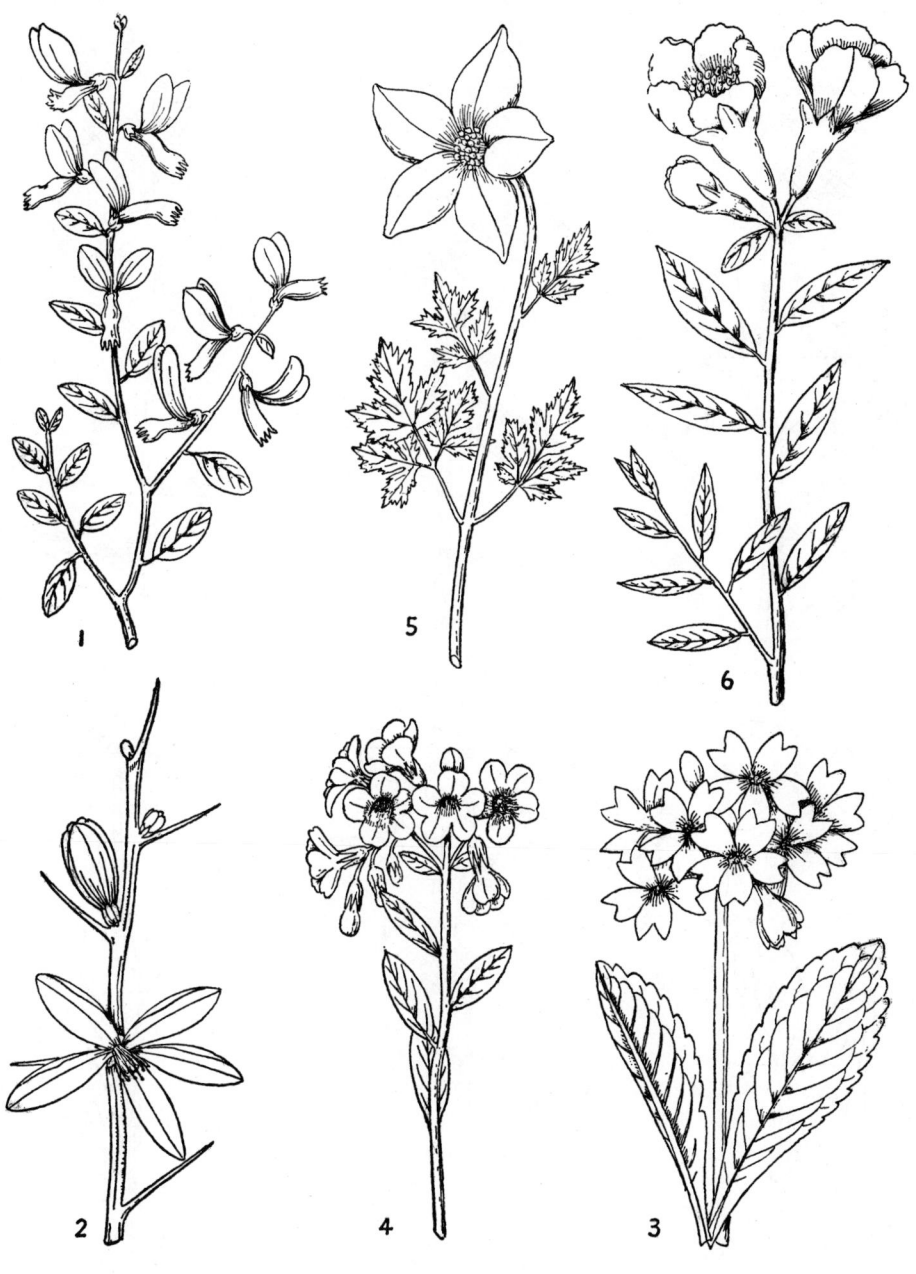

PLATE 33

1. *Polygala chamaebuxus* 2. *Poncirus trifoliata* 3. *Primula auricula*
4. *Pulmonaria augustifolia var. azurea* 5. *Pulsatilla alpina var. sulphurea*
6. *Punica granatum var. nana*

PLATE 34

1. *Ranunculus calandrinioides*
3. *Rhazya orientalis*
5. *Rhododendron campylocarpum*
2. *Ranunculus amplexicaulis*
4. *Rhexia virginica*
6. *Rhododendron williamsianum*

root-stock, similar to a tap-root, well supplied with fleshy roots. This produces a rather sparse tuft of comparatively small, lance-shaped to ovate, glaucous leaves, which are usually wavy on their margins. The flower-stems reach a height of 3 to 5 inches and bear from 1 to 3, white, pink-flushed blossoms, each about 2 inches across. Care should be taken to secure specimens with broad, rounded petals as there are some poor forms in cultivation. This species flowers in March and April and is increased by seeds and division.

RANUNCULUS CRETICUS [PLATE 34]

The amateur gardener when intending to purchase this very handsome buttercup should make sure that the plant offered is true to type as there are forms in cultivation whose flowers are but little larger than those of our *R. bulbosus*. To retain it in vigorous health it is advisable to divide and replant it in fresh soil every two or three years, for if left in the same position for several years it usually deteriorates and the flowers become smaller.

Ranunculus creticus is a perfectly hardy herbaceous perennial and breaks into growth in the spring, however hard the winter may have been. It has thick roots and erect, branched, many-flowered stems, from 1 to $1\frac{1}{2}$ foot tall, sparsely clothed with rather large, deeply lobed and toothed leaves, much resembling those of our bulbous buttercup in shape but not in size. The flower is of a rich golden yellow and frequently measures 3 inches in diameter. This species is a native of the Grecian Islands and flowers in April and May. If possible it should be planted at the foot of a south wall and does best in good, loamy soil.

Ranunculus amplexicaulis is one of the most desirable of the crowfoots. It is a native of the Pyrenees and is not so common in gardens these days. Its stem reaches a height of 3 to 12 inches and is furnished with ovate, stem clasping glaucous leaves. The lovely white flowers, from 1 to 2 inches in diameter are freely produced in May. There is a rare form with appleblossom pink flowers. Increase is by division and seeds.

RHAZYA ORIENTALIS (*Apocynaceae*) [PLATE 34]

The genus Rhazya apparently contains two species only. The above mentioned species is at present the only one in cultivation and although it has been available for a considerable number of years it is quite unfamiliar to most gardeners and is rarely seen outside botanical gardens. When seen in full flower in the herbaceous border in midsummer it is certainly one of the most desirable herbaceous plants that flower at that period. It is closely related to the periwinkles, but most unlike them in habit.

It is of erect habit and under some conditions forms a permanently shrubby base, especially in the warmer counties. The numerous stems reach a height of 2 to 3 feet and are furnished with alternate, ovate-lance-shaped, smooth, bright green leaves. Each stem normally terminates in a loose or densely many-flowered cyme of pretty flowers varying from violet to blue and lilac. The individual flower has a narrow tube which is expanded into 5, oblong lobes and measures about a $\frac{1}{4}$ inch across. This species flowers in June and July and is a native of Greece and Asia Minor. It is not particular with regard to soil but thrives best in a deep friable medium loam in full sun and is easily increased by seeds.

RHEXIA VIRGINICA *(Melastomaceae)* [PLATE 34]

The majority of the trees, shrubs and herbaceous plants contained in the family Melastomaceae are natives of the tropics and it is unusual for any of the genera it contains to be sufficiently hardy to enable them to be successfully cultivated in the open air in this country. In the genus Rhexia, which comprises perennial herbaceous plants and sub-shrubs, at least two of its members are very decorative subjects and should certainly be more frequently cultivated than they are at present. They have showy flowers, are neat in habit and are not difficult to grow.

Rhexia virginica is known in Virginia as Meadow Beauty and Deer Grass and is almost confined to that State. It is of erect habit with a slowly creeping, branched root-stock, which takes a long time to become invasive and is quite easily eradicated if it does. The upright, 4-angled stems, which are usually unbranched, reach a height of 6 to 12 inches and are furnished with medium-sized, bright green leaves, which are rounded, on the lower part of the stems, gradually passing into ovate and finally to ovate-lance-shape at the top. The purple-violet 4-petaled blossoms have a touch of magenta and are either solitary or borne in few-flowered cymes, opening in succession over a long period from June to the autumn. The hardy rhexias thrive best in a compost of peat, leaf-soil and sand and should never be allowed to dry out. They die down to small visible tubers in the winter; these offer a ready means of increase.

RHODODENDRON CAMPYLOCARPUM
(Ericaceae) [PLATE 34]

Comparatively few of the vast number of species of Rhododendron in cultivation in this country are suitable to include in gardens of limited area. Most of them are too robust and occupy too much space when they are fully developed. A few of the dwarf and slow-growing kinds, especially the alpine species, should be grown in every garden where the soil meets their requirements. The four species described below are amongst the best of these rhododendrons and are hardy and easy to grow.

In *Rhododendron campylocarpum* we have the best of the yellow-flowered species, suitable for cultivation in the open air in this country. Like many other very desirable rhododendrons it is a native of the Himalaya and has been in cultivation for over a hundred years. It is an evergreen species from 3 to 4 feet tall, with medium-sized leaves of the usual rhododendron shape. The fragrant, clear yellow flowers are bell-shaped and measure about 3 inches across. They are borne in loose, terminal clusters of 6 to 8 in April and May.

Rhododendron ciliatum is a charming, very dwarf species, native in the Sikkim Himalaya. It is an evergreen of compact habit, apparently but little over 2 feet high in its native habitat. The rather small lance-shaped, blue-green leaves are covered with long brown hairs as are the branches. The beautiful lilac-purple, bell-shaped flowers measure about 2 inches in width and are borne in terminal clusters of 4 to 6 in May.

RHODENDRON MUCRONULATUM [PLATE 34]

In purchasing this delightful little deciduous species care should be taken to see the plant in bloom, as the colour of its flowers varies considerably. The most desirable form is that in which the blossoms are a delightful shade of pure pink. In an open position it forms a neat little, loosely branched but twiggy bush, from 2 to 4 feet high, with small, oblong, rich green leaves clustered towards the ends of the branchlets. The salver-shaped blossoms, which measure about $1\frac{3}{4}$ inch in diameter, are borne on the tips of the branchlets, from December to February, when the shrub is perfectly leafless. It belongs to the azalea section of the genus and is a native of the mountainous districts of central Asia.

Rhododendron williamsianum is a very desirable little evergreen species, of dense, rounded, compact habit and slow growth, and is rarely more than 4 feet tall. Its short branches are densely clothed with small, orbicular or ovate or heart-shaped, very dark green leaves which are glaucous beneath. The flowers have bell-shaped corollas of a rich rosy red, each measuring about $2\frac{1}{2}$ inches in width. They are borne singly or in twos, threes and fours, on the tips of the branchlets in April. This species is a native of western China and is quite hardy. All the above mentioned rhododendrons thrive in peat or good, light loam, kept moist in dry weather. Increase is by seeds, cuttings and inarching.

RHUS AROMATICA *(Anacardiaceae)* [PLATE 35]

The true species of Rhus are valued mostly for the vivid tints their foliage assumes before it falls in the autumn. The inflorescence is frequently conspicuous but rarely brightly coloured. Several species of rhus are in cultivation, the best known is of course the Stag's Horn Sumach, *Rhus typhina*.

The species under consideration is eminently suitable for small gardens, for it is dwarf, compact and well-behaved and very desirable in every way, yet is but rarely seen. It is a most delightful deciduous shrub, rarely more than 3 feet high when grown in light soils. The stoutish branches are clothed with rather large, bright green, pinnate, downy leaves, composed of ovate leaflets with coarsely toothed margins. The leaves assume most beautiful tints of gold, purple and crimson before they fall in late autumn. The flower buds are formed in late summer and are sometimes destroyed by frosts when they are about to open. The small, bright yellow flowers are borne in catkin-like racemes terminating the branches or in the leaf-axils of the upper leaves during February and March.

It is found wild in Ontario and Vermont, on dry banks in open situations and is of course perfectly hardy, but should be given a position where it is not exposed to the early morning sun in the winter. It thrives in any well-drained soil and is increased by layers and cuttings.

RIBES AUREUM *(Grossulariaceae)* [PLATE 35]

There are three outstanding species of Ribes in cultivation in this country. They are: *R. sanguineum* of which there are many poor forms in cultivation; *R. speciosum*, and *R. aureum*. *Ribes speciosum*, sometimes known as *R. fuchsioides*, is not definitely hardy and although a handsome shrub is perhaps not worth including in small gardens in cold districts where wall space is limited. There are many more beautiful shrubs needing wall protection, the best of which should certainly be tried out.

Ribes aureum is a native of North America and is known as Golden Currant and Buffalo Currant. When allowed to develop naturally it is a deciduous bush of loose habit from 6 to 8 feet tall and nearly the same measurement in width. The spreading and erect dark brown branches are well clothed with comparatively small, wide, usually 3-lobed, coarsely toothed leaves of a rather dull yellowish-green. The bright golden yellow flowers, which emit a spicy odour, are borne in drooping racemes from 1 to 2 inches long, composed of from 6 to 12 blossoms. Like all those of the currant family the most conspicuous portion of the flower is the 5, spreading, oblong lobes of the calyx which form a flower about 1 inch in

PLATE 35

1. *Rhus aromatica*   2. *Ribes aureum*   3. *Robinia kelseyi*
4. *Romneya coulteri*   5. *Roscoea cautleoides*
6. *Salvia involucrata var. bethelii*

PLATE 36

1. *Sanguinaria canadensis* 2. *Saponaria ocymoides*
3. *Sarcococca hookeriana var. digyna*
4. *Sarracenia purpurea* 5. *Schizandra chinensis* 6. *Schizopetalon walkeri*

diameter, the petals being very small. The flowers are usually produced in April and in a normal season are followed by a crop of globose black fruits. This shrub is not particular as to soil and is increased by seeds and cuttings.

ROBINIA KELSEYI (*Leguminosae*) [PLATE 35]
Of the four species of Rose Acacia in cultivation in this country the above mentioned is perhaps the best where space is limited. *R. hispida* is also a very beautiful species but has a tendency to sucker.

Robinia kelseyi was introduced into cultivation here about sixty years ago from North Carolina and is quite hardy. In cultivation it is usually a fairly dwarf deciduous shrub but will sometimes become tree-like and reach a height of 10 feet. The slender, brittle, prickly branches arch gracefully and are clothed with fairly long pinnate leaves, composed of from 9 to 11, oblong or ovate, smooth, pointed leaflets of an attractive shade of green. The very beautiful bright rose coloured flowers measure about ¾ inch long and about 1 inch wide and are borne in short clusters of 3 to 8 blossoms on slender flower-stems springing from the upper leaf-axils. They are produced in June and are usually followed by bristly pods about 2 inches long.

Robinia hartwigii is rather similar in habit to the preceding species but its leaves have a greater number of leaflets and the white to rosy purple flowers are larger and are borne in crowded racemes composed of as many as 30 blossoms. In order to keep these two shrubs compact they should be cut back severely immediately after they have flowered as both mostly flower on the previous season's wood and thrive in a light, loamy soil in a sunny, sheltered position. Increase is by cuttings taken in September and by seeds.

ROMNEYA COULTERI (*Papaveraceae*) [PLATE 35]
This genus of Californian semi-shrubby perennials is comprised of two species only and a cross between them; they have two faults. Firstly they are liable to be cut to the ground in severe winters, but new growths will invariably shoot up from the roots in the spring. Secondly they possess the habit of spreading extensively by means of underground stolons and eventually occupying considerable space, which is perhaps not altogether desirable where it is limited. Both the above mentioned species and *R. trichocalyx* are exceedingly beautiful plants both in foliage and flower and it is certainly worthwhile to attempt their successful cultivation. The two species differ one from the other in particulars of botanical interest only.

The creeping roots of *Romneya coulteri* produce a number of erect, somewhat fleshy, semi-shrubby stems from 5 to nearly 10 feet in height. They are clothed with numerous large, pale glaucous green leaves composed of lance-shaped leaflets, the terminal one being large and usually 3-lobed. The exquisite, 6-petaled white flowers measure from 5 to 6 inches in diameter and their petals resemble silk crepe in texture, their beauty being enhanced by the tuft of golden stamens in the centre of blossom. It flowers in July and August and should be planted if possible at the base of a wall facing west, in light loam and is increased by root cuttings, inserted in pots of peaty soil and placed in a greenhouse or frame.

ROSCOEA CAUTLEOIDES (*Zingiberaceae*) [PLATE 35]

The roscoeas, or Mock Orchids as I like to call them, have very delightful flowers, which very closely resemble those of several genera of orchids. Indeed, they are very closely related to the Orchidaceae and in the natural sequence of the plant families are placed immediately before them. They form a comparatively small genus of Himalayan and Chinese herbaceous perennials, inhabiting open situations on the mountains in rather moist soil.

Roscoea cautleoides when in full flower is remarkably orchid-like and its blossoms are very beautiful and delicate. It possesses long cylindrical tuberous roots and a rather stout, stiff, erect stem from 9 to 18 inches high, usually sheathed at the base with 2 lance-shaped reduced leaves and clothed upwards with comparatively large deep-green, strap-shaped, rather blunt leaves, which become more sheath-like towards the top of the stem. The flowers are of a delicate primrose-yellow and are borne in a crowded spike composed of 3 to 7 blossoms, each composed of 6 oblong segments springing from a slender tube and measuring about 2 inches long. This species is a native of western China and has been in cultivation in this country for over fifty years and flowers in May and June. It thrives in good, light loam and leaf-soil in a cool position with plenty of moisture about its roots when in growth. Increase is usually by seeds which set freely, the seedlings taking 2 years to produce flowering plants.

ROSCOEA HUMEANA

This extremely beautiful Roscoea has larger and more delicately coloured flowers than any other species in cultivation. It has even more orchid-like flowers than the preceding species, and like that plant it is a native of western China. Both were introduced into cultivation here about the same time.

The root-stock is a fairly stout spindle-shaped tuber, with but few fibrous roots. The stout stem, which is rarely more than 8 to 9 inches high is almost completely clothed with from 4 to 6, large, broadly lance-shaped or ovate-lance-shaped rich green leaves, recurving considerably at their points at flowering time. The flowers, 2 to 4 in number, are borne in a similar manner to those of the preceding species. They vary in colour from pale pinkish-purple to violet-purple and measure fully 3 inches in diameter when quite mature. The flower consists of a slender tube which expands at its mouth into 6 segments, the lowermost being the largest. The tuber of this species should be planted at a depth of at least 6 inches, in light fibrous loam and leaf-soil with plenty of moisture at the root when growth is active. Increase is usually by seeds.

Roscoea purpurea var. capitata is a moisture-loving plant with bright lilac coloured flowers and pale green leaves margined at their tips with red. It is an excellent bog plant and will also thrive in the border if well supplied with water.

SALVIA INVOLUCRATA (*Labiatae*) [PLATE 35]

Mexico is the native habitat of a number of brilliantly beautiful sages. Most are greenhouse plants and only fit for summer bedding. Several of the most beautiful species are on the border line of hardiness and can only be grown out of doors in this country in sheltered localities in the southern and western maritime counties with any hope of success. Fortunately the two very beautiful salvias described below are practically hardy and only need slight protection, even in cold districts.

Salvia involucrata is a sub-shrub from 2 to 4 feet high, of sparsely branched, fairly compact habit. Its square branches are furnished with handsome, medium-sized, ovate, long-pointed, rich green leaves, margined with rounded teeth. The beautiful rose-coloured flowers are borne in whorls of about 6, subtended by coloured bracts, the whole inflorescence forming a spike-like raceme several inches long. The corolla, which measures over an inch in length, has an inflated tube, expanding upwards into 2 lips, the lower being 3-lobed.

The variety *bethelii* appears to be of garden origin and is a remarkably showy sage. It grows to a height of 2 to 3 feet and has large ovate leaves, heart-shaped at the base and bears long spikes of large rosy crimson flowers, similar in shape to those of the type. Each whorl when in the bud stage is subtended by 2, large coloured bracts. The species and its variety thrive in any friable loam in full sun and are increased by division and cuttings.

SALVIA ULIGINOSA

As the greater part of Brazil is within the tropics and there are no very high mountain ranges within the hinterland, but few gardeners would imagine that any plant from this enormous country could be successfully cultivated in the open air here, especially if they are familiar with the numerous beautiful room plants, now so popular, many of which are natives of Brazil.

The species under consideration is found in the extreme south-eastern Provinces of Brazil, bordering on Uruguay of which it is also a native. When in a thriving condition and well established it is a noble and very decorative species, sometimes reaching a height of 8 feet or more, but is usually 3 to 4 feet. The hairy, 4-angled stems are branched upwards and are clothed with medium-sized, oblong-lance-shaped, deeply toothed leaves, sprinkled with black dots beneath and slightly hairy. The lower ones are stalked and the upper are sessile. The beautiful azure blue flowers are borne in crowded whorls at the ends of the branchlets and are both terminal and lateral, forming a large and very striking inflorescence. The flower measures about ¾ inch long and is very similar in shape to that of the preceding species.

This species is a purely herbaceous perennial and produces suckers from the roots all around the plant which of course offer a ready means of increase. It flowers from July to November and seems to appreciate a good, moist loam in full sun in cultivation in this country.

SANGUINARIA CANADENSIS (*Papaveraceae*) [PLATE 36]

Many members of the poppywort family possess a coloured juice or sap in various parts of their structure, mostly in their roots, stems and seed-vessels. That of our native Greater Celandine (*Chelidonium majus*) is orange or orange-red and when the roots of the Sanguinaria are bruised or broken a bright red juice soon makes its appearance: hence the popular name of Blood Root by which it is known in northern U.S.A. and Canada. It is a perfectly hardy perennial and is subjected to a zero temperature for several months in its native habitat.

It possesses a long stout root-stock, which extends horizontally very slowly. Buds form at its nodes, each of which usually produces a solitary, rather large leaf. It is palmate, deeply veined and is toothed or lobed on its margins. It is a beautiful bluish-grey and rosy green and is borne on a stalk about 6 inches long. The leaf slowly unfolds and discloses a snow white blossom whose lengthening stem bears it well above the mature leaf. The rather fugacious blossom is composed of from 7 to 12, egg-shaped or ovate petals and measures about 1 inch across. This exquisite herbaceous plant is not particular as to soil but is at its best in a deep, cool compost of almost pure leaf-soil, in a bed facing north or in a cool, shady corner. It flowers in April and is usually increased by seeds as it resents disturbance. There is a form known as *grandiflora* and one with very many petals.

SAPONARIA OCYMOIDES (*Caryophyllaceae*) [PLATE 36]

I am inclined to bracket the Soapwort (*Saponaris officinalis*) as almost as pestilent as the Bindweed (*Convolvulus sepium*) and would advise my readers with small gardens to admire it in the gardens of others. I must admit that the pink-flowered form is very beautiful but from my own experience it is one of the most difficult plants to eradicate when its creeping roots produce growths among plants of greater value. The Rock Soapwort, as *Saponaria ocymoides* is called, is not an invasive species and has equally beautiful pink flowers in its best forms. It is a common plant in the Alps of Switzerland and is also found in the Jura mountains in France and is perfectly hardy.

It is a perennial with a woody, branching root-stock and prostrate stems which branch from the base, forming an elegant mat of yellowish-green foliage. The slender stems reach a height of 3 to 6 inches and are furnished below with egg-shaped or egg-shaped-lance-shaped leaves with a wide stalk. The upper leaves are stalkless and oblong-lance-shaped. The rose-pink or rosy purple, 5-petaled flowers measure about $\frac{5}{8}$ inch in diameter and are borne in umbel-like clusters on the tips of the stems and are produced in June and July. This little saponaria thrives in a raised bed of gritty soil in an open sunny position with some granite chippings placed around its root-stock after it is established. Propagation is by cuttings and seeds.

SARCOCOCCA HOOKERIANA (*Buxaceae*) [PLATE 36]

The sarcococcas very much resemble our Butcher's Broom in appearance and have the same habit of slowly increasing their girth by pushing up suckers. They are valuable subjects for shady places and will thrive under trees, also their flowers are fragrant, but are by no means showy. Being dwarf and compact they take up but little room and are very suitable for odd shady corners in small gardens. The species under consideration is a native of Afghanistan and the western Himalaya. Its flowers are probably more fragrant than those of any other species in cultivation and its variety *digyna* is the most colourful with regard to the tinting of its young branchlets and leaves.

The type is a leafy, much-branched, hardy, evergreen shrub from 3 to 4 feet high. Its slender branches and branchlets are clothed with fairly small, somewhat leathery, shortly-stalked dark green, narrowly lance-shaped, pointed leaves. The flowers are either male or female and are produced in short terminal and axillary racemes. The flowers lack petals; the males are composed of 4 creamy-white, petal-like stamens and the females of a solitary style. They are produced from January to March and are followed by black berries. In the Chinese variety *digyna* the young shoots are purplish, the leaf-margins are pink and the female flower has 2 styles. It is easily increased by division.

SARRACENIA PURPUREA (*Sarraceniaceae*) [PLATE 36]

Specimens of several species of these insectivorous plants may usually be seen at Kew in the annexe to the hot-house in which the Giant Water Lily is housed. It is devoted to plants growing in a state of nature in wet sphagnum moss, with very poorly developed roots, which never penetrate the moss to the soil beneath it. They are thus unable to obtain the nitrogen necessary to their existence, except by trapping insects by means of sticky glands on their leaves and stems, as in the droseras, or in their hollow, trumpet-shaped leaves as in the sarracenias. In both cases a digestive fluid is secreted and the juices of the insects absorbed, thus supplying the necessary nitrogen to the plant.

Sarracenia purpurea is known by several popular names in its native country, such as Indian Cup, Pitcher Plant, Side Saddle Flower and Trumpet Leaf, and is a native of eastern North America. It is a perennial with a short, thick root-stock, furnished with a few slender roots, beset with many very short rootlets. The large, very remarkable pitcher-like leaves arise directly from the root-stock and are tinted with dull green, dark red and purple. The rather stout, naked flower-stem reaches a height of 8 to 16 inches and bears a solitary nodding flower about $2\frac{1}{2}$ inches wide, with large green sepals and a very large umbrella-like style, which is the most conspicuous part of the blossom, which is produced in May. It should be planted in a low, swampy position in living sphagnum moss and peat and is increased by seeds.

SCHIZANDRA CHINENSIS (*Magnoliaceae*) [PLATE 36]

The genus Schizandra contains a few species of stove, greenhouse and half-hardy shrubs, related to the magnolias. The species described is probably the only perfectly hardy member of the genus and has withstood thirty degrees of frost and remained unscathed. It has been in cultivation in this country for a considerable number of years but is still an unfamiliar plant in small gardens and is certainly not a difficult subject to cultivate. It is a very graceful, deciduous, climbing shrub and is eminently suitable for clothing a wall or pergola.

Its very slender branches and branchlets will reach a height of 20 to 30 feet on a wall or unwanted tree and are furnished towards their tips with very attractive, medium-sized, rich green, ovate, pointed leaves, margined with small, widely spaced teeth and somewhat resemble the leaf of an apple. They are borne on rather long stalks and are attractively tinted before they fall in the autumn. The very pretty rose coloured blossoms are borne on slender, curved stalks of varying length, in the leaf-axils, towards the tips of the branchlets, all over the plant during April and May. They are sweetly fragrant and are composed of about 5, egg-shaped or ovate segments, forming an almost globose blossom $\frac{1}{2}$ to $\frac{3}{4}$ inch across. The scarlet fruits are borne in clusters and are very decorative. It is a native of China and Japan and thrives in a compost of peat and loam and is increased by seeds and layers.

SCHIZOPETALON WALKERI (*Cruciferae*) [PLATE 36]

There are several annuals which, although of no great decorative value, are worth growing where space can be afforded, for the sake of the delightful fragrance of their blossoms, which like those of the Night-scented Stock are only scented towards and after sun-down. Many such annuals have white or pale coloured flowers to attract the night-flying insects. The plant in cultivation with the most fragrant flowers is probably a shrub closely allied to the magnolias and is known as *Michelia fuscata*. It is a native of Hong Kong and it is said that the fragrance emitted by a solitary blossom can be distinctly detected in perfectly still air from a distance of one hundred yards.

Schizopetalon walkeri is the sole member of its genus and is a native of Chile. Although the seeds are offered by several seedsmen it is but rarely seen. It has a thong-like root with only a few rootlets and a sparse tuft or rosette of long, sinuately pinnate leaves which soon shrivel as the season advances. The stem is erect, slightly branched and up to $1\frac{1}{2}$ foot high; the stem leaves are much smaller than the root-leaves and are of an uncommon shape; they are irregularly escalloped and waved on their margins, blunt at the apex and taper abruptly to the base. The pure white, 4-petaled fragrant flowers are borne in terminal leafy racemes, from August onwards, and measure about $\frac{3}{4}$ inch wide; their petals are deeply cut on their edges giving them a feathery look. Seeds should be sown in late May in a position where the plants are to flower.

SCHIZOSTYLIS COCCINEA (*Iridaceae*) [PLATE 37]

Although this brilliant member of the iris family was quite frequently cultivated years ago it is now rarely seen except in botanical and large private gardens. Possibly its lack of complete hardiness is the main reason for its neglect. It is however, a very valuable subject for the decoration of the garden in the autumn as it produces its lovely flowers from October onwards well into December and spikes in full flower may frequently be cut for table decoration at Christmas in mild seasons. It is known as the Kaffir Lily or Crimson Flag and is a native of South Africa.

It is a robust perennial herbaceous plant with handsome fan-shaped tufts of sword-shaped, sheathing, grey-green leaves which frequently attain a length of 4 feet or more and degenerate into bracts on the flower-stem which usually overtops the leaves. The brilliantly tinted flowers are borne in long spikes, composed of 10 to 15 blossoms or more; they measure about $2\frac{1}{2}$ inches in diameter and have a slightly curved, funnel-shaped golden yellow tube which expands at its mouth into 6, oval, brilliant vermilion-scarlet lobes. There are two garden forms: Mrs Hegarty with salmon-pink flowers, and Viscountess Byng with flesh-pink ones. All require a moist rich soil and are increased by offsets and seeds.

SEDUM PILOSUM (*Crassulaceae*)

Unfortunately this little stonecrop is of biennial duration only, but self-sown seeds germinate freely and in light, stony soil the lateral rosettes frequently survive, thus rendering the plant more or less perennial. It is perhaps the most beautiful of all the hardy stonecrops in cultivation, and was introduced into cultivation in this country in 1910, but has long been known to botanical science. It is perfectly hardy in well-drained soil and is a native of Asia Minor and the Caucasus.

In the first year of its existence it forms a dense, almost globose rosette of rather small, incurved, hairy foliage and then bears a resemblance to a sempervivum. The leaves of the rosette are linear-spoon-shaped, rather blunt, imbricated, stalkless, very fleshy and of a dark green colour. Those on the flower-stems are larger and oblong-egg-shaped. The flower-stems are completely hidden by the leaves and are about 2 inches long. The inflorescence is a much-branched, panicled cyme up to 3 inches across, convex at the top. The lovely bright rose coloured flowers measure about $\frac{3}{8}$ inch across and have spreading, oblong, pointed petals and linear dark green sepals, about half the length of the petals. This delightful little stonecrop flowers in May and June in normal seasons and thrives perfectly in a raised bed of stony soil in full sun. A foot wide mat of this Sedum when in full flower is indeed a most beautiful and uncommon sight.

SEDUM PULCHELLUM [PLATE 37]

This very handsome species is one of the few hardy sedums that do not creep and is one of the most desirable stonecrops in cultivation, for its large, claw-like inflorescence of brightly coloured flowers is very decorative. This species somewhat resembles the well-known, yellow flowered *Sedum reflexum* in habit but not in foliage or flower.

S. *pulchellum* is a native of the United States, and ranges from Missouri to Virginia and Texas and is perfectly hardy in this country. It is a compact evergreen perennial forming attractive tufts of bright green foliage 2 to 4 inches high. The usually erect stems are well clothed with linear, ascending, cylindrical leaves of medium length, with a forked spur at the base. The inflorescence which measures from 3 to 4 inches across is borne on an erect leafy stem from 4 to 6 inches long, and is composed of 3 to 5, down-curved, terminal, divided, leafy branches, crowded with more or less erect, 5-petaled blossoms of a beautiful rosy purple tint, with red anthers, each flower measuring about ½ inch in diameter. They are produced freely over a long period from June to the end of August.

This species is one of the few stonecrops that thrive best in a damp soil but should have a sunny position. It is a failure in hot, dry soils and where the garden soil is sandy loam must be planted on the edge of a pool or in the bog garden. It is easily increased by division and by seeds.

SHORTIA UNIFLORA
var. GRANDIFLORA (*Diapensiaceae*) [PLATE 37]

The distribution of the five or six species of dwarf perennials which constitute the genus Shortia is most remarkable. All but one of its members are natives of China, Japan and Formosa. The remaining species—S. *galacifolia*—is found on the mountains of north and south Carolina, usually on the banks of rivulets and nowhere else. Thus many thousands of miles separates it from the other members of the genus native in north-eastern Asia. *Shortia galacifolia* is not a very common plant in small gardens but is perhaps familiar to many a keen gardener who can give the plant the conditions it requires.

In *Shortia uniflora* var. *grandiflora* we have one of the most beautiful of the lovely Japanese plants which grace our gardens to-day. It is found in the clefts in rocks on the mountains of both the north and south islands of Japan and is quite hardy in this country. The fibrous root-stock produces a comparatively small tuft of medium-sized, leathery, wedge-shaped or broadly egg-shaped, pointed leaves, which are coarsely toothed above the middle. They are of a rich, dark green and are frequently tinted crimson. The lovely flowers vary in colour from white to pale pink and are produced during May and June on stalks 2 to 3 inches long. The corolla which measures about 2 inches across has a short, broad tube and 5, spreading, toothed lobes. The species and its variety should be grown in a damp, semi-shady position in a compost of peat, leaf-soil and sand and is increased by division.

SILENE SCHAFTA (*Caryophyllaceae*) [PLATE 37]

Many members of this genus possess stems furnished with glands or glandular hairs which secrete a resinous, viscid substance, which entraps insects attempting to alight upon the stems; hence the popular name of Catchfly for these plants. The genus contains a number of annual, biennial and perennial herbs, several of which are of much value for garden decoration and occupy but little space.

Silene schafta is one of the most desirable of our rock-plants, especially on account of its late-flowering habit, for it is frequently in full bloom in early October. In habit it is neat and attractive and although it possesses creeping roots it remains compact and almost carpet-like. It is a perennial herb with numerous, slender, purplish, branching stems from 2 to 3 inches high, well clothed with opposite lance-shaped, deep green leaves tapering to a narrow base. The 5-petaled vivid, magenta-rose blossom is about 1 inch in diameter and has wedge-shaped petals, shallowly cleft and finely toothed on their front margins. This silene is perfectly hardy and is a native of the high mountains of south-eastern Russia, Armenia and Persia. It is not particular as to soil and is increased by seeds and division. *Silene caroliniana* is also an attractive perennial, native in eastern U.S.A. It is of densely tufted habit, from 4 to 6 inches high, with deep pink flowers, each $1\frac{1}{2}$ inch across and is perfectly hardy, thriving in light soil in full sun.

SISYRINCHIUM DOUGLASII (*Iridaceae*)

Several popular names have been bestowed on this very beautiful member of the iris family in its native country and also in this, such as Violet-eyed Grass, Spring Satin Flower and Spring Bell-flower, all of which are quite appropriate. It is a native of north America and is found in practically the same sort of localities as *S. filifolium*. It has always been a great favourite of

PLATE 37

1. *Schizostylis coccinea*   2. *Sedum pulchellum*
3. *Shortia uniflora var. grandiflora*
4. *Silene caroliniana*   5. *Sisyrinchium filifolium*   6. *Sophora viciifolia*

PLATE 38

1. *Stachyurus praecox* 2. *Staphylea holocarpa* 3. *Sternbergia lutea*
4. *Stewartia ovata* 5. *Stylomecon heterophylla* 6. *Styrax hemsleyana*

mine and it is surprising how few lovers of beautiful flowers are familiar with it.

It is a perennial whose foliage dies away in late summer and if its position is not marked it is liable to be dug up and consigned to the rubbish heap in the autumn clean-up. The root-stock is a short rhizome, furnished with a few fleshy roots; it produces a wiry erect, unbranched flower-stem from 6 to 12 inches long, clothed with 3 to 4 grass-like, very pointed, deep green sheathing leaves, which are much shorter than the flower-stem. The richly tinted pendant flowers are borne 2 to 3 at a time over a long period, normally in May and June, on slender stalks springing from the top of the stem between 2 bracts. The flower is rich purple veined with reddish-purple and has a satin-like sheen. It is about 1½ inch wide when fully open. This species is perfectly hardy and needs a light, rich, moist soil and is increased by seeds and division.

SISYRINCHIUM FILIFOLIUM [PLATE 37]

This delicately beautiful member of an extensive genus of American herbaceous perennials is one of the two most desirable species. More than a few of the other species of Sisyrinchium are worthy of cultivation in gardens where space is not unduly restricted. This delightful plant is a native of the Falkland Islands and is endemic, or in other words is not found anywhere else in the world. It inhabits open situations among grasses and short herbage and is known to the inhabitants of these far away isles as Fair Maidens, a delightful name for a beautiful plant.

It is a perennial herbaceous plant, with short rhizomes, which produce tufts of narrow, grass-like, pointed, deep green leaves. The slender, erect flower-stem reaches a height of from 6 to 15 inches and is clothed with a few pointed, stem-clasping sheaths. The lovely, bell-shaped fragrant blossoms are borne in clusters of 2 to 3, each on a slender, curving stalk, which springs from between bracts on the upper part of the stem. The individual flower measures about 1 inch across and is composed of 6 ovate or egg-shaped, pure white segments, veined with reddish-purple. They are produced in succession during April and May. It is hardy and thrives in good, light, moist loam in full sun and is increased by division and seeds.

SOPHORA VICIIFOLIA (*Leguminosae*) [PLATE 37]

The genus Sophora contains a number of stove, greenhouse, half-hardy and hardy trees, shrubs and herbs, several of which are very desirable garden plants and among these is the above mentioned species. It is a member of the pea-flower family and is a very pretty species, very suitable for small gardens.

In an open situation in poor soil it is a deciduous, bushy shrub from 4 to 6 feet tall, well furnished with vetch-like, medium-sized, bright green leaves, composed of from 11 to 15, elliptic, stalk-less leaflets; they are very attractive and enhance the beauty of the plant. The delicately tinted blossoms are borne in short racemes, composed of 6 to 12 flowers, on short shoots of the previous season's growths and at the bases of each of these branchlets a slender, curved spine is usually to be found. The pea-shaped flowers which measure about ½ inch long, have white segments, tinged with blue and white filaments, capped with orange-yellow anthers. The cup-shaped, blue calyx adds to their attractiveness.

It is a native of China and has been collected in the Provinces of Hupeh, Shensi, Yunnan and Szechuan and is quite hardy, flowering in June. Like most of the pea-flower family it thrives in a light, well-drained soil, in a sunny position and is increased by cuttings and seeds.

STACHYURUS PRAECOX (*Stachyuraceae*) [PLATE 38]

In mild winters this desirable deciduous shrub opens its first blossoms in the middle of January and continues to do so throughout February and March. On account of its habit of producing its beautiful flowers in the dull days of winter, it deserves to be widely grown, but is at present rarely seen. According to some authorities it is up to 10 feet in height, but I have never seen it more than 5 and often in full flower when only 3 feet tall.

The reddish or brownish-green branches and twigs are quite smooth; they are clothed with rather large, oval or ovate-lance-shaped leaves, tapering to a slender point, prominently veined and toothed on their margins. The dainty pale yellow, pendant blossoms are composed of 4 erect petals about a ¼ inch long, forming a bell-shaped corolla with a cluster of golden anthers in the centre. The flowers are borne in stiff, drooping racemes 2 to 4 inches long, all along the bare shoots; each raceme contains from 10 to 20 flowers. The globose, greenish-yellow fruit measures about a ¼ inch in diameter and is not commonly produced. It is a native of Japan and is quite hardy, thriving in any good, light loam in a position sheltered from the early morning sun in the winter. It is increased by layers and cuttings of half-ripened shoots in a sand frame. *S. chinensis* has more open flowers and abruptly pointed leaves.

STAPHYLEA HOLOCARPA (*Staphyleaceae*) [PLATE 38]

The staphyleas are collectively known as Bladder Nut Trees on account of their curiously inflated fruits. Two species are fairly well known, namely *S. pinnata* and *S. colchica*. The former is the one most frequently seen and is said to be naturalised in one or two localities in England, and the latter is frequently used as a pot-plant for early forcing. Both have pure white flowers and are desirable shrubs.

Staphylea holocarpa has been in cultivation for over fifty years and is practically unknown outside the larger private and botanical gardens. From a decorative point of view it is superior to the other two species as its flowers are charmingly tinted. It is found in the province of Hupeh in central China and is a perfectly hardy deciduous shrub from 15 to 20 feet high when fully developed, but flowers freely when quite small. The spreading branches are clothed with medium-sized, rich green, trifoliate leaves with oblong-lance-shaped leaflets with serrated margins. The flowers measure about ½ inch long and have 4 or sometimes 5 narrow petals of a beautiful shade of pink; they are borne in rather flat corymbs 2 to 3 inches long in April and May. The curious 3-celled, inflated, pear-shaped fruits contain hard, brown seeds. This species is not particular as to soil but thrives best in a good light loam and is increased by seeds, cuttings and layers.

STERNBERGIA LUTEA (*Amaryllidaceae*) [PLATE 38]

All the species of this small genus of bulbous plants are very desirable and should be better known to amateur gardeners as they have been in cultivation for a considerable number of years. My first experience with this very beautiful Sternbergia was many years ago when I purchased half a dozen bulbs from a well-known firm in London. All flowered in the autumn of the year they were planted, but two years passed before they flowered again, after which they flowered annually until I moved to another district.

Sternbergia lutea is a native of Asia Minor and is quite hardy. It has a long-necked bulb about 2 inches long, rather like that of a daffodil. The rich green, strap-shaped, recurved leaves are about a foot in length and are contemporary with the flowers, which are produced in October and November and stand rough weather well as there is much more substance in their blossoms than those of the crocus, which they very much resemble in shape, but are distinctly stalked; they are of a rich golden yellow and frequently measure over 4 inches across when fully open in the sunshine. The sternbergias require a good, well-drained, loamy soil in the hottest part of the garden and are at their best in counties with sunshine records above the average. Increase is by offsets and seeds.

STEWARTIA OVATA (*Theaceae*) [PLATE 38]
The stewartias are closely related to the camellias and number four or five species. All are very beautiful shrubs or small trees, with large white flowers resembling those of a single camellia. Several have been in cultivation in this country for a great number of years and are yet rarely seen outside the large private gardens or botanical establishments. The genus is represented in North America, China and Japan. The species under consideration is a native of southern U.S.A. and although quite hardy seems to thrive better and flower more freely in counties with a high sunshine record.

It is deciduous and forms a wide-spread bush or small tree from 8 to 12 feet high and rather more in diameter when full grown, but is of slow growth and flowers freely when only half that height. The spreading branches are clothed with large, handsome, ovate, bright green leaves, often suffused with bronze and assuming tints of crimson in the autumn, sometime before they fall. The creamy white, 5-petaled flowers measure from 3 to 4 inches in diameter and sometimes have one deformed petal. They have yellow stamens and are produced singly in the upper leaf-axils in August when most shrubs have finished flowering. In the variety *grandiflora* the stamens are purple and the flowers frequently measure 5 inches across. The stewartias thrive in a good, light, well-drained soil, but should never suffer from want of water and dislike lime. Propagation is by seeds and layers.

STYLOMECON HETEROPHYLLA
(*Papaveraceae*) [PLATE 38]
Formerly known as *Meconopsis heterophylla* this uniquely tinted half-hardy annual should be more frequently cultivated by amateurs for it is of very considerable decorative value and its flowers are pleasantly fragrant, a most unusual occurrence amongst the poppy family. The scent is said to resemble that of the lily-of-the-valley.

It is a native of California, frequenting light soils in open, sunny situations. When allowed sufficient room to develop freely it forms a fairly large rosette composed of a dozen or more pale green pinnate, remotely and deeply toothed leaves. The slender, erect flower-stem which springs from the centre of the rosette to a height of about 12 inches is branched upwards and furnished with a few linear, entire or toothed leaves. The 4-petaled poppy-like flowers are borne on the apex of the stem and its branches on very long slender stalks. They measure from $1\frac{1}{2}$ to 2 inches in width and are of a brilliant coppery orange with a deep crimson or maroon blotch at the base of the petals which are sometimes asymmetrical. The yellow anthers are borne on purple filaments and are usually inclined to one side of the flower in a tassel-like cluster. Unlike those of most of the poppy family the flowers are long-lasting. The seeds should be sown in a warm, sunny border in May and the seedlings thinned so that they are 9 to 12 inches apart. In the more favoured counties with regard to climate it will maintain itself by self-sown seeds.

STYRAX HEMSLEYANA (*Styracaceae*) [PLATE 38]
Several members of this most attractive genus of shrubs and trees produce substances of economic value, notably *S. benzoin*, which produces benzoin resin used in 'Friar's Balsam' and *S. officinale*, storax resin. The species under consideration is in my opinion the most desirable for garden decoration for it is both handsome in leaf and very beautiful in flower. In a well sheltered but not shady position it forms a very graceful deciduous tree from 20 to 30 feet high of somewhat open habit.

The rather stout, spreading branches are clothed with large, alternate, strongly veined egg-shaped or oval leaves, smooth and pale green on the upper surface and slightly downy and paler beneath. They taper slightly towards the base and are pointed at the tip and their margins are obscurely toothed. They assume a bright yellow tint before they fall in the autumn. The lovely pure white pendant flowers are borne in terminal and axillary racemes or panicles from 4 to 6 inches long in June and July. Each is composed of from 15 to 20 fragrant blossoms borne on short, curved stalks. The flower is composed of 5, spreading, ovate petals and is about 1 inch across. It is a native of central and western China and needs a compost of sandy loam, peat and leaf soil and is increased by seeds, layers and cuttings.

SUTHERLANDIA FRUTESCENS (*Leguminosae*) [PLATE 39]
Many years ago I bought a packet of seeds of this brilliantly beautiful member of the pea-flower family. They were planted in pots of sand and peat and germinated in a greenhouse. The seedlings were planted out in the warmest part of my garden in light loam when the danger from frost was over. They grew quickly as it was a warm spring and summer and were in full flower in August. They were planted 18 inches apart in threes and were an unforgettable sight of handsome glaucous foliage and brilliantly tinted blossoms, remaining decorative until they were destroyed by the first hard frost.

It is common over the greater part of South Africa, usually being found in open situations in rather dry soil and has been in cultivation in this country for a very long time, in fact since 1683. It is known as the Cape Bladder Senna on account of the inflated, pale green seed vessel's resemblance to a senna pod.

It is an evergreen shrub forming a small, erect bush from 2 to 6 feet high. The stiff, grooved, brownish branches are somewhat sparsely furnished with long pinnate leaves composed of from 6 to 10 pairs and an odd terminal one of narrowly oblong leaflets, each with a notch at its apex. The brilliant vermilion blossoms measure about an inch long and are borne in crowded racemes 3 to 4 inches long springing from the upper leaf-axils. It must be treated as a tender annual and given a position in full sun in good light loam.

SYRINGA PERSICA (*Oleaceae*) [PLATE 39]

I have a bush of this elegant lilac in my garden in a position facing south, where it has been for the past forty years to my knowledge. It is growing in poor, sandy loam over gravel and is now not more than 7 feet tall and about the same measurement in width. Year after year in May its foliage is almost hidden by great panicles of lilac coloured blossom with an extremely pleasant spicy odour, quite different from that of the common lilac. Apart from the removal of dead flower-panicles and the cutting out of a few crowded branches to the ground level it has never been pruned.

This delightful shrub should be given a place in every amateur's garden however small, but is far from frequently seen. It is deciduous and forms a compact, much-branched bush, which will cover itself with blossom when only 2 to 3 feet high. The small, lance-shaped, deep green leaves are narrowed to a point and in some specimens are cut into several narrow lobes. The flowers are borne in panicles 6 to 12 inches long and 6 inches wide on the tips of the slender branchlets, which are borne down by their weight. They vary in tint from lilac to lilac-pink and there is a very beautiful variety with pure white flowers. Some authorities state that this lilac is a native of China, not Persia, others that it is indigenous in Afghanistan. An open position in light, sandy loam suits this shrub. Propagation is by seeds, layers and cuttings.

TRACHYMENE CAERULEA (*Umbelliferae*) [PLATE 39]

Trachymene caerulea or *Didiscus caeruleus*, as this very attractive member of the carrot family is termed, comes from Western Australia, the native habitat of very many brilliantly beautiful plants that have from time to time been introduced into this country. Unfortunately only a few of these are sufficiently hardy to enable them to be grown successfully in the open air in this country except perhaps in the very mild coastal districts of south-western England and western Scotland. It has been given the very pretty popular name of Blue Lace Flower and is apparently the sole member of its genus.

It is a half-hardy annual of sparse habit, with rather stout, erect, thinly branched stems from 1 to 2 feet high, sparsely clothed with bright green, broadly wedge-shaped leaves of medium size, tapering below and divided upwards into 3, spreading lobes, which are again lobed and sharply toothed. The flowers are borne on the tip of the stem and its lateral branches in dense, many-flowered umbels, from 1 to 2 inches in diameter. The individual flower is about ⅜ inch across and is of a delicate lilac-blue tint. They are composed of 5 ovate-oblong, blunt petals. This annual flowers in July and August if its seeds are sown under glass and the seedlings are given a sunny position in good, light soil.

TRICYRTIS MACROPODA (*Liliaceae*) [PLATE 39]
The name of Toad Lily has been given to this interesting but not showy plant, presumably on account of its speckled and spotted blossoms. The Toad Lilies have only a little decorative value but should appeal to those amateurs who like to cultivate plants rarely seen outside botanical gardens and can appreciate their quaint and curiously constructed flowers. They number only a few species and are much alike in habit and appearance and there is not much to choose between them for garden purposes. *T. macropoda* is probably the best if only one species is desired, although *T. hirta* in its pink-flowered form is also desirable. All are natives of China or Japan and are hardy over the greater part of this country but it is advisable in very cold districts to cover the clumps with ashes or some other protective material in the autumn.

Tricyrtis macropoda is a herbaceous perennial, with a shortly creeping rhizome and numerous erect stems from 2 to 4 feet high, furnished with rather large, oblong, rich green leaves, pointed at the apex, rounded at the base and either sessile and slightly stem-clasping or very shortly stalked. The quaint flowers are borne erect in a branching inflorescence measuring 4 to 6 inches across from September until they are cut down by frost. The flower which measures from ¾ to 1 inch in length is formed of 6, erect, broadly lance-shaped segments, either white or very pale purple, thickly covered with small purple spots. Increase is by division in spring.

TRILLIUM GRANDIFLORUM (*Liliaceae*) [PLATE 39]
Some thirty species constitute the genus Trillium, several of which are of decorative value, but unfortunately the majority have green or purple tinted blossoms, which are not very attractive and would only appeal to specialists. They are found in Japan, China and north America and are all quite hardy in this country. The above mentioned species is by far the most decorative of these members of the lily family and is known in its native country as Wake Robin probably on account of the early appearance of its growths above the surface of the soil.

The root-stock is a short, thick rhizome, which produces a solitary, rather stout stem from 1 to 1½ foot tall, it is naked below and bears a whorl of 3 large, spreading, rich, deep green, usually ovate leaves, abruptly narrowed at the tip and almost stalkless, at its apex in the manner of our native Herb Paris, to which it is closely related. The solitary flower is borne on a rather long slender, erect or curved stalk springing from the tip of the stem. It measures from 2 to 2½ inches in width and is composed of 3 ovate, pointed, spreading white petals, which are tinted with rose colour as they age. There are two notable forms, *roseum* which always has pink flowers and *rubrum* in which they are deep pink. This species is a native of north America and needs a rather shady position and a deep moist, peaty or woodland soil and is increased by division and seeds.

TROLLIUS ACAULIS (*Ranunculaceae*) [PLATE 39]
The more robust florist's forms of such species of Globe Flower as *T. europaeus* and *T. asiaticus* etc., are deservedly popular with gardeners whose soil meets their requirements but one rarely sees the more dwarf growing kinds, although several equal in beauty the garden forms and sometimes have larger flowers.

Trollius acaulis forms attractive tufts of 3 to 7 lobed leaves with much divided and toothed margins. The rich golden yellow flowers measure from 1 to 2 inches in diameter and are composed of about 9, lance-shaped, pointed sepals which form the decorative part of the flower, for the spoon-shaped petals are shorter than the conspicuous stamens. The flowers are borne on very short stems and are produced in June and July. This charming and neat little Globe Flower is a native of the Himalaya and is quite hardy.

Trollius ranunculinus, perhaps better known as *T. patulus* is another charming little species of comparatively dwarf habit, native in the Caucasus and Armenia and some of the mountainous districts of Asia Minor. It forms tufts of palmately divided root-leaves with much cut and

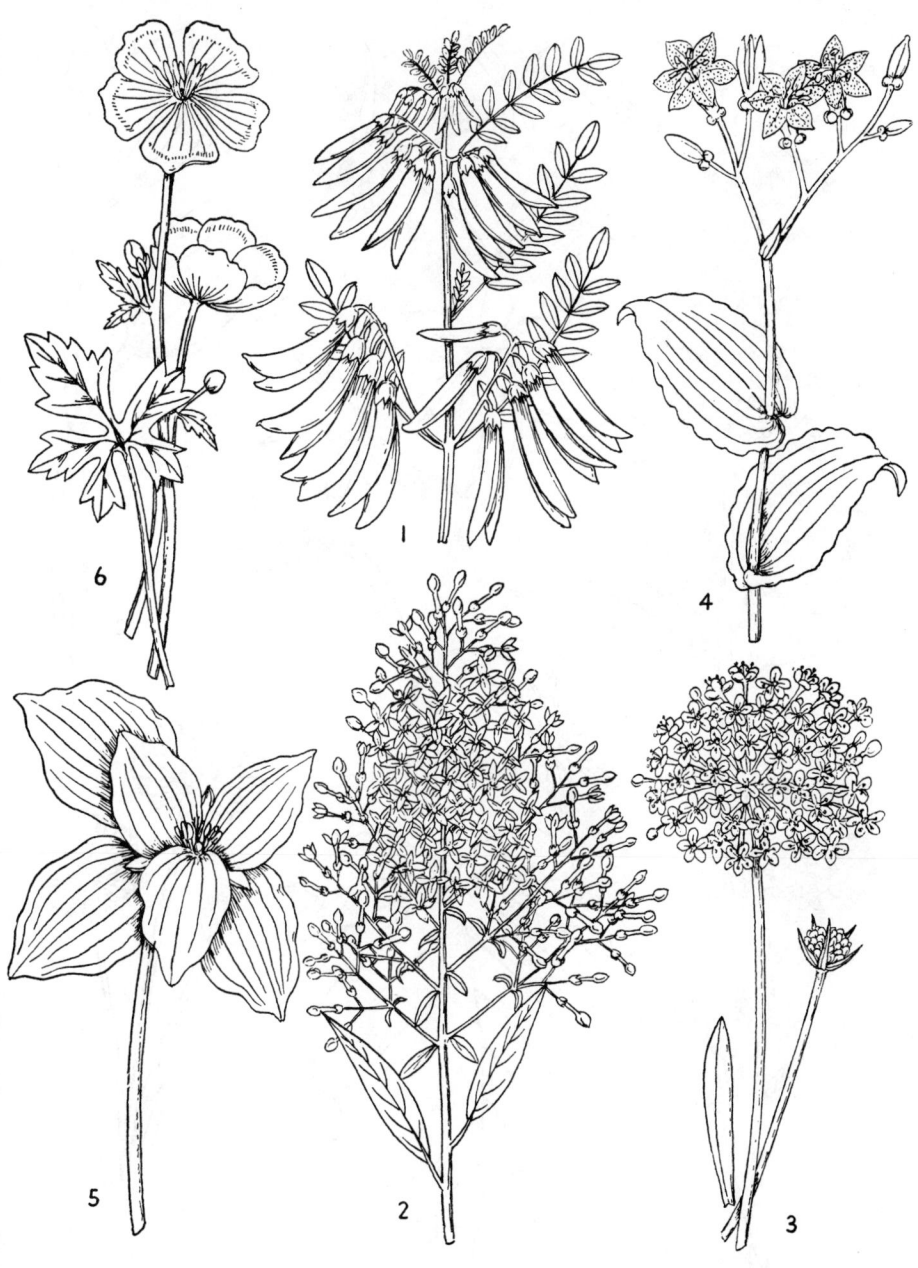

PLATE 39

1. *Sutherlandia frutescens* 2. *Syringa persica* 3. *Trachymene caerulea*
4. *Tricyrtis macropoda* 5. *Trillium grandiflorum* 6. *Trollius acaulis*

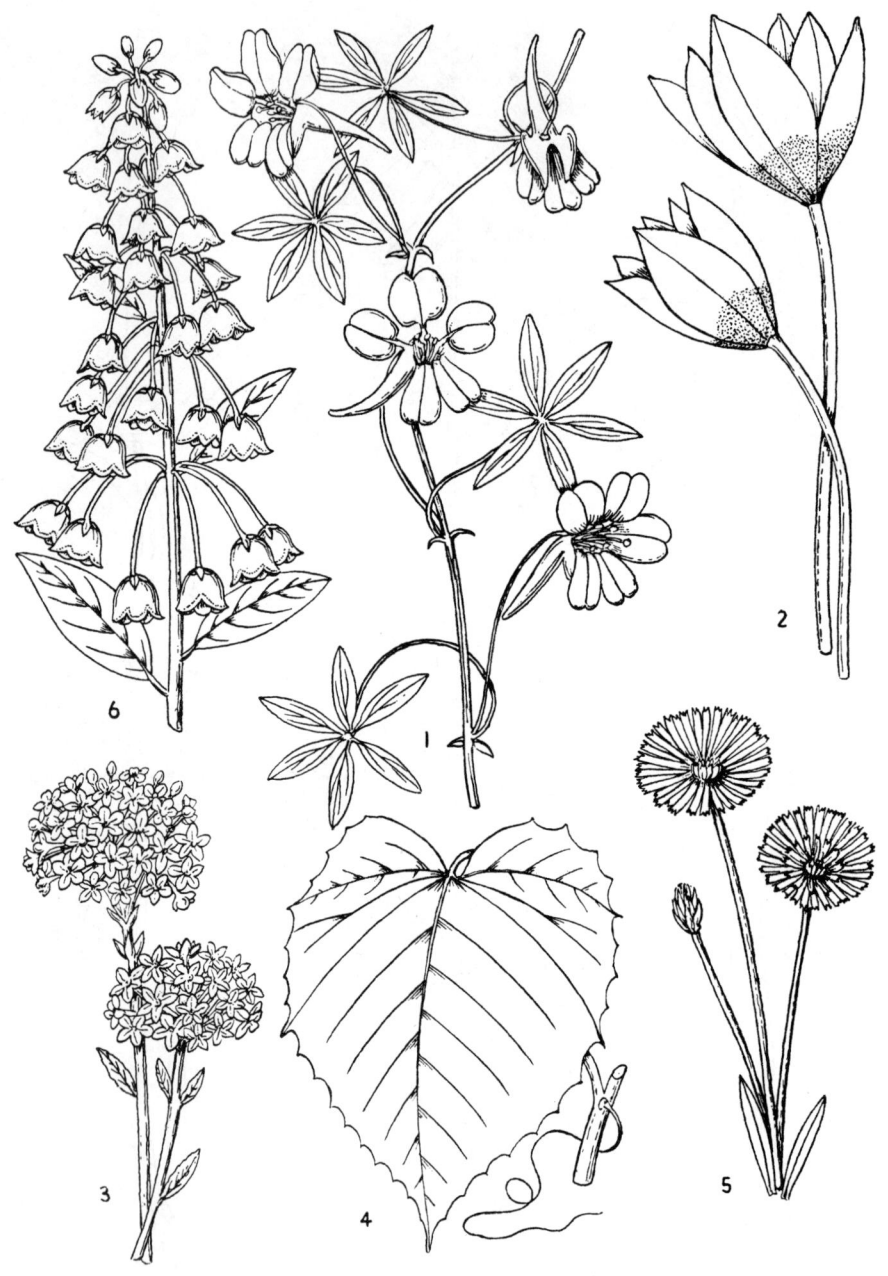

PLATE 40

1. *Tropaeolum speciosum*   2. *Tulipa saxatilis*   3. *Viburnun fragrans*
4. *Vitis coignetiae*   5. *Xeranthemum annuum*   6. *Zenobia pulverulenta*

toothed segments. The bright golden yellow flowers are produced singly; each measures from 1 to 1½ inch across and is formed of 5 to 10 ovate or egg-shaped, spreading sepals. The small petals are spoon-shaped. Both species need similar cultural treatment, preferring a good, moist friable loam in a sunny position. They are increased by division and seeds which are usually tardy in germinating.

TROPAEOLUM SPECIOSUM (*Tropaeolaceae*) [PLATE 40]
More advice has probably been given in gardening periodicals with regard to the cultivation of this glorious Chilean climber than perhaps any plant of a similar nature. When seen climbing amongst the branches of a holly or yew and in full flower it is indeed a very beautiful sight. Popularly known as the Flame Flower, a name which it thoroughly deserves, this herbaceous climber is said to flourish better in the counties north-west of the Midlands and Scotland than in the South. Nevertheless, I have seen some very fine specimens south of the Thames.

Nurserymen normally supply specimens of this Tropaeolum in pots in April or May. The plant should be given a shady position but not under the drip of trees and requires a deep, cool rooting medium, composed of fibrous lime-free loam, leaf-soil and coarse sand, or peat, leaf-soil, and coarse grit or small gravel. It should be planted firmly and never be allowed to suffer from drought. A mulch of half rotten leaves is beneficial in the summer. It possesses a rather fleshy rhizome which produces slender, branching stems from 12 to 15 feet long, clothed with numerous comparatively small fresh green leaves, composed of about 6 egg-shaped lobes, borne on a slender, twining stalk. The brilliant vermilion flowers are borne singly on slender stalks from July to October and are of the usual nasturtium shape with deeply jagged petals and measure about 1½ inch across. The bright blue fruits take rather a long time to germinate.

TULIPA SAXATILIS (*Liliaceae*) [PLATE 40]
Of all the tulips in cultivation, at least three are of outstanding merit either on account of the size and brilliancy of their flowers or on their tintings. They are *T. fosteriana*, *T. kaufmanniana* and *T. saxatilis*. The first and second of the above mentioned species are fairly well known and appreciated by those who grow them, but *T. saxatilis* is very rarely seen and is quite unique in the tinting of its blossoms and is very lovely. It has the reputation of producing many leaves and none or but few flowers. This is undoubtedly the case unless it is treated differently to the two above mentioned species.

T. saxatilis produces stolons, which send up leaves indefinitely. In order to induce this tulip to flower freely its roots must be confined to a very narrow border, by means of slates or tiles, sunk at a depth in the soil to restrict the plant completely to a very small area. This together with a position in full sun and a porous soil usually proves satisfactory. The bulbs should remain undisturbed for years. A hand-light placed over them when they are going to rest is very helpful. This species is a native of Crete and flowers from late February to April. It has a small, globose bulb and an erect stem about 10 inches high, furnished with 2 long, pale green leaves and bears a solitary bloom up to $4\frac{1}{2}$ inches across, of a pale rose colour or bright mauve in the upper two-thirds of its length, the basal third is bright golden yellow. The blue-black anthers are borne on yellow filaments. Increase is by offsets.

VIBURNUM FRAGRANS (*Caprifoliaceae*) [PLATE 40]

There are many experienced gardeners who prefer *V. carlesii* to the species under consideration, on account of its habit of producing its flowers in April, thus usually escaping damage by severe frost, which rather frequently happens to the winter-flowering *V. fragrans* when the shrub is planted in an unsuitable position. With a little forethought much can be done to prevent such damage occurring. The flowers of *V. fragrans* are perhaps a little smaller than those of *V. carlesii*, but they are more highly coloured and seem to me to be much more fragrant, also its habit of growth eminently fits it for small gardens.

It is a deciduous bush of loose, open but compact habit, eventually reaching a height of 8 or 10 feet, but will flower profusely when only a foot or two high. The rather stout branches are clothed with medium-sized, oval or lance-shaped, rich green leaves. The lovely flowers are borne in many-flowered clusters or heads 2 to $2\frac{1}{2}$ inches in diameter on the tips of the naked branchlets, commencing to open at the fall of the leaf and continuing to do so until the spring. They are bright almond-blossom pink and measure about $\frac{3}{8}$ inch across. With age they become paler in tint. This viburnum is a native of south-western China and is not particular as to soil, but should be given a sheltered position where the sun in the winter does not reach it before noon. It is increased by cuttings rooted in heat and also by grafts on the common viburnum.

VIBURNUM GRANDIFLORUM

The genus Viburnum contains some of the most beautiful hardy shrubs in cultivation. Some are treasured for the beauty of their inflorescences, others for the exquisite fragrance of their flowers. *Viburnum grandiflorum* combines both of these desirable qualities and is certainly the most decorative of the winter-flowering species.

When fully developed it forms a large deciduous bush up to 10 feet high, of rather loose but of more or less erect habit. The branchlets are clothed with large, handsome, elliptic-oblong, dark green leaves with a bronzy sheen. They are densely hairy on their under surface and are borne on red stalks. The lovely blossoms measure up to ¾ inch in diameter and are of a rich rose-pink in the bud and white, tinged with rose-pink when fully open; they are not damaged by frost. They resemble those of the laurustinus in shape but are very much larger. They are borne from Mid-December to the end of February, on short, spur-like growths on the bare twigs in dense heads.

This species is a native of the Himalaya and has been in cultivation for nearly sixty years. A good, well-drained loam and a half-shady position meets its needs. The strong leading shoots should be shortened in order to obtain a more compact bush. It is usually grafted on a *Viburnum opulus* stock.

VIBURNUM TOMENTOSUM var. PLICATUM

This Viburnum is known as the Japanese Guelder Rose and is considered to be one of the finest deciduous shrubs in cultivation in this country. Like so many of our horticultural treasures it was introduced in the form of seeds by Robert Fortune, that indefatigable collector of Chinese and Japanese plants during the middle of the last century. A well-grown bush in full flower is one of the most beautiful sights imaginable. The innumerable heads of snowy blossoms almost completely hide the foliage. It is an ideal plant for the amateur's garden where space is limited for it can be trained on a wall or close fence, preferably a west one, and in this position will flower abundantly.

It is a graceful shrub of neat habit, usually from 4 to 6 feet tall. The slender, spreading branches are well clothed with rather large, dark green, oblong or oval, rather plaited leaves, which are downy beneath. The blossoms are produced in rounded heads or trusses, 3 to 4 inches in diameter, during the month of May; these are composed of very numerous sterile flowers, each a ½ to ¾ inch across. They are produced on short branchlets which arise along the whole length of the branches in the autumn. It thrives in any good friable loam and needs plenty of water in dry weather, and is usually increased by grafting, the stock being the Snow-ball tree.

VITIS COIGNETIAE (*Vitaceae*) [PLATE 40]
The glory of this ornamental vine lies in the vivid tints its huge leaves assume in the autumn, which they retain for many weeks before they fall in early winter. For hiding unsightly objects and also for clothing a damp wall, it is one of the best of the climbing plants for this purpose, with ornamental foliage. Like so many other valuable plants that decorate our gardens it is a native of Japan and is, fortunately, quite hardy.

The stout, long-branched stems may reach a length of 20 feet or more and are clothed with thick, heart-shaped, dark, rich green leaves, frequently more than 9 inches in length and nearly the same measurement in width. They change from dark green to brilliant tints of orange, crimson and claret colour in September and October and a well-placed specimen is then a very beautiful sight. The inflorescence much resembles that of a grape vine and the small, greenish-yellow flowers have no decorative value. This grand climber is not particular as to soil, but a good, deep, loam seems to suit it best. It should be pruned in the same manner as a grape vine and is usually increased by layers and cuttings. For those who desire to include in their gardens a more dwarf member of the grape vine family, *Ampelopsis heterophylla var. humulifolia* (formerly one of the *Vitis* genus), is available. It is quite hardy and has elegant foliage and delightful china-blue, spotted berries and is known as the Turquoise Berry. There is an attractive variegated form.

XERANTHEMUM ANNUUM (*Compositae*) [PLATE 40]
In the last century nearly every suburban garden had a small portion of its area devoted to the cultivation of Everlasting Flowers to be cut and dried for house decoration in the winter. They were mostly forms of *Helichrysum monstrosum*, which even in those days could be had in many brilliant shades of yellow and red. Most of the Everlastings belong to the Compositae family and are usually natives of hot dry countries such as Australia and South Africa, both of which supply us with numerous beautiful species. Several genera containing species with flowers of this nature and formerly considered distinct are now included in the genera Xeranthemum and Helichrysum.

Xeranthemum annuum is a hardy, erect, branched annual from 1 to $2\frac{1}{2}$ feet high. The fairly long linear-lance-shaped or narrowly oblong, grey-green leaves are rather flaccid and have revolute margins. The numerous flower-heads terminate each branch and branchlet, each measuring about $1\frac{3}{4}$ inch across, and are composed of about 25, narrowly lance-shaped outer florets, normally of a beautiful rose-magenta. The tubular inner or disc florets are of a much deeper colour which adds to the beauty of the flower. The florets are borne in a hemispheric involucre composed of numerous scale-like bracts. There are several colour forms ranging from white to purple. It is not particular as to soil but does best in a rich sandy one. The seeds may be sown in autumn or spring, where the plants are to bloom.

ZENOBIA PULVERULENTA (*Ericaceae*) [PLATE 40]
This extremely beautiful shrub should be given a place in every amateur's garden and in my opinion is the best of all the hardy, white-flowered members of the heath family. It was formerly made a variety of *Z. speciosa* but has now been raised to specific rank and *speciosa* has been made a variety of it under the name of *nuda*.

Zenobia pulverulenta is evergreen, semi-evergreen or deciduous, according to the climatic conditions of the locality in which it is growing. It is a graceful shrub of loose habit from 3 to 6 feet tall, with slender, arching branches, clothed with medium-size, leathery, oblong-oval leaves toothed or shallowly lobed on their margins and borne on short stalks. Both surfaces are covered with a beautiful grey-green 'bloom'. The lovely waxy, white blossoms resemble those of the lily-of-the-valley but measure over $\frac{1}{2}$ inch across. They are borne in clusters of 3 to 5 in the leaf-axils, each on a long, curving stalk and forming a leafy raceme over a foot long. The flowers are produced in July and are usually followed by glaucous, berry-like fruits.

It is a native of U.S.A. from North Carolina to Florida and is perfectly hardy. It needs a lime-free soil and will thrive in light loam but likes a peaty soil and should be cut well back after flowering to promote new growths which will bear next year's flowers. Increase is by seeds, layers and cuttings.

Glossary

Alternate, when only one leaf springs from a node or joint and the other is placed above or below it on the opposite side of the stem; this applies to the branches.
Annual, a plant which lives but one season.
Anther, the lobes of the stamen, which contain the pollen.

Appressed or *adpressed*, when hairs are pressed closely to a leaf or fruit to a branch.
Ascending, when stems spread horizontally and then turn upwards and become erect.
Axil, the angle between the leaf and the stem or between two branches.
Bidentate, two-toothed.
Biennial, a plant which lives for two seasons only.
Bipinnate, twice divided to the base.
Biternate, twice divided into threes.
Blade, the broad or upper portion of a leaf.
Bloom, the wax-like substance which coats a ripe plum or grape.
Bract, an undeveloped leaf.
Branchlet, a minor branch, twig or shoot.
Bulb, buds consisting of fleshy scales.
Bulbil, a small bulb found in the leaf-axils or in the inflorescence.
Bush, a much-branched shrub.
Calyx, the outer whorl of the segments of a flower.
Capsule, a more or less dry, hollow seed-vessel.
Cluster, a close head of flowers as in the lilac.
Collar, the part of a plant from which the stem springs.
Compound umbel, an umbel in which the flower stalks are branched.
Corm, a fleshy, solid, bulb-like, underground stem as in the crocus.
Corolla, the petals of a flower.
Corymb, when the flower stems of an inflorescence although starting from different points all attain the same level at the top.
Creeping, when prostrate stems extend and emit roots at the joints.
Crown, the apex of the root-stock.
Deciduous, applied to plants which loose their leaves annually.
Decumbent, lying horizontally, but with a tendency to become erect at their tips.
Diffuse, scattered, widely spread.
Dioecious, when the male and female organs are on different plants.
Drupe, a stone fruit.
Entire, when the margins of a leaf are undivided.
Filament, the thread-like portion of the stamen bearing the anther.
Floret, usually applied to an individual flower in the flower-head of the compositae.
Flower-head, florets collected several together in a head surrounded by scaly bracts.
Fruit, the structure enclosing one or more seeds.

Fugacious, soon dying, short-lasting, fleeting.
Glaucous, bluish-green.
Glands, wart-like bodies, secreting oil and resin.
Glandular hairs, gland-tipped hairs.
Herbaceous perennial, a plant in which the greater portion of its growth above ground dies down to a persistent root.
Inarching, grafting one shrub or tree on another without separating the graft or scion from its parent.
Inflorescence, the flowering branches and the flowers they bear.
Internodal cutting, a cutting severed between two joints of a stem, retaining a portion of the stem below the joint.
Internode, the portion of the stem between two joints.
Layer, a shoot or branch pegged down to ground level, with a notch in a joint in order to induce it to produce roots at that point.
Leaflet, small leaves making up a compound leaf.
Linear, narrow, grass-like.
Keel, the projecting lower petals of a pea-shaped flower.
Mealy, when a portion of a plant is coated with a meal-like dust.
Naked, when a stem is not clothed with bracts or leaves.
Node, the joint in the stem of a plant.
Obovate, egg-shaped, with the broad end upwards.
Opposite, when leaves are placed opposite to another in the same plane.
Orbicular, almost circular in outline, when applied to leaves.
Oval, rounded at both ends but widest in the middle.
Ovate, egg-shaped with the broad end downwards.
Ovoid, egg-shaped.
Palmate, when several lobes of a leaf diverge from the same point, like the fingers of a hand.
Panicle, an inflorescence with its branches irregularly arranged.
Perennial, a plant which lives for several years.
Perfoliate, when a stem apparently runs through a leaf, owing to the joining of the basal lobes.
Perianth, a flower in which there is no apparent calyx.
Pinnate, when the lobes of a leaf are arranged in a regular manner on each side of the midrib.
Procumbent, prostrate on the ground as in the trailing plants.
Raceme, when flowers have stalks and are arranged along an unbranched flower stem.
Rhizome, an underground stem, fleshy or woody, producing roots.

Root-stock, the portion of a plant from which the stem arises and the roots descend.

Rotate, like the spokes of a wheel.

Sand-frame, a cold frame in which the lower portion of the compost consists of leaf-mould and peat to the depth of about 1 foot and the upper portion of 4 to 6 inches of sand.

Scattered, when leaves are arranged irregularly around a stem.

Secund, parts of a plant directed to one side only.

Sepals, the lobes of the calyx.

Serrate, like the teeth of a saw.

Sessile, when the blade of a leaf has no stalk where it joins a stem.

Sheathing, when the blade of a leaf or bract forms a sheath around the stem, this also applies to a leaf stalk.

Shrub, a woody plant that branches at or near its base.

Simple, unbranched.

Spadix, the poker-like structure bearing the male and female organs of the members of the arum family.

Spathe, a bract subtending or enclosing the inflorescence of a member of the arum family.

Spike, when flowers have no stalks and are arranged along an unbranched flower stem.

Stamens, the structure bearing the male organs of a flower.

Stolon, an underground stem proceeding horizontally from the root-stock or collar of a plant, frequently with a bud at its apex.

Style or *pistil*, the structure which bears the female organs of a flower.

Subtended, when a bract or leaf is placed immediately at the base of a flower or fruit.

Suckers, young plants on the ends of creeping, underground root-stocks.

Tap-root, when the chief root descends perpendicularly into the ground.

Ternate, when a leaf is divided into three lobes.

Thrice pinnate, or *tripinnate*, when each primary division of a pinnate leaf is deeply divided into three lobes.

Tree, a woody plant with a single stem, trunk or bole.

Trifoliate, composed of three leaflets.

Tuber, a soft, fleshy or somewhat woody structure, frequently forming a root-stock.

Twice pinnate or bipinnate, when each primary division of a pinnate leaf is divided into two lobes.

Umbel, when several flower stalks start from the same point on the flower stem and are all of about the same length.

Undershrub, a dwarf shrub, permanently woody at its base, but the flowering branches die annually.

Whorl or *whorled*, when several branches, stems or leaves spring from the same joint or node and are arranged in a regular manner around the stem.

Index
to popular and catalogue names

Alpine Toad-flax, 98
American Cowslip, 59

Balloon Flower, 122
Barrenwort, 64
Beauty Bush, 91
Belladonna Lily, 14
Bell-flower, Chinese, 122
Bellflowers, 31, 32
Bindweed, 43
Bladder Nut Tree, 142
Blazing Star, 95
Bleeding Heart, 57
Blood Root, 134
Blue Lace Flower, 147
Blue Marguerite, 70
Bluets, 82
Buffalo Currant, 130
Buffalo Rose, 29
Burning Bush, 57
Bush Clover, 93
Button Snake-root, 95

Californian Tree Poppy, 55
Cape Bladder Senna, 146
Cape Figwort, 119, 120
Catchfly, 140
Chilean Barberry, 25
Chinese Bell-flower, 122
Chinese Honeysuckle, 100
Chinese Poppywort, 63
Cloth of Silver Crocus, 48
Coral Plant, 24
Cornelian Cherry, 44
Crimson Flag, 138
Cupidone, 35

Currant, Buffalo, 130
Currant, Golden, 130
Cyclamen Poppy, 63

Deer Grass, 128
Devil's Poppy, 19
Dog's-tooth Violet, 66
Dorset Heath, 65
Dove Tree, 52
Dragon's Head, 60

Evening Primrose, 108, 109
Everlasting Flowers, 152

Fair Maidens, 141
False Dittany, 57
False Dragon's Head, 121
Flame Flower, 149
Fraxinella, 57
French Honeysuckle, 80
Fringe Tree, 38

Globe Flower, 148
Golden Club, 112
Golden Currant, 130
Golden Drop, 111
Guelder Rose, Japanese, 151

Harebell Poppy, 104
Honeysuckle, Chinese, 100
Honeysuckle, French, 80
Hounds-tongue, 49

Immortelle, 16
Indian Cup, 136
Italian Jasmine, 89

Japanese Guelder Rose, 151
Jerusalem Cross, 100
Jew's Cherry, 44
Judas Tree, 37

Kaffir Lily, 138
Kingfisher Daisy, 69

Lungwort, 124, 125
Lyre-flower, 57

Meadow Beauty, 128
Meadow Saffron, 42
Mexican Orange-flower, 39
Mexican Wood-sorrel, 113
Milkwort, 122
Moccasin Flower, 50
Mock Orchid, 132
Monkey Flower, 105
Monk's Hood, 9
Mount Etna Broom, 74

Navelwort, 109

Obedient Plant, 121

Pearl Bush, 68
Pimpernel, 16
Pitcher Plant, 136
Pocket Handerchief Tree, 52
Pomegranate, 126
Poppywort, 134
Prickly Poppy, 19
Prickly Thrift, 9
Prophet's Flower, 21

Quamash, 29

Rock Cress, 18
Rock Soapwort, 135

Rose Acacia, 131

St Bernard's Lily, 17, 116
St Bruno's Lily, 116
St Johnsworts, 84
Sage, 133
Shamrock Pea, 116
Side Saddle Flower, 136
Silver-bell Tree, 78
Skunk Cabbage, 101
Slipper Orchid, 50
Snowdrop Tree, 78
Snow Flower Tree, 38
Soapwort, 135
Soapwort, Rock, 135
Southernwood, 22
Spanish Hyacinth, 83
Spindle Tree, Broad-leaved, 68
Spring Adonis, 11
Spring Bell-flower, 140
Spring Satin Flower, 140
Spring Snowflake, 94
Spring Star-flower, 87
Stonecrop, 138, 139
Swallow-wort, 23

Thrift, 21
Thrift, Prickly, 9
Tidy Tips, 93
Toad Lily, 147
Trumpet Leaf, 136
Turquoise Berry, 152

Violet Cress, 86
Violet-eyed Grass, 140

Wake Robin, 148
Wand Flower, 58
Winter Sweet, 38
Witch Hazel, 79

**A CATALOGUE OF SELECTED DOVER BOOKS
IN ALL FIELDS OF INTEREST**

A CATALOGUE OF SELECTED DOVER BOOKS
IN ALL FIELDS OF INTEREST

AMERICA'S OLD MASTERS, James T. Flexner. Four men emerged unexpectedly from provincial 18th century America to leadership in European art: Benjamin West, J. S. Copley, C. R. Peale, Gilbert Stuart. Brilliant coverage of lives and contributions. Revised, 1967 edition. 69 plates. 365pp. of text.
21806-6 Paperbound $3.00

FIRST FLOWERS OF OUR WILDERNESS: AMERICAN PAINTING, THE COLONIAL PERIOD, James T. Flexner. Painters, and regional painting traditions from earliest Colonial times up to the emergence of Copley, West and Peale Sr., Foster, Gustavus Hesselius, Feke, John Smibert and many anonymous painters in the primitive manner. Engaging presentation, with 162 illustrations. xxii + 368pp.
22180-6 Paperbound $3.50

THE LIGHT OF DISTANT SKIES: AMERICAN PAINTING, 1760-1835, James T. Flexner. The great generation of early American painters goes to Europe to learn and to teach: West, Copley, Gilbert Stuart and others. Allston, Trumbull, Morse; also contemporary American painters—primitives, derivatives, academics—who remained in America. 102 illustrations. xiii + 306pp.
22179-2 Paperbound $3.50

A HISTORY OF THE RISE AND PROGRESS OF THE ARTS OF DESIGN IN THE UNITED STATES, William Dunlap. Much the richest mine of information on early American painters, sculptors, architects, engravers, miniaturists, etc. The only source of information for scores of artists, the major primary source for many others. Unabridged reprint of rare original 1834 edition, with new introduction by James T. Flexner, and 394 new illustrations. Edited by Rita Weiss. 6⅝ x 9⅝.
21695-0, 21696-9, 21697-7 Three volumes, Paperbound $15.00

EPOCHS OF CHINESE AND JAPANESE ART, Ernest F. Fenollosa. From primitive Chinese art to the 20th century, thorough history, explanation of every important art period and form, including Japanese woodcuts; main stress on China and Japan, but Tibet, Korea also included. Still unexcelled for its detailed, rich coverage of cultural background, aesthetic elements, diffusion studies, particularly of the historical period. 2nd, 1913 edition. 242 illustrations. lii + 439pp. of text.
20364-6, 20365-4 Two volumes, Paperbound $6.00

THE GENTLE ART OF MAKING ENEMIES, James A. M. Whistler. Greatest wit of his day deflates Oscar Wilde, Ruskin, Swinburne; strikes back at inane critics, exhibitions, art journalism; aesthetics of impressionist revolution in most striking form. Highly readable classic by great painter. Reproduction of edition designed by Whistler. Introduction by Alfred Werner. xxxvi + 334pp.
21875-9 Paperbound $3.00

CATALOGUE OF DOVER BOOKS

JOHANN SEBASTIAN BACH, Philipp Spitta. One of the great classics of musicology, this definitive analysis of Bach's music (and life) has never been surpassed. Lucid, nontechnical analyses of hundreds of pieces (30 pages devoted to St. Matthew Passion, 26 to B Minor Mass). Also includes major analysis of 18th-century music. 450 musical examples. 40-page musical supplement. Total of xx + 1799pp.
(EUK) 22278-0, 22279-9 Two volumes, Clothbound $25.00

MOZART AND HIS PIANO CONCERTOS, Cuthbert Girdlestone. The only full-length study of an important area of Mozart's creativity. Provides detailed analyses of all 23 concertos, traces inspirational sources. 417 musical examples. Second edition. 509pp. 21271-8 Paperbound $4.50

THE PERFECT WAGNERITE: A COMMENTARY ON THE NIBLUNG'S RING, George Bernard Shaw. Brilliant and still relevant criticism in remarkable essays on Wagner's Ring cycle, Shaw's ideas on political and social ideology behind the plots, role of Leitmotifs, vocal requisites, etc. Prefaces. xxi + 136pp.
(USO) 21707-8 Paperbound $1.75

DON GIOVANNI, W. A. Mozart. Complete libretto, modern English translation; biographies of composer and librettist; accounts of early performances and critical reaction. Lavishly illustrated. All the material you need to understand and appreciate this great work. Dover Opera Guide and Libretto Series; translated and introduced by Ellen Bleiler. 92 illustrations. 209pp.
21134-7 Paperbound $2.00

BASIC ELECTRICITY, U. S. Bureau of Naval Personel. Originally a training course, best non-technical coverage of basic theory of electricity and its applications. Fundamental concepts, batteries, circuits, conductors and wiring techniques, AC and DC, inductance and capacitance, generators, motors, transformers, magnetic amplifiers, synchros, servomechanisms, etc. Also covers blue-prints, electrical diagrams, etc. Many questions, with answers. 349 illustrations. x + 448pp. 6½ x 9¼.
20973-3 Paperbound $3.50

REPRODUCTION OF SOUND, Edgar Villchur. Thorough coverage for laymen of high fidelity systems, reproducing systems in general, needles, amplifiers, preamps, loudspeakers, feedback, explaining physical background. "A rare talent for making technicalities vividly comprehensible," R. Darrell, *High Fidelity*. 69 figures iv + 92pp. 21515-6 Paperbound $1.35

HEAR ME TALKIN' TO YA: THE STORY OF JAZZ AS TOLD BY THE MEN WHO MADE IT, Nat Shapiro and Nat Hentoff. Louis Armstrong, Fats Waller, Jo Jones, Clarence Williams, Billy Holiday, Duke Ellington, Jelly Roll Morton and dozens of other jazz greats tell how it was in Chicago's South Side, New Orleans, depression Harlem and the modern West Coast as jazz was born and grew. xvi + 429pp.
21726-4 Paperbound $3.95

FABLES OF AESOP, translated by Sir Roger L'Estrange. A reproduction of the very rare 1931 Paris edition; a selection of the most interesting fables, together with 50 imaginative drawings by Alexander Calder. v + 128pp. 6½x9¼.
21780-9 Paperbound $1.50

CATALOGUE OF DOVER BOOKS

AGAINST THE GRAIN (A REBOURS), Joris K. Huysmans. Filled with weird images, evidences of a bizarre imagination, exotic experiments with hallucinatory drugs, rich tastes and smells and the diversions of its sybarite hero Duc Jean des Esseintes, this classic novel pushed 19th-century literary decadence to its limits. Full unabridged edition. Do not confuse this with abridged editions generally sold. Introduction by Havelock Ellis. xlix + 206pp. 22190-3 Paperbound $2.50

VARIORUM SHAKESPEARE: HAMLET. Edited by Horace H. Furness; a landmark of American scholarship. Exhaustive footnotes and appendices treat all doubtful words and phrases, as well as suggested critical emendations throughout the play's history. First volume contains editor's own text, collated with all Quartos and Folios. Second volume contains full first Quarto, translations of Shakespeare's sources (Belleforest, and Saxo Grammaticus), Der Bestrafte Brudermord, and many essays on critical and historical points of interest by major authorities of past and present. Includes details of staging and costuming over the years. By far the best edition available for serious students of Shakespeare. Total of xx + 905pp.
21004-9, 21005-7, 2 volumes, Paperbound $7.00

A LIFE OF WILLIAM SHAKESPEARE, Sir Sidney Lee. This is the standard life of Shakespeare, summarizing everything known about Shakespeare and his plays. Incredibly rich in material, broad in coverage, clear and judicious, it has served thousands as the best introduction to Shakespeare. 1931 edition. 9 plates. xxix + 792pp. 21967-4 Paperbound $4.50

MASTERS OF THE DRAMA, John Gassner. Most comprehensive history of the drama in print, covering every tradition from Greeks to modern Europe and America, including India, Far East, etc. Covers more than 800 dramatists, 2000 plays, with biographical material, plot summaries, theatre history, criticism, etc. "Best of its kind in English," *New Republic.* 77 illustrations. xxii + 890pp.
20100-7 Clothbound $10.00

THE EVOLUTION OF THE ENGLISH LANGUAGE, George McKnight. The growth of English, from the 14th century to the present. Unusual, non-technical account presents basic information in very interesting form: sound shifts, change in grammar and syntax, vocabulary growth, similar topics. Abundantly illustrated with quotations. Formerly *Modern English in the Making.* xii + 590pp.
21932-1 Paperbound $3.50

AN ETYMOLOGICAL DICTIONARY OF MODERN ENGLISH, Ernest Weekley. Fullest, richest work of its sort, by foremost British lexicographer. Detailed word histories, including many colloquial and archaic words; extensive quotations. Do not confuse this with the Concise Etymological Dictionary, which is much abridged. Total of xxvii + 830pp. 6½ x 9¼.
21873-2, 21874-0 Two volumes, Paperbound $7.90

FLATLAND: A ROMANCE OF MANY DIMENSIONS, E. A. Abbott. Classic of science-fiction explores ramifications of life in a two-dimensional world, and what happens when a three-dimensional being intrudes. Amusing reading, but also useful as introduction to thought about hyperspace. Introduction by Banesh Hoffmann. 16 illustrations. xx + 103pp. 20001-9 Paperbound $1.00

CATALOGUE OF DOVER BOOKS

POEMS OF ANNE BRADSTREET, edited with an introduction by Robert Hutchinson. A new selection of poems by America's first poet and perhaps the first significant woman poet in the English language. 48 poems display her development in works of considerable variety—love poems, domestic poems, religious meditations, formal elegies, "quaternions," etc. Notes, bibliography. viii + 222pp.
22160-1 Paperbound $2.50

THREE GOTHIC NOVELS: THE CASTLE OF OTRANTO BY HORACE WALPOLE; VATHEK BY WILLIAM BECKFORD; THE VAMPYRE BY JOHN POLIDORI, WITH FRAGMENT OF A NOVEL BY LORD BYRON, edited by E. F. Bleiler. The first Gothic novel, by Walpole; the finest Oriental tale in English, by Beckford; powerful Romantic supernatural story in versions by Polidori and Byron. All extremely important in history of literature; all still exciting, packed with supernatural thrills, ghosts, haunted castles, magic, etc. xl + 291pp.
21232-7 Paperbound $3.00

THE BEST TALES OF HOFFMANN, E. T. A. Hoffmann. 10 of Hoffmann's most important stories, in modern re-editings of standard translations: Nutcracker and the King of Mice, Signor Formica, Automata, The Sandman, Rath Krespel, The Golden Flowerpot, Master Martin the Cooper, The Mines of Falun, The King's Betrothed, A New Year's Eve Adventure. 7 illustrations by Hoffmann. Edited by E. F. Bleiler. xxxix + 419pp. 21793-0 Paperbound $3.00

GHOST AND HORROR STORIES OF AMBROSE BIERCE, Ambrose Bierce. 23 strikingly modern stories of the horrors latent in the human mind: The Eyes of the Panther, The Damned Thing, An Occurrence at Owl Creek Bridge, An Inhabitant of Carcosa, etc., plus the dream-essay, Visions of the Night. Edited by E. F. Bleiler. xxii + 199pp. 20767-6 Paperbound $2.00

BEST GHOST STORIES OF J. S. LEFANU, J. Sheridan LeFanu. Finest stories by Victorian master often considered greatest supernatural writer of all. Carmilla, Green Tea, The Haunted Baronet, The Familiar, and 12 others. Most never before available in the U. S. A. Edited by E. F. Bleiler. 8 illustrations from Victorian publications. xvii + 467pp. 20415-4 Paperbound $3.00

MATHEMATICAL FOUNDATIONS OF INFORMATION THEORY, A. I. Khinchin. Comprehensive introduction to work of Shannon, McMillan, Feinstein and Khinchin, placing these investigations on a rigorous mathematical basis. Covers entropy concept in probability theory, uniqueness theorem, Shannon's inequality, ergodic sources, the E property, martingale concept, noise, Feinstein's fundamental lemma, Shanon's first and second theorems. Translated by R. A. Silverman and M. D. Friedman. iii + 120pp. 60434-9 Paperbound $2.00

SEVEN SCIENCE FICTION NOVELS, H. G. Wells. The standard collection of the great novels. Complete, unabridged. *First Men in the Moon, Island of Dr. Moreau, War of the Worlds, Food of the Gods, Invisible Man, Time Machine, In the Days of the Comet.* Not only science fiction fans, but every educated person owes it to himself to read these novels. 1015pp. (USO) 20264-X Clothbound $6.00

CATALOGUE OF DOVER BOOKS

LAST AND FIRST MEN AND STAR MAKER, TWO SCIENCE FICTION NOVELS, Olaf Stapledon. Greatest future histories in science fiction. In the first, human intelligence is the "hero," through strange paths of evolution, interplanetary invasions, incredible technologies, near extinctions and reemergences. Star Maker describes the quest of a band of star rovers for intelligence itself, through time and space: weird inhuman civilizations, crustacean minds, symbiotic worlds, etc. Complete, unabridged. v + 438pp. (USO) 21962-3 Paperbound $3.00

THREE PROPHETIC NOVELS, H. G. WELLS. Stages of a consistently planned future for mankind. *When the Sleeper Wakes*, and *A Story of the Days to Come*, anticipate *Brave New World* and *1984*, in the 21st Century; *The Time Machine*, only complete version in print, shows farther future and the end of mankind. All show Wells's greatest gifts as storyteller and novelist. Edited by E. F. Bleiler. x + 335pp. (USO) 20605-X Paperbound $3.00

THE DEVIL'S DICTIONARY, Ambrose Bierce. America's own Oscar Wilde—Ambrose Bierce—offers his barbed iconoclastic wisdom in over 1,000 definitions hailed by H. L. Mencken as "some of the most gorgeous witticisms in the English language." 145pp. 20487-1 Paperbound $1.50

MAX AND MORITZ, Wilhelm Busch. Great children's classic, father of comic strip, of two bad boys, Max and Moritz. Also Ker and Plunk (Plisch und Plumm), Cat and Mouse, Deceitful Henry, Ice-Peter, The Boy and the Pipe, and five other pieces. Original German, with English translation. Edited by H. Arthur Klein; translations by various hands and H. Arthur Klein. vi + 216pp.
20181-3 Paperbound $2.00

PIGS IS PIGS AND OTHER FAVORITES, Ellis Parker Butler. The title story is one of the best humor short stories, as Mike Flannery obfuscates biology and English. Also included, That Pup of Murchison's, The Great American Pie Company, and Perkins of Portland. 14 illustrations. v + 109pp. 21532-6 Paperbound $1.50

THE PETERKIN PAPERS, Lucretia P. Hale. It takes genius to be as stupidly mad as the Peterkins, as they decide to become wise, celebrate the "Fourth," keep a cow, and otherwise strain the resources of the Lady from Philadelphia. Basic book of American humor. 153 illustrations. 219pp. 20794-3 Paperbound $2.00

PERRAULT'S FAIRY TALES, translated by A. E. Johnson and S. R. Littlewood, with 34 full-page illustrations by Gustave Doré. All the original Perrault stories—Cinderella, Sleeping Beauty, Bluebeard, Little Red Riding Hood, Puss in Boots, Tom Thumb, etc.—with their witty verse morals and the magnificent illustrations of Doré. One of the five or six great books of European fairy tales. viii + 117pp. 8⅛ x 11. 22311-6 Paperbound $2.00

OLD HUNGARIAN FAIRY TALES, Baroness Orczy. Favorites translated and adapted by author of the *Scarlet Pimpernel*. Eight fairy tales include "The Suitors of Princess Fire-Fly," "The Twin Hunchbacks," "Mr. Cuttlefish's Love Story," and "The Enchanted Cat." This little volume of magic and adventure will captivate children as it has for generations. 90 drawings by Montagu Barstow. 96pp.
(USO) 22293-4 Paperbound $1.95

CATALOGUE OF DOVER BOOKS

THE RED FAIRY BOOK, Andrew Lang. Lang's color fairy books have long been children's favorites. This volume includes Rapunzel, Jack and the Bean-stalk and 35 other stories, familiar and unfamiliar. 4 plates, 93 illustrations x + 367pp.
21673-X Paperbound $2.50

THE BLUE FAIRY BOOK, Andrew Lang. Lang's tales come from all countries and all times. Here are 37 tales from Grimm, the Arabian Nights, Greek Mythology, and other fascinating sources. 8 plates, 130 illustrations. xi + 390pp.
21437-0 Paperbound $2.75

HOUSEHOLD STORIES BY THE BROTHERS GRIMM. Classic English-language edition of the well-known tales — Rumpelstiltskin, Snow White, Hansel and Gretel, The Twelve Brothers, Faithful John, Rapunzel, Tom Thumb (52 stories in all). Translated into simple, straightforward English by Lucy Crane. Ornamented with headpieces, vignettes, elaborate decorative initials and a dozen full-page illustrations by Walter Crane. x + 269pp.
21080-4 Paperbound **$2.00**

THE MERRY ADVENTURES OF ROBIN HOOD, Howard Pyle. The finest modern versions of the traditional ballads and tales about the great English outlaw. Howard Pyle's complete prose version, with every word, every illustration of the first edition. Do not confuse this facsimile of the original (1883) with modern editions that change text or illustrations. 23 plates plus many page decorations. xxii + 296pp.
22043-5 Paperbound $2.75

THE STORY OF KING ARTHUR AND HIS KNIGHTS, Howard Pyle. The finest children's version of the life of King Arthur; brilliantly retold by Pyle, with 48 of his most imaginative illustrations. xviii + 313pp. 6⅛ x 9¼.
21445-1 Paperbound $2.50

THE WONDERFUL WIZARD OF OZ, L. Frank Baum. America's finest children's book in facsimile of first edition with all Denslow illustrations in full color. The edition a child should have. Introduction by Martin Gardner. 23 color plates, scores of drawings. iv + 267pp.
20691-2 Paperbound $3.50

THE MARVELOUS LAND OF OZ, L. Frank Baum. The second Oz book, every bit as imaginative as the Wizard. The hero is a boy named Tip, but the Scarecrow and the Tin Woodman are back, as is the Oz magic. 16 color plates, 120 drawings by John R. Neill. 287pp.
20692-0 Paperbound $2.50

THE MAGICAL MONARCH OF MO, L. Frank Baum. Remarkable adventures in a land even stranger than Oz. The best of Baum's books not in the Oz series. 15 color plates and dozens of drawings by Frank Verbeck. xviii + 237pp.
21892-9 Paperbound $2.25

THE BAD CHILD'S BOOK OF BEASTS, MORE BEASTS FOR WORSE CHILDREN, A MORAL ALPHABET, Hilaire Belloc. Three complete humor classics in one volume. Be kind to the frog, and do not call him names . . . and 28 other whimsical animals. Familiar favorites and some not so well known. Illustrated by Basil Blackwell. 156pp.
(USO) 20749-8 Paperbound $1.50

CATALOGUE OF DOVER BOOKS

EAST O' THE SUN AND WEST O' THE MOON, George W. Dasent. Considered the best of all translations of these Norwegian folk tales, this collection has been enjoyed by generations of children (and folklorists too). Includes True and Untrue, Why the Sea is Salt, East O' the Sun and West O' the Moon, Why the Bear is Stumpy-Tailed, Boots and the Troll, The Cock and the Hen, Rich Peter the Pedlar, and 52 more. The only edition with all 59 tales. 77 illustrations by Erik Werenskiold and Theodor Kittelsen. xv + 418pp. 22521-6 Paperbound $3.50

GOOPS AND HOW TO BE THEM, Gelett Burgess. Classic of tongue-in-cheek humor, masquerading as etiquette book. 87 verses, twice as many cartoons, show mischievous Goops as they demonstrate to children virtues of table manners, neatness, courtesy, etc. Favorite for generations. viii + 88pp. 6½ x 9¼.
22233-0 Paperbound $1.50

ALICE'S ADVENTURES UNDER GROUND, Lewis Carroll. The first version, quite different from the final *Alice in Wonderland,* printed out by Carroll himself with his own illustrations. Complete facsimile of the "million dollar" manuscript Carroll gave to Alice Liddell in 1864. Introduction by Martin Gardner. viii + 96pp. Title and dedication pages in color. 21482-6 Paperbound $1.25

THE BROWNIES, THEIR BOOK, Palmer Cox. Small as mice, cunning as foxes, exuberant and full of mischief, the Brownies go to the zoo, toy shop, seashore, circus, etc., in 24 verse adventures and 266 illustrations. Long a favorite, since their first appearance in St. Nicholas Magazine. xi + 144pp. 6⅝ x 9¼.
21265-3 Paperbound $1.75

SONGS OF CHILDHOOD, Walter De La Mare. Published (under the pseudonym Walter Ramal) when De La Mare was only 29, this charming collection has long been a favorite children's book. A facsimile of the first edition in paper, the 47 poems capture the simplicity of the nursery rhyme and the ballad, including such lyrics as I Met Eve, Tartary, The Silver Penny. vii + 106pp. (USO) 21972-0 Paperbound $1.25

THE COMPLETE NONSENSE OF EDWARD LEAR, Edward Lear. The finest 19th-century humorist-cartoonist in full: all nonsense limericks, zany alphabets, Owl and Pussycat, songs, nonsense botany, and more than 500 illustrations by Lear himself. Edited by Holbrook Jackson. xxix + 287pp. (USO) 20167-8 Paperbound $2.00

BILLY WHISKERS: THE AUTOBIOGRAPHY OF A GOAT, Frances Trego Montgomery. A favorite of children since the early 20th century, here are the escapades of that rambunctious, irresistible and mischievous goat—Billy Whiskers. Much in the spirit of *Peck's Bad Boy,* this is a book that children never tire of reading or hearing. All the original familiar illustrations by W. H. Fry are included: 6 color plates, 18 black and white drawings. 159pp. 22345-0 Paperbound $2.00

MOTHER GOOSE MELODIES. Faithful republication of the fabulously rare Munroe and Francis "copyright 1833" Boston edition—the most important Mother Goose collection, usually referred to as the "original." Familiar rhymes plus many rare ones, with wonderful old woodcut illustrations. Edited by E. F. Bleiler. 128pp. 4½ x 6⅜. 22577-1 Paperbound $1.00

CATALOGUE OF DOVER BOOKS

Two Little Savages; Being the Adventures of Two Boys Who Lived as Indians and What They Learned, Ernest Thompson Seton. Great classic of nature and boyhood provides a vast range of woodlore in most palatable form, a genuinely entertaining story. Two farm boys build a teepee in woods and live in it for a month, working out Indian solutions to living problems, star lore, birds and animals, plants, etc. 293 illustrations. vii + 286pp.
20985-7 Paperbound $2.50

Peter Piper's Practical Principles of Plain & Perfect Pronunciation. Alliterative jingles and tongue-twisters of surprising charm, that made their first appearance in America about 1830. Republished in full with the spirited woodcut illustrations from this earliest American edition. 32pp. 4½ x 6⅜.
22560-7 Paperbound $1.00

Science Experiments and Amusements for Children, Charles Vivian. 73 easy experiments, requiring only materials found at home or easily available, such as candles, coins, steel wool, etc.; illustrate basic phenomena like vacuum, simple chemical reaction, etc. All safe. Modern, well-planned. Formerly *Science Games for Children*. 102 photos, numerous drawings. 96pp. 6⅛ x 9¼.
21856-2 Paperbound $1.25

An Introduction to Chess Moves and Tactics Simply Explained, Leonard Barden. Informal intermediate introduction, quite strong in explaining reasons for moves. Covers basic material, tactics, important openings, traps, positional play in middle game, end game. Attempts to isolate patterns and recurrent configurations. Formerly *Chess*. 58 figures. 102pp. (USO) 21210-6 Paperbound $1.25

Lasker's Manual of Chess, Dr. Emanuel Lasker. Lasker was not only one of the five great World Champions, he was also one of the ablest expositors, theorists, and analysts. In many ways, his Manual, permeated with his philosophy of battle, filled with keen insights, is one of the greatest works ever written on chess. Filled with analyzed games by the great players. A single-volume library that will profit almost any chess player, beginner or master. 308 diagrams. xli x 349pp.
20640-8 Paperbound $2.75

The Master Book of Mathematical Recreations, Fred Schuh. In opinion of many the finest work ever prepared on mathematical puzzles, stunts, recreations; exhaustively thorough explanations of mathematics involved, analysis of effects, citation of puzzles and games. Mathematics involved is elementary. Translated by F. Göbel. 194 figures. xxiv + 430pp.
22134-2 Paperbound $4.00

Mathematics, Magic and Mystery, Martin Gardner. Puzzle editor for Scientific American explains mathematics behind various mystifying tricks: card tricks, stage "mind reading," coin and match tricks, counting out games, geometric dissections, etc. Probability sets, theory of numbers clearly explained. Also provides more than 400 tricks, guaranteed to work, that you can do. 135 illustrations. xii + 176pp.
20335-2 Paperbound $2.00

CATALOGUE OF DOVER BOOKS

"ESSENTIAL GRAMMAR" SERIES

All you really need to know about modern, colloquial grammar. Many educational shortcuts help you learn faster, understand better. Detailed cognate lists teach you to recognize similarities between English and foreign words and roots—make learning vocabulary easy and interesting. Excellent for independent study or as a supplement to record courses.

ESSENTIAL FRENCH GRAMMAR, Seymour Resnick. 2500-item cognate list. 159pp.
(EBE) 20419-7 Paperbound $1.50

ESSENTIAL GERMAN GRAMMAR, Guy Stern and Everett F. Bleiler. Unusual shortcuts on noun declension, word order, compound verbs. 124pp.
(EBE) 20422-7 Paperbound $1.25

ESSENTIAL ITALIAN GRAMMAR, Olga Ragusa. 111pp.
(EBE) 20779-X Paperbound $1.25

ESSENTIAL JAPANESE GRAMMAR, Everett F. Bleiler. In Romaji transcription; no characters needed. Japanese grammar is regular and simple. 156pp.
21027-8 Paperbound $1.50

ESSENTIAL PORTUGUESE GRAMMAR, Alexander da R. Prista. vi + 114pp.
21650-0 Paperbound $1.35

ESSENTIAL SPANISH GRAMMAR, Seymour Resnick. 2500 word cognate list. 115pp.
(EBE) 20780-3 Paperbound $1.25

ESSENTIAL ENGLISH GRAMMAR, Philip Gucker. Combines best features of modern, functional and traditional approaches. For refresher, class use, home study. x + 177pp.
21649-7 Paperbound $1.75

A PHRASE AND SENTENCE DICTIONARY OF SPOKEN SPANISH. Prepared for U. S. War Department by U. S. linguists. As above, unit is idiom, phrase or sentence rather than word. English-Spanish and Spanish-English sections contain modern equivalents of over 18,000 sentences. Introduction and appendix as above. iv + 513pp.
20495-2 Paperbound $3.50

A PHRASE AND SENTENCE DICTIONARY OF SPOKEN RUSSIAN. Dictionary prepared for U. S. War Department by U. S. linguists. Basic unit is not the word, but the idiom, phrase or sentence. English-Russian and Russian-English sections contain modern equivalents for over 30,000 phrases. Grammatical introduction covers phonetics, writing, syntax. Appendix of word lists for food, numbers, geographical names, etc. vi + 573 pp. 6⅛ x 9¼.
20496-0 Paperbound $5.50

CONVERSATIONAL CHINESE FOR BEGINNERS, Morris Swadesh. Phonetic system, beginner's course in Pai Hua Mandarin Chinese covering most important, most useful speech patterns. Emphasis on modern colloquial usage. Formerly *Chinese in Your Pocket*. xvi + 158pp.
21123-1 Paperbound $1.75

CATALOGUE OF DOVER BOOKS

How to Know the Wild Flowers, Mrs. William Starr Dana. This is the classical book of American wildflowers (of the Eastern and Central United States), used by hundreds of thousands. Covers over 500 species, arranged in extremely easy to use color and season groups. Full descriptions, much plant lore. This Dover edition is the fullest ever compiled, with tables of nomenclature changes. 174 full-page plates by M. Satterlee. xii + 418pp. 20332-8 Paperbound $3.00

Our Plant Friends and Foes, William Atherton DuPuy. History, economic importance, essential botanical information and peculiarities of 25 common forms of plant life are provided in this book in an entertaining and charming style. Covers food plants (potatoes, apples, beans, wheat, almonds, bananas, etc.), flowers (lily, tulip, etc.), trees (pine, oak, elm, etc.), weeds, poisonous mushrooms and vines, gourds, citrus fruits, cotton, the cactus family, and much more. 108 illustrations. xiv + 290pp. 22272-1 Paperbound $2.50

How to Know the Ferns, Frances T. Parsons. Classic survey of Eastern and Central ferns, arranged according to clear, simple identification key. Excellent introduction to greatly neglected nature area. 57 illustrations and 42 plates. xvi + 215pp. 20740-4 Paperbound $2.00

Manual of the Trees of North America, Charles S. Sargent. America's foremost dendrologist provides the definitive coverage of North American trees and tree-like shrubs. 717 species fully described and illustrated: exact distribution, down to township; full botanical description; economic importance; description of subspecies and races; habitat, growth data; similar material. Necessary to every serious student of tree-life. Nomenclature revised to present. Over 100 locating keys. 783 illustrations. lii + 934pp. 20277-1, 20278-X Two volumes, Paperbound $7.00

Our Northern Shrubs, Harriet L. Keeler. Fine non-technical reference work identifying more than 225 important shrubs of Eastern and Central United States and Canada. Full text covering botanical description, habitat, plant lore, is paralleled with 205 full-page photographs of flowering or fruiting plants. Nomenclature revised by Edward G. Voss. One of few works concerned with shrubs. 205 plates, 35 drawings. xxviii + 521pp. 21989-5 Paperbound $3.75

The Mushroom Handbook, Louis C. C. Krieger. Still the best popular handbook: full descriptions of 259 species, cross references to another 200. Extremely thorough text enables you to identify, know all about any mushroom you are likely to meet in eastern and central U. S. A.: habitat, luminescence, poisonous qualities, use, folklore, etc. 32 color plates show over 50 mushrooms, also 126 other illustrations. Finding keys. vii + 560pp. 21861-9 Paperbound $4.50

Handbook of Birds of Eastern North America, Frank M. Chapman. Still much the best single-volume guide to the birds of Eastern and Central United States. Very full coverage of 675 species, with descriptions, life habits, distribution, similar data. All descriptions keyed to two-page color chart. With this single volume the average birdwatcher needs no other books. 1931 revised edition. 195 illustrations. xxxvi + 581pp. 21489-3 Paperbound $5.00

CATALOGUE OF DOVER BOOKS

AMERICAN FOOD AND GAME FISHES, David S. Jordan and Barton W. Evermann. Definitive source of information, detailed and accurate enough to enable the sportsman and nature lover to identify conclusively some 1,000 species and sub-species of North American fish, sought for food or sport. Coverage of range, physiology, habits, life history, food value. Best methods of capture, interest to the angler, advice on bait, fly-fishing, etc. 338 drawings and photographs. 1 + 574pp. 6⅝ x 9⅜.
22196-2 Paperbound $5.00

THE FROG BOOK, Mary C. Dickerson. Complete with extensive finding keys, over 300 photographs, and an introduction to the general biology of frogs and toads, this is the classic non-technical study of Northeastern and Central species. 58 species; 290 photographs and 16 color plates. xvii + 253pp.
21973-9 Paperbound $4.00

THE MOTH BOOK: A GUIDE TO THE MOTHS OF NORTH AMERICA, William J. Holland. Classical study, eagerly sought after and used for the past 60 years. Clear identification manual to more than 2,000 different moths, largest manual in existence. General information about moths, capturing, mounting, classifying, etc., followed by species by species descriptions. 263 illustrations plus 48 color plates show almost every species, full size. 1968 edition, preface, nomenclature changes by A. E. Brower. xxiv + 479pp. of text. 6½ x 9¼.
21948-8 Paperbound $6.00

THE SEA-BEACH AT EBB-TIDE, Augusta Foote Arnold. Interested amateur can identify hundreds of marine plants and animals on coasts of North America; marine algae; seaweeds; squids; hermit crabs; horse shoe crabs; shrimps; corals; sea anemones; etc. Species descriptions cover: structure; food; reproductive cycle; size; shape; color; habitat; etc. Over 600 drawings. 85 plates. xii + 490pp.
21949-6 Paperbound $4.00

COMMON BIRD SONGS, Donald J. Borror. 33⅓ 12-inch record presents songs of 60 important birds of the eastern United States. A thorough, serious record which provides several examples for each bird, showing different types of song, individual variations, etc. Inestimable identification aid for birdwatcher. 32-page booklet gives text about birds and songs, with illustration for each bird.
21829-5 Record, book, album. Monaural. $3.50

FADS AND FALLACIES IN THE NAME OF SCIENCE, Martin Gardner. Fair, witty appraisal of cranks and quacks of science: Atlantis, Lemuria, hollow earth, flat earth, Velikovsky, orgone energy, Dianetics, flying saucers, Bridey Murphy, food fads, medical fads, perpetual motion, etc. Formerly "In the Name of Science." x + 363pp.
20394-8 Paperbound $3.00

HOAXES, Curtis D. MacDougall. Exhaustive, unbelievably rich account of great hoaxes: Locke's moon hoax, Shakespearean forgeries, sea serpents, Loch Ness monster, Cardiff giant, John Wilkes Booth's mummy, Disumbrationist school of art, dozens more; also journalism, psychology of hoaxing. 54 illustrations. xi + 338pp.
20465-0 Paperbound $3.50

CATALOGUE OF DOVER BOOKS

THE PRINCIPLES OF PSYCHOLOGY, William James. The famous long course, complete and unabridged. Stream of thought, time perception, memory, experimental methods—these are only some of the concerns of a work that was years ahead of its time and still valid, interesting, useful. 94 figures. Total of xviii + 1391pp.
20381-6, 20382-4 Two volumes, Paperbound $9.00

THE STRANGE STORY OF THE QUANTUM, Banesh Hoffmann. Non-mathematical but thorough explanation of work of Planck, Einstein, Bohr, Pauli, de Broglie, Schrödinger, Heisenberg, Dirac, Feynman, etc. No technical background needed. "Of books attempting such an account, this is the best," Henry Margenau, Yale. 40-page "Postscript 1959." xii + 285pp. 20518-5 Paperbound $3.00

THE RISE OF THE NEW PHYSICS, A. d'Abro. Most thorough explanation in print of central core of mathematical physics, both classical and modern; from Newton to Dirac and Heisenberg. Both history and exposition; philosophy of science, causality, explanations of higher mathematics, analytical mechanics, electromagnetism, thermodynamics, phase rule, special and general relativity, matrices. No higher mathematics needed to follow exposition, though treatment is elementary to intermediate in level. Recommended to serious student who wishes verbal understanding. 97 illustrations. xvii + 982pp. 20003-5, 20004-3 Two volumes, Paperbound $10.00

GREAT IDEAS OF OPERATIONS RESEARCH, Jagjit Singh. Easily followed non-technical explanation of mathematical tools, aims, results: statistics, linear programming, game theory, queueing theory, Monte Carlo simulation, etc. Uses only elementary mathematics. Many case studies, several analyzed in detail. Clarity, breadth make this excellent for specialist in another field who wishes background. 41 figures. x + 228pp. 21886-4 Paperbound $2.50

GREAT IDEAS OF MODERN MATHEMATICS: THEIR NATURE AND USE, Jagjit Singh. Internationally famous expositor, winner of Unesco's Kalinga Award for science popularization explains verbally such topics as differential equations, matrices, groups, sets, transformations, mathematical logic and other important modern mathematics, as well as use in physics, astrophysics, and similar fields. Superb exposition for layman, scientist in other areas. viii + 312pp.
20587-8 Paperbound $2.75

GREAT IDEAS IN INFORMATION THEORY, LANGUAGE AND CYBERNETICS, Jagjit Singh. The analog and digital computers, how they work, how they are like and unlike the human brain, the men who developed them, their future applications, computer terminology. An essential book for today, even for readers with little math. Some mathematical demonstrations included for more advanced readers. 118 figures. Tables. ix + 338pp. 21694-2 Paperbound $2.50

CHANCE, LUCK AND STATISTICS, Horace C. Levinson. Non-mathematical presentation of fundamentals of probability theory and science of statistics and their applications. Games of chance, betting odds, misuse of statistics, normal and skew distributions, birth rates, stock speculation, insurance. Enlarged edition. Formerly "The Science of Chance." xiii + 357pp. 21007-3 Paperbound $2.50

CATALOGUE OF DOVER BOOKS

PLANETS, STARS AND GALAXIES: DESCRIPTIVE ASTRONOMY FOR BEGINNERS, A. E. Fanning. Comprehensive introductory survey of astronomy: the sun, solar system, stars, galaxies, universe, cosmology; up-to-date, including quasars, radio stars, etc. Preface by Prof. Donald Menzel. 24pp. of photographs. 189pp. 5¼ x 8¼.
21680-2 Paperbound $2.50

TEACH YOURSELF CALCULUS, P. Abbott. With a good background in algebra and trig, you can teach yourself calculus with this book. Simple, straightforward introduction to functions of all kinds, integration, differentiation, series, etc. "Students who are beginning to study calculus method will derive great help from this book." Faraday House Journal. 308pp. 20683-1 Clothbound $2.50

TEACH YOURSELF TRIGONOMETRY, P. Abbott. Geometrical foundations, indices and logarithms, ratios, angles, circular measure, etc. are presented in this sound, easy-to-use text. Excellent for the beginner or as a brush up, this text carries the student through the solution of triangles. 204pp. 20682-3 Clothbound $2.00

BASIC MACHINES AND HOW THEY WORK, U. S. Bureau of Naval Personnel. Originally used in U.S. Naval training schools, this book clearly explains the operation of a progression of machines, from the simplest—lever, wheel and axle, inclined plane, wedge, screw—to the most complex—typewriter, internal combustion engine, computer mechanism. Utilizing an approach that requires only an elementary understanding of mathematics, these explanations build logically upon each other and are assisted by over 200 drawings and diagrams. Perfect as a technical school manual or as a self-teaching aid to the layman. 204 figures. Preface. Index. vii + 161pp. 6½ x 9¼. 21709-4 Paperbound $2.50

THE FRIENDLY STARS, Martha Evans Martin. Classic has taught naked-eye observation of stars, planets to hundreds of thousands, still not surpassed for charm, lucidity, adequacy. Completely updated by Professor Donald H. Menzel, Harvard Observatory. 25 illustrations. 16 x 30 chart. x + 147pp. 21099-5 Paperbound $2.00

MUSIC OF THE SPHERES: THE MATERIAL UNIVERSE FROM ATOM TO QUASAR, SIMPLY EXPLAINED, Guy Murchie. Extremely broad, brilliantly written popular account begins with the solar system and reaches to dividing line between matter and nonmatter; latest understandings presented with exceptional clarity. Volume One: Planets, stars, galaxies, cosmology, geology, celestial mechanics, latest astronomical discoveries; Volume Two: Matter, atoms, waves, radiation, relativity, chemical action, heat, nuclear energy, quantum theory, music, light, color, probability, antimatter, antigravity, and similar topics. 319 figures. 1967 (second) edition. Total of xx + 644pp. 21809-0, 21810-4 Two volumes, Paperbound $5.75

OLD-TIME SCHOOLS AND SCHOOL BOOKS, Clifton Johnson. Illustrations and rhymes from early primers, abundant quotations from early textbooks, many anecdotes of school life enliven this study of elementary schools from Puritans to middle 19th century. Introduction by Carl Withers. 234 illustrations. xxxiii + 381pp.
21031-6 Paperbound $4.00

CATALOGUE OF DOVER BOOKS

THE PHILOSOPHY OF THE UPANISHADS, Paul Deussen. Clear, detailed statement of upanishadic system of thought, generally considered among best available. History of these works, full exposition of system emergent from them, parallel concepts in the West. Translated by A. S. Geden. xiv + 429pp.
21616-0 Paperbound $3.50

LANGUAGE, TRUTH AND LOGIC, Alfred J. Ayer. Famous, remarkably clear introduction to the Vienna and Cambridge schools of Logical Positivism; function of philosophy, elimination of metaphysical thought, nature of analysis, similar topics. "Wish I had written it myself," Bertrand Russell. 2nd, 1946 edition. 160pp.
20010-8 Paperbound $1.50

THE GUIDE FOR THE PERPLEXED, Moses Maimonides. Great classic of medieval Judaism, major attempt to reconcile revealed religion (Pentateuch, commentaries) and Aristotelian philosophy. Enormously important in all Western thought. Unabridged Friedländer translation. 50-page introduction. lix + 414pp.
(USO) 20351-4 Paperbound $4.50

OCCULT AND SUPERNATURAL PHENOMENA, D. H. Rawcliffe. Full, serious study of the most persistent delusions of mankind: crystal gazing, mediumistic trance, stigmata, lycanthropy, fire walking, dowsing, telepathy, ghosts, ESP, etc., and their relation to common forms of abnormal psychology. Formerly *Illusions and Delusions of the Supernatural and the Occult.* iii + 551pp. 20503-7 Paperbound $4.00

THE EGYPTIAN BOOK OF THE DEAD: THE PAPYRUS OF ANI, E. A. Wallis Budge. Full hieroglyphic text, interlinear transliteration of sounds, word for word translation, then smooth, connected translation; Theban recension. Basic work in Ancient Egyptian civilization; now even more significant than ever for historical importance, dilation of consciousness, etc. clvi + 377pp. $6\frac{1}{2}$ x $9\frac{1}{4}$.
21866-X Paperbound $4.95

PSYCHOLOGY OF MUSIC, Carl E. Seashore. Basic, thorough survey of everything known about psychology of music up to 1940's; essential reading for psychologists, musicologists. Physical acoustics; auditory apparatus; relationship of physical sound to perceived sound; role of the mind in sorting, altering, suppressing, creating sound sensations; musical learning, testing for ability, absolute pitch, other topics. Records of Caruso, Menuhin analyzed. 88 figures. xix + 408pp.
21851-1 Paperbound $3.50

THE I CHING (THE BOOK OF CHANGES), translated by James Legge. Complete translated text plus appendices by Confucius, of perhaps the most penetrating divination book ever compiled. Indispensable to all study of early Oriental civilizations. 3 plates. xxiii + 448pp. 21062-6 Paperbound $3.50

THE UPANISHADS, translated by Max Müller. Twelve classical upanishads: Chandogya, Kena, Aitareya, Kaushitaki, Isa, Katha, Mundaka, Taittiriyaka, Brhadaranyaka, Svetasvatara, Prasna, Maitriyana. 160-page introduction, analysis by Prof. Müller. Total of 670pp. 20992-X, 20993-8 Two volumes, Paperbound $7.50

CATALOGUE OF DOVER BOOKS

JIM WHITEWOLF: THE LIFE OF A KIOWA APACHE INDIAN, Charles S. Brant, editor. Spans transition between native life and acculturation period, 1880 on. Kiowa culture, personal life pattern, religion and the supernatural, the Ghost Dance, breakdown in the White Man's world, similar material. 1 map. xii + 144pp.
22015-X Paperbound $1.75

THE NATIVE TRIBES OF CENTRAL AUSTRALIA, Baldwin Spencer and F. J. Gillen. Basic book in anthropology, devoted to full coverage of the Arunta and Warramunga tribes; the source for knowledge about kinship systems, material and social culture, religion, etc. Still unsurpassed. 121 photographs, 89 drawings. xviii + 669pp.
21775-2 Paperbound $5.00

MALAY MAGIC, Walter W. Skeat. Classic (1900); still the definitive work on the folklore and popular religion of the Malay peninsula. Describes marriage rites, birth spirits and ceremonies, medicine, dances, games, war and weapons, etc. Extensive quotes from original sources, many magic charms translated into English. 35 illustrations. Preface by Charles Otto Blagden. xxiv + 685pp.
21760-4 Paperbound $4.00

HEAVENS ON EARTH: UTOPIAN COMMUNITIES IN AMERICA, 1680-1880, Mark Holloway. The finest nontechnical account of American utopias, from the early Woman in the Wilderness, Ephrata, Rappites to the enormous mid 19th-century efflorescence; Shakers, New Harmony, Equity Stores, Fourier's Phalanxes, Oneida, Amana, Fruitlands, etc. "Entertaining and very instructive." *Times Literary Supplement*. 15 illustrations. 246pp.
21593-8 Paperbound $2.00

LONDON LABOUR AND THE LONDON POOR, Henry Mayhew. Earliest (c. 1850) sociological study in English, describing myriad subcultures of London poor. Particularly remarkable for the thousands of pages of direct testimony taken from the lips of London prostitutes, thieves, beggars, street sellers, chimney-sweepers, street-musicians, "mudlarks," "pure-finders," rag-gatherers, "running-patterers," dock laborers, cab-men, and hundreds of others, quoted directly in this massive work. An extraordinarily vital picture of London emerges. 110 illustrations. Total of lxxvi + 1951pp. 6⅝ x 10.
21934-8, 21935-6, 21936-4, 21937-2 Four volumes, Paperbound $16.00

HISTORY OF THE LATER ROMAN EMPIRE, J. B. Bury. Eloquent, detailed reconstruction of Western and Byzantine Roman Empire by a major historian, from the death of Theodosius I (395 A.D.) to the death of Justinian (565). Extensive quotations from contemporary sources; full coverage of important Roman and foreign figures of the time. xxxiv + 965pp. 20398-0, 20399-9 Two volumes, Paperbound $7.00

AN INTELLECTUAL AND CULTURAL HISTORY OF THE WESTERN WORLD, Harry Elmer Barnes. Monumental study, tracing the development of the accomplishments that make up human culture. Every aspect of man's achievement surveyed from its origins in the Paleolithic to the present day (1964); social structures, ideas, economic systems, art, literature, technology, mathematics, the sciences, medicine, religion, jurisprudence, etc. Evaluations of the contributions of scores of great men. 1964 edition, revised and edited by scholars in the many fields represented. Total of xxix + 1381pp. 21275-0, 21276-9, 21277-7 Three volumes, Paperbound $10.50